VINE DELORIA, JR.

"Into each life, it is said, some rain must fall. Some people have bad horoscopes, others take tips on the stock market. McNamara created the TFX and the Edsel. But Indians have been cursed above all other people. Indians have anthropologists.

The origin of the anthropologist is hidden in the historical mists. Indians are certain that all societies of the Near East had anthropologists at one time because all those societies are now defunct."

"Deloria is a Sioux, an ex-marine, an ex-divinity student, a soon-to-be lawyer, a savage wit. . . . Real people are embarrassments. When, beyond their personal embarrassment, they can, like Mr. Deloria, remind us of moral embarrassments, they frighten therapeutically."

John Leonard, *The New York Times*

CUSTER DIED FOR YOUR SINS

AN INDIAN MANIFESTO

VINE DELORIA, JR.

AVON
PUBLISHERS OF
DISCUS • CAMELOT • BARD

AVON BOOKS
A division of
The Hearst Corporation
959 Eighth Avenue
New York, New York 10019

First Avon Printing, October, 1970

Printed in Canada

CONTENTS

CUSTER DIED FOR YOUR SINS

AN INDIAN MANIFESTO

1 ✦ INDIANS TODAY,

THE REAL

AND THE UNREAL

INDIANS ARE LIKE the weather. Everyone knows all about the weather, but none can change it. When storms are predicted, the sun shines. When picnic weather is announced, the rain begins. Likewise, if you count on the unpredictability of Indian people, you will never be sorry.

One of the finest things about being an Indian is that people are always interested in you and your "plight." Other groups have difficulties, predicaments, quandaries, problems, or troubles. Traditionally we Indians have had a "plight."

Our foremost plight is our transparency. People can tell just by looking at us what we want, what should be done to help us, how we feel, and what a "real" Indian is really like. Indian life, as it relates to the real world, is a continuous attempt not to disappoint people who know us. Unfulfilled expectations cause grief and we have already had our share.

Because people can see right through us, it becomes impossible to tell truth from fiction or fact from mythology. Experts paint us as they would like us to be. Often we paint ourselves as we wish we were or as we might have been.

9

The more we try to be ourselves the more we are forced to defend what we have never been. The American public feels most comfortable with the mythical Indians of stereotype-land who were always THERE. These Indians are fierce, they wear feathers and grunt. Most of us don't fit this idealized figure since we grunt only when overeating, which is seldom.

To be an Indian in modern American society is in a very real sense to be unreal and ahistorical. In this book we will discuss the other side—the unrealities that face *us* as Indian people. It is this unreal feeling that has been welling up inside us and threatens to make this decade the most decisive in history for Indian people. In so many ways, Indian people are re-examining themselves in an effort to redefine a new social structure for their people. Tribes are reordering their priorities to account for the obvious discrepancies between their goals and the goals whites have defined for them.

Indian reactions are sudden and surprising. One day at a conference we were singing "My Country 'Tis of Thee" and we came across the part that goes:

> Land where our fathers died
> Land of the Pilgrims' pride . . .

Some of us broke out laughing when we realized that our fathers undoubtedly died trying to keep those Pilgrims from stealing our land. In fact, many of our fathers died because the Pilgrims killed them as witches. We didn't feel much kinship with those Pilgrims, regardless of who they did in.

We often hear "give it back to the Indians" when a gadget fails to work. It's a terrible thing for a people to realize that society has set aside all non-working gadgets for their exclusive use.

During my three years as Executive Director of the National Congress of American Indians it was a rare day when some white didn't visit my office and proudly proclaim that he or she was of Indian descent.

Cherokee was the most popular tribe of their choice and many people placed the Cherokees anywhere from Maine to Washington State. Mohawk, Sioux, and Chippewa were next in popularity. Occasionally I would be told about some mythical tribe from lower Pennsylvania, Virginia, or Massachusetts which had spawned the white standing before me.

At times I became quite defensive about being a Sioux when these white people had a pedigree that was so much more respectable than mine. But eventually I came to understand their need to identify as partially Indian and did not resent them. I would confirm their wildest stories about their Indian ancestry and would add a few tales of my own hoping that they would be able to accept themselves someday and leave us alone.

Whites claiming Indian blood generally tend to reinforce mythical beliefs about Indians. All but one person I met who claimed Indian blood claimed it on their grandmother's side. I once did a projection backward and discovered that evidently most tribes were entirely female for the first three hundred years of white occupation. No one, it seemed, wanted to claim a male Indian as a forebear.

It doesn't take much insight into racial attitudes to understand the real meaning of the Indian-grandmother complex that plagues certain whites. A male ancestor has too much of the aura of the savage warrior, the unknown primitive, the instinctive animal, to make him a respectable member of the family tree. But a young Indian princess? Ah, there was royalty for the taking. Somehow the white was linked with a noble house of gentility and culture if his grandmother was an Indian princess who ran away with an intrepid pioneer. And royalty has always been an unconscious but all-consuming goal of the European immigrant.

The early colonists, accustomed to life under benevolent despots, projected their understanding of the European political structure onto the Indian tribe in trying to explain its political and social structure. European royal houses were closed to ex-convicts and indentured servants, so the colonists made all Indian maidens princesses, then proceeded to climb a social ladder of their own creation. Within the next generation, if the trend continues, a large portion of the American population will eventually be related to Powhattan.

While a real Indian grandmother is probably the nicest

thing that could happen to a child, why is a remote Indian princess grandmother so necessary for many whites? Is it because they are afraid of being classed as foreigners? Do they need some blood tie with the frontier and its dangers in order to experience what it means to be an American? Or is it an attempt to avoid facing the guilt they bear for the treatment of the Indian?

The phenomenon seems to be universal. Only among the Jewish community, which has a long tribal-religious tradition of its own, does the mysterious Indian grandmother, the primeval princess, fail to dominate the family tree. Otherwise, there's not much to be gained by claiming Indian blood or publicly identifying as an Indian. The white believes that there is a great danger the lazy Indian will eventually corrupt God's hard-working people. He is still suspicious that the Indian way of life is dreadfully wrong. There is, in fact, something *un-American* about Indians for most whites.

I ran across a classic statement of this attitude one day in a history book which was published shortly after the turn of the century. Often have I wondered how many Senators, Congressmen, and clergymen of the day accepted the attitudes of that book as a basic fact of life in America. In no uncertain terms did the book praise God that the Indian had not yet been able to corrupt North America as he had South America:

> It was perhaps fortunate for the future of America that the Indians of the North rejected civilization. Had they accepted it the whites and Indians might have intermarried to some extent as they did in Mexico. That would have given us a population made up in a measure of shiftless half-breeds.

I never dared to show this passage to my white friends who had claimed Indian blood, but I often wondered why they were so energetic if they did have some of the bad seed in them.

Those whites who dare not claim Indian blood have an asset of their own. They *understand* Indians.

Understanding Indians is not an esoteric art. All it takes

is a trip through Arizona or New Mexico, watching a documentary on TV, having known *one* in the service, or having read a popular book on *them*.

There appears to be some secret osmosis about Indian people by which they can magically and instantaneously communicate complete knowledge about themselves to these interested whites. Rarely is physical contact required. Anyone and everyone who knows an Indian or who is *interested,* immediately and thoroughly understands them.

You can verify this great truth at your next party. Mention Indians and you will find a person who saw some in a gas station in Utah, or who attended the Gallup ceremonial celebration, or whose Uncle Jim hired one to cut logs in Oregon, or whose church had a missionary come to speak last Sunday on the plight of Indians and the mission of the church.

There is no subject on earth so easily understood as that of the American Indian. Each summer, work camps disgorge teenagers on various reservations. Within one month's time the youngsters acquire a knowledge of Indians that would astound a college professor.

Easy knowledge about Indians is a historical tradition. After Columbus "discovered" America he brought back news of a great new world which he assumed to be India and, therefore, filled with Indians. Almost at once European folklore devised a complete explanation of the new land and its inhabitants which featured the Fountain of Youth, the Seven Cities of Gold, and other exotic attractions. The absence of elephants apparently did not tip off the explorers that they weren't in India. By the time they realized their mistake, instant knowledge of Indians was a cherished tradition.

Missionaries, after learning some of the religious myths of tribes they encountered, solemnly declared that the inhabitants of the new continent were the Ten Lost Tribes of Israel. Indians thus received a religious-historical identity far greater than they wanted or deserved. But it was an impossible identity. Their failure to measure up to Old Testament standards doomed them to a fall from grace and they were soon relegated to the status of a picturesque species of wildlife.

Like the deer and the antelope, Indians seemed to play

rather than get down to the serious business of piling up treasures upon the earth where thieves break through and steal. Scalping, introduced prior to the French and Indian War by the English,* confirmed the suspicion that Indians

* Notice, for example the following proclamation:

Given at the Council Chamber in Boston this third day of November 1755 in the twenty-ninth year of the Reign of our Sovereign Lord George the Second by the Grace of God of Great Britain, France, and Ireland, King Defender of the Faith.

By His Honour's command
J. Willard, Secry.
God Save the King

Whereas the tribe of Penobscot Indians have repeatedly in a perfidious manner acted contrary to their solemn submission unto his Majesty long since made and frequently renewed.

I have, therefore, at the desire of the House of Representatives . . . thought fit to issue this Proclamation and to declare the Penobscot Tribe of Indians to be enemies, rebels and traitors to his Majesty. . . . And I do hereby require his Majesty's subjects of the Province to embrace all opportunities of pursuing, captivating, killing and destroy-all and every of the aforesaid Indians.

And whereas the General Court of this Province have voted that a bounty . . . be granted and allowed to be paid out of the Province Treasury . . . the premiums of bounty following viz:

For every scalp of a male Indian brought in as evidence of their being killed as aforesaid, forty pounds.

For every scalp of such female Indian or male Indian under the age of twelve years that shall be killed and brought in as evidence of their being killed as aforesaid, twenty pounds.

were wild animals to be hunted and skinned. Bounties were set and an Indian scalp became more valuable than beaver, otter, marten, and other animal pelts.

American blacks had become recognized as a species of human being by amendments to the Constitution shortly after the Civil War. Prior to emancipation they had been counted as three-fifths of a person in determining population for representation in the House of Representatives. Early Civil Rights bills nebulously state that other people shall have the same rights as "white people," indicating there *were* "other people." But Civil Rights bills passed during and after the Civil War systematically excluded Indian people. For a long time an Indian was not presumed capable of initiating an action in a court of law, of owning property, or of giving testimony against whites in court. Nor could an Indian vote or leave his reservation. Indians were America's captive people without any defined rights whatsoever.

Then one day the white man discovered that the Indian tribes still owned some 135 million acres of land. To his horror he learned that much of it was very valuable. Some was good grazing land, some was farm land, some mining land, and some covered with timber.

Animals could be herded together on a piece of land, but they could not sell it. Therefore it took no time at all to discover that Indians were really people and should have the right to sell their lands. Land was the means of recognizing the Indian as a human being. It was the method whereby land could be stolen legally and not blatantly.

Once the Indian was thus acknowledged, it was fairly simple to determine what his goals were. If, thinking went, the Indian was just like the white, he must have the same outlook as the white. So the future was planned for the Indian people in public and private life. First in order was allotting them reservations so that they could sell their lands. God's foreordained plan to repopulate the continent fit exactly with the goals of the tribes as they were defined by their white friends.

It is fortunate that we were never slaves. We gave up land instead of life and labor. Because the Negro labored, he was considered a draft animal. Because the Indian occupied large areas of land, he was considered a wild animal. Had we given up anything else, or had anything else to give up, it is certain that we would have been considered some other thing.

Whites have had different attitudes toward the Indians and the blacks since the Republic was founded. Whites have always refused to give non-whites the respect which they have been found to legally possess. Instead there has always been a contemptuous attitude that although the law says one thing, "we all know better."

Thus whites steadfastly refused to allow blacks to enjoy the fruits of full citizenship. They systematically closed schools, churches, stores, restaurants, and public places to blacks or made insulting provisions for them. For one hundred years every program of public and private white America was devoted to the exclusion of the black. It was, perhaps, embarrassing to be rubbing shoulders with one who had not so long before been defined as a field animal.

The Indian suffered the reverse treatment. Law after law was passed requiring him to conform to white institutions. Indian children were kidnapped and forced into boarding schools thousands of miles from their homes to learn the white man's ways. Reservations were turned over to different Christian denominations for governing. Reservations were for a long time church operated. Everything possible was done to ensure that Indians were forced into American life. The wild animal was made into a household pet whether or not he wanted to be one.

Policies for both black and Indian failed completely. Blacks eventually began the Civil Rights movement. In doing so they assured themselves some rights in white society. Indians continued to withdraw from the overtures of white society and tried to maintain their own communities and activities.

Actually both groups had little choice. Blacks, trapped in a world of white symbols, retreated into themselves. And people thought comparable Indian withdrawal unnatural because they expected Indians to behave like whites.

The white world of abstract symbols became a nightmare for Indian people. The words of the treaties, clearly stating that Indians should have "free and undisturbed" use of their lands under the protection of the federal government, were cast aside by the whites as if they didn't exist. The Sioux once had a treaty plainly stating that it would take the signatures or marks of three-fourths of the adult males to amend it. Yet through force the govern-

ment obtained only 10 percent of the required signatures
and declared the new agreement valid.

Indian solutions to problems which had been defined by
the white society were rejected out of hand and obvious
solutions discarded when they called for courses of action
that were not proper in white society. When Crow Dog assassinated Spotted Tail the matter was solved under traditional Sioux customs. Yet an outraged public, furious because Crow Dog had not been executed, pressured for the
Seven Major Crimes Act for the federal government to assume nearly total criminal jurisdiction over the reservations. Thus foreign laws and customs using the basic concepts of justice came to dominate Indian life. If, Indians
reasoned, justice is for society's benefit, why isn't our justice accepted? Indians became convinced they were the
world's stupidest people.

Words and situations never seemed to fit together. Always, it seemed, the white man chose a course of action
that did not work. The white man preached that it was
good to help the poor, yet he did nothing to assist the poor
in his society. Instead he put constant pressure on the Indian people to hoard their worldly goods, and when they
failed to accumulate capital but freely gave to the poor,
the white man reacted violently.

The failure of communication created a void into which
poured the white do-gooder, the missionary, the promoter,
the scholar, and every conceivable type of person who believed he could help. White society failed to understand
the situation because this conglomerate of assistance
blurred the real issues beyond recognition.

The legend of the Indian was embellished or tarnished
according to the need of the intermediates to gain leverage
in their struggle to solve problems that never existed outside of their own minds. The classic example, of course, is
the old-time missionary box. People were horrified that Indians continued to dress in their traditional garb. Since
whites did not wear buckskin and beads, they equated
such dress with savagery. So do-gooders in the East held
fantastic clothing drives to supply the Indians with civilized clothes. Soon boxes of discarded evening gowns, tux-
edos, tennis shoes, and uniforms flooded the reservations.
Indians were made to dress in these remnants so they

could be civilized. Then, realizing the ridiculous picture presented by the reservation people, neighboring whites made fun of the Indian people for having the presumption to dress like whites.

But in the East, whites were making great reputations as "Indian experts," as people who devoted their lives to helping the savages. Whenever Indian land was needed, the whites pictured the tribes as wasteful people who refused to develop their natural resources. Because the Indians did not "use" their lands, argued many land promoters, the lands should be taken away and given to people who knew what to do with them.

White society concentrated on the individual Indian to the exclusion of his group, forgetting that any society is merely a composite of individuals. Generalizations by experts universalized "Indianness" to the detriment of unique Indian values. Indians with a common cultural base shared behavior patterns. But they were expected to behave like a similar group of whites and rarely did. Whites, on the other hand, generally came from a multitude of backgrounds and shared only the need for economic subsistence. There was no way, therefore, to combine white values and Indian behavior into a workable program or intelligible subject of discussion.

One of the foremost differences separating white and Indian was simply one of origin. Whites derived predominantly from western Europe. The earliest settlers on the Atlantic seaboard came from England and the low countries. For the most part they shared the common experiences of their peoples and dwelt within the world view which had dominated western Europe for over a millenium.

Conversely Indians had always been in the western hemisphere. Life on this continent and views concerning it were not shaped in a post-Roman atmosphere. The entire outlook of the people was one of simplicity and mystery, not scientific or abstract. The western hemisphere produced wisdom, western Europe produced knowledge.

Perhaps this distinction seems too simple to mention. It is not. Many is the time I have sat in Congressional hearings and heard the chairman of the committee crow about "our" great Anglo-Saxon heritage of law and order.

Looking about the hearing room I saw row after row of full-blood Indians with blank expressions on their faces. As far as they were concerned, Sir Walter Raleigh was a brand of pipe tobacco that you got at the trading post.

When we talk about European background, we are talking about feudalism, kings, queens, their divine right to rule their subjects, the Reformation, Christianity, the Magna Charta and all of the events that went to make up European history.

American Indians do not share that heritage. They do not look wistfully back across the seas to the old country. The Apache were not at Runymede to make King John sign the Magna Charta. The Cherokee did not create English common law. The Pima had no experience with the rise of capitalism and industrialism. The Blackfeet had no monasteries. No tribe has an emotional, historical, or political relationship to events of another continent and age.

Indians have had their own political history which has shaped the outlook of the tribes. There were great confederacies throughout the country before the time of the white invader. The eastern Iroquois formed a strong league because as single tribes they had been weak and powerless against larger tribes. The Deep South was controlled by three confederacies: the Creeks with their town system, the Natchez, and the Powhattan confederation which extended into tidelands Virginia. The Pequots and their cousins the Mohicans controlled the area of Connecticut, Massachusetts, Rhode Island, and Long Island.

True democracy was more prevalent among Indian tribes in pre-Columbian days than it has been since. Despotic power was abhorred by tribes that were loose combinations of hunting parties rather than political entities.

Conforming their absolute freedom to fit rigid European political forms has been very difficult for most tribes, but on the whole they have managed extremely well. Under the Indian Reorganization Act Indian people have generally created a modern version of the old tribal political structure and yet have been able to develop comprehensive reservation programs which compare favorably with governmental structures anywhere.

The deep impression made upon American minds by the Indian struggle against the white man in the last century has made the contemporary Indian somewhat invisible compared with his ancestors. Today Indians are not conspicuous by their absence from view. Yet they should be.

In *The Other America,* the classic study of poverty by Michael Harrington, the thesis is developed that the poor are conspicuous by their invisibility. There is no mention of Indians in the book. A century ago, Indians would have dominated such a work.

Indians are probably invisible because of the tremendous amount of misinformation about them. Most books about Indians cover some abstract and esoteric topic of the last century. Contemporary books are predominantly by whites trying to solve the "Indian problem." Between the two extremes lives a dynamic people in a social structure of their own, asking only to be freed from cultural oppression. The future does not look bright for the attainment of such freedom because the white does not understand the Indian and the Indian does not wish to understand the white.

Understanding Indians means understanding so-called Indian Affairs. Indian Affairs, like Gaul, is divided into three parts: the government, the private organizations, and the tribes themselves. Mythological theories about the three sectors are as follows: paternalism exists in the governmental area, assistance is always available in the private sector, and the tribes dwell in primitive splendor. All three myths are false.

The government has responsibility for the Indian estate because of treaty commitments and voluntary assumption of such responsibility. It allegedly cares for Indian lands and resources. Education, health services, and technical assistance are provided to the major tribes by the Bureau of Indian Affairs, which is in the Department of the Interior.

But the smaller tribes get little or nothing from the Interior Department. Since there are some 315 distinct tribal communities and only about 30 get any kind of federal services, there is always a Crisis in Indian Affairs. Interior could solve the problems of 250 small tribes in one year if it wanted to. It doesn't want to.

The name of the game in the government sector is TASK FORCE REPORT. Every two years some reporter causes a great uproar about how Indians are treated by the Bureau of Indian Affairs. This, in turn, causes great consternation among Senators and Congressmen who have to answer mail from citizens concerned about Indians. So a TASK FORCE REPORT is demanded on Indian problems.

The conclusion of every TASK FORCE REPORT is that Congress is not appropriating enough money to do an adequate job of helping Indians. Additionally, these reports find that while Indians are making some progress, the fluctuating policy of Congress is stifling Indian progress. The reports advise that a consistent policy of self-help with adequate loan funds for reservation development be initiated.

Since Congress is not about to appropriate any more money than possible for Indian Affairs, the TASK FORCE REPORT is filed away for future reference. Rumor has it that there is a large government building set aside as a storage bin for TASK FORCE REPORTS.

This last year saw the results of a number of TASK FORCE REPORTS. In 1960, when the New Frontier burst upon the scene, a TASK FORCE REPORT was prepared. It made the recommendations listed above. In 1966 two additional TASK FORCES went abroad in search of the solution to the "Indian problem." One was a secret Presidential TASK FORCE. One was a semi-secret Interior TASK FORCE. In March of 1968 the President asked for a 10 percent increase in funds for Indian programs and after eight years of Democratic rule, a TASK FORCE recommendation was actually carried out.

Government agencies always believe that their TASK FORCES are secret. They believe that anonymous experts can ferret out the esoteric answers to an otherwise insoluble problem. Hence they generally keep secret the names of people serving on their TASK FORCES until after the report is issued. Only they make one mistake. They always have the same people on the TASK FORCE. So when Indians learn there is a TASK FORCE abroad they automatically know who are on it and what they are thinking.

Paternalism is always a favorite subject of the TASK FORCES. They make it one of the basic statements of their preambles. It has therefore become an accepted tenet that paternalism dominates government-Indian relationships.

Congress always wants to do away with paternalism. So it has a policy designed to do away with Indians. If there are no Indians, there cannot be any paternalism.

But governmental paternalism is not a very serious problem. If an employee of the Bureau of Indian Affairs gives any tribe any static the problem is quickly resolved. The tribal chairman gets on the next plane to Washington. The next morning he walks into the Secretary of the Interior's office and raises hell. Soon a number of bureaucrats are working on the problem. The tribal chairman has a good dinner, goes to a movie, and takes the late plane back to his reservation. Paternalism by field men is not very popular in the Department of the Interior in Washington. Consequently, there is very little paternalism in the governmental sector if the tribe knows what it is doing. And most tribes know what they are doing.

In the private sector, however, paternalism is a fact of life. Nay, it is the standard operating procedure. Churches, white interest organizations, universities, and private firms come out to the reservations asking only to be of service IN THEIR OWN INIMITABLE WAY. No one asks them to come out. It is very difficult, therefore, to get them to leave.

Because no chairman has the time to fly into New York weekly and ask the national churches to stop the paternalistic programs of their missionaries, the field is ripe for paternalism. Most of them are not doing much anyway.

But, people in the private area are working very hard to keep Indians happy. When Indians get unhappy they begin to think about kicking out the white do-gooders, paternalism or not. And if the private organizations were kicked out of a reservation, where would they work? What would they claim as their accomplishments at fund-raising time?

Churches, for example, invest great amounts to train white men for Indian missions. If there were ever too great a number of Indian missionaries, Indians might think they should have their own churches. Then there would be no opportunity to convert the pagans. Where, then, would clergy misfits go if not to Indian missions?

So paternalism is very sophisticated in the private sector. It is disguised by a board of "Indian advisors," selected from among the Indians themselves on the reservation. These "advisors" are put to use to make it appear as if all is well. Pronouncements by Indian advisory boards generally commend the private organization for its work. They ask it to do even more work, for only in that way, they declare, can justice be done to their people.

To hear some people talk, Indians are simultaneously rich from oil royalties and poor as church mice. To hear others, Indians have none of the pleasures of the mainstream, like riots, air pollution, snipers, ulcers, and traffic. Consequently, they class Indians among the "underprivileged" in our society.

Primitive purity is sometimes attributed to tribes. Some tribes keep their rituals and others don't. The best characterization of tribes is that they stubbornly hold on to what they feel is important to them and discard what they feel is irrelevant to their current needs. Traditions die hard and innovation comes hard. Indians have survived for thousands of years in all kinds of conditions. They do not fly from fad to fad seeking novelty. That is what makes them Indian.

Three books, to my way of thinking, give a good idea of the intangible sense of reality that pervades the Indian people. *When the Legends Die* by Hal Borland gives a good picture of Indian youth. *Little Big Man* by Thomas Berger gives a good idea of Indian attitudes toward life. *Stay Away, Joe,* by Dan Cushman, the favorite of Indian people, gives a humorous but accurate idea of the problems caused by the intersection of two ways of life. Anyone who can read, appreciate, and understand the spiritual forces brought out in these books will have a good idea of what Indians are all about.

Other books may be nice, accurate, and historical but they are not really about Indians. In general, they twist Indian reality into a picture which is hard to understand and consequently greatly in error.

Statistical information on Indians can easily be found in other books. What is important, for understanding the present state of Indian Affairs, is to know how tribes are organized today, how they work together, and what they anticipate for the future. And there is no easy way to broach the subject. So let us begin.

In 1934 the Indian Reorganization Act was passed. Under the provisions of this act reservation people were enabled to organize for purposes of self-government. Nearly three-quarters of the reservations organized. These reservations are not known as tribes. Often the remnants of larger historical tribal groups that were located on different pieces of land, they became under IRA officially recognized as "tribes."

There are nineteen different Chippewa tribes, fifteen Sioux tribes, four Potawatomi tribes, a number of Paiute tribes, and several consolidated tribes which encompass two different groups that happened to land on the same reservation.

Examples of consolidated tribes are the Salish and Kootenai of Montana, the Cheyenne-Arapaho of Oklahoma, the Kiowa-Comanche-Apache of Oklahoma, and the Mandan, Hidatsa, and Arikara of the Fort Berthold reservation in North Dakota.

Over the past generation tribes have discovered that they must band together to make themselves heard. Consequently most states have inter-tribal councils, composed of the tribes in that state, that meet regularly and exchange ideas. In some areas, particularly in the Northwest, tribal representation is on a regional basis. The Northwest Affiliated Tribes is an organization made up of tribes from Montana, Idaho, Washington, and Oregon. Its counterpart, the Western Washington Inter-tribal Coordinating Council consists of tribes that live in the Puget Sound area.

Rarely do tribes overlap across state boundaries. While there are fifteen Sioux tribes, the United Sioux is an organization of only South Dakota tribes. Sioux groups in North Dakota, Nebraska, or Minnesota are not invited.

Indians have two "mainstream" organizations, the National Congress of American Indians and the National Indian Youth Council. The NCAI is open to tribes, organizations, and individuals, both red and white. Its major emphasis is on strong tribal membership because it works primarily with legislation and legislation is handled on an individual tribal basis.

The NIYC is the SNCC of Indian Affairs. Organized in

1962, it has been active among the post-college group just entering Indian Affairs. Although NIYC has a short history, it has been able to achieve recognition as a force to be reckoned with in national Indian Affairs. Generally more liberal and more excitable than the NCAI, the NIYC inclines to the spectacular short-term project rather than the extended program. The rivalry between the two groups is intense.

Lesser known but with great potential for the future are the traditional organizations. Primary among these is the oldest continuous Indian-run organization: the League of Nations, Pan American Indians. Its President, Alfred Gagne, incorporates the best of traditional Indian life and national problems into a coherent working philosophy. Should this group ever receive sufficient funding to have field workers, it could very well overturn established government procedures in Indian Affairs. It has long fought the Bureau of Indian Affairs and seeks a return to traditional Indian customs.

From the work of the League of Nations has come the alliance of the traditional Indians of each tribe. In June of 1968 they met in Oklahoma to form the National Aborigine Conference. Discussions ranging from religious prophecies to practical politics were held. From this conference is expected to come a strong nationalistic push on the reservations in the next several years.

Another group well worthy of mention is the American Indian Historical Society of San Francisco. Begun by Rupert Costo a Cauhilla man, the society has become the publishers of the finest contemporary material on Indians. Excellent research and wide knowledge of Indian people makes it an influential voice in Indian Affairs.

Recently, during the Poor People's March, Indian participants formed the Coalition of American Indian Citizens. A loose and perhaps temporary alliance of disgruntled young people, the Coalition brought to Indian Affairs a sense of urgency. Whether it will continue to function depends on the commitment of its members to goals which they originally stated.

Regional groups are occasionally formed around a specific issue. In the Northwest the Survivors of American Indians, Inc., works exclusively on the issue of fishing rights.

In Oklahoma the Original Cherokee Community Organization has been formed to defend hunting and treaty rights of the Cherokees.

Most urban areas have urban centers or clubs composed of Indian people. For the most part these centers provide a place where urban Indians can meet and socialize. The best-known centers are in Los Angeles, Oakland, Chicago, and Minneapolis. New centers are always springing up in different cities. There are probably in excess of thirty functioning centers or clubs at any one time. The urban areas show the most potential for strong lasting organizations, however, and once the urban Indians stabilize themselves they will experience phenomenal growth.

All of these groups are primarily interested in issues and policies. The Indian Council Fire of Chicago works primarily in the field of public relations and Indian culture. The American Indian Development, Inc., works in the field of youth work and economic development of Indian communities.

There are a number of white organizations that attempt to help Indian people. Since we would be better off without them I will not mention them, except to comment that they do exist.

Movement occurs easily in Indian Affairs. Tribes are generally quite alert to issues and policies advocated by red and white alike. It is a rare event that goes unnoticed. Careful observation of the effects of the moccasin telegraph indicates a tendency by the Indian people to organize and coalesce around certain issues rather than according to any set pattern.

The National Congress of American Indians is the best example of this tendency. Membership fluctuates in the NCAI according to the urgency of national issues affecting member tribes. The NCAI attracts only those tribes that are interested in its programs. Unity for unity's sake is not yet a concept that has been accepted by the tribes. Nor has unity for future action been understood.

Within the NCAI personal leadership determines policies and programs. In 1954 Congress began the great push to abrogate Indian rights in a series of "termination bills" by which federal services and protections would be denied to tribes. Fortunately the northwestern tribes under the leadership of Joseph Garry, Chairman of the Coeur d'Alenes of Idaho, were then in control of the NCAI. Garry succeeded in uniting enough tribes under his leadership to bring the policy to a stalemate. It has remained in a deadlock ever since, with Congress waiting for the tribes to lose interest and the tribes remaining on the alert against any termination move by Congress.

Garry served as President of the NCAI from 1953–1959. He established a tradition in the Northwest of political cooperation between the tribes. National Indian Affairs has ever since been haunted by the memory of the powerful coalition of that era. Since Garry's days few decisions are made in Indian Affairs without first checking with northwestern tribal leadership. The recent alliance of the Northwest with the Alaskan natives will shortly result in a total takeover of the NCAI by the northwestern tribes as the Indian political balance is once again achieved.

The power of the Northwest has been balanced by the leadership and political ability of the Sioux. During twenty-five years of NCAI existence the Sioux have held the Executive Directorship for fourteen years. The Sioux reign is nearly at an end, however, as other tribes achieve more political sophistication and begin to exert more influence on the total national scene. The rise of the Wisconsin-Minnesota groups of Chippewas as a potent force was noted at the NCAI convention in Omaha in 1968. Since the Chippewas and the Sioux are traditional enemies and the Chippewa are now allied with the northwestern tribes, the Chippewa should be able to take over the entire field of Indian Affairs within a period of three years. They now lack only that charismatic leader who can articulate critical issues to other tribes.

The tribes from California, Kansas, and Nevada have traditionally been slow to rise to the challenge of national Indian political combat. Yet they could unite and take over the organization completely if they were to join it en masse. With the current inroads being made into national Indian Affairs by the Coalition of Indian Citizens and the National Indian Youth Council, California and Nevada may yet exert tremendous influence over other tribes by attending an NCAI convention with full voting power.

The NCAI is important to the Indian people only when

it provides a forum in which issues can be discussed. Occasionally it has come to be dominated by a few tribes and then it has rapidly gone downhill. At the Omaha convention of 1968 nontribal groups attended the meeting hoping to be allowed to participate. Instead they were rebuffed, and during the convention all non-tribal forces became allied outside the normal channels of Indian Affairs. This tragic blunder by the NCAI could cause a great conflict between reservation and non-reservation groups in the future. There is little doubt that urban Indians have more sophistication than do reservation people, and now urban Indians and the National Indian Youth Council have formed together as cooperating organizations to work for urban and young Indian people. It will probably take several years for Indian tribes to absorb the meaning of this new coalition. By then it may be too late for them to survive.

Individual tribes show incredible differences. No single aspect seems to be as important as tribal solidarity. Tribes that can handle their reservation conflicts in traditional Indian fashion generally make more progress and have better programs than do tribes that continually make adaptations to the white value system. The Pueblos of New Mexico have a solid community life and are just now, with the influx of college-educated Pueblos, beginning large development projects. In spite of the vast differences between the generations, the Pueblos have been able to maintain a sense of tribal purpose and solidarity, and developments are undertaken by the consensus of all the people of the community.

Even more spectacular are the Apaches of the Southwest—the Mescalero, San Carlos, White Mountain, and Jicarilla tribes. Numbering probably less than a dozen college graduates among them, the four tribes have remained close to their traditions, holding ancient ceremonies to be of utmost importance to the future of the tribe. Without the benefit of the white man's vaunted education, these four Apache groups have developed their reservations with amazing skill and foresight. Mescalero Apache owns a ski resort worth over one million dollars. Jicarilla has a modern shopping center. White Mountain has a tremendous tourism development of some twenty-six artificial lakes stocked with trout. San Carlos has a fine cattle industry and is presently developing an industrial park.

Contrast the Chippewas with the Apaches and the picture is not as bright. The Chippewas are located in Minnesota, Wisconsin, and Michigan. They have access to the large cities of Chicago, Minneapolis, Milwaukee, and Detroit. The brain drain of leadership from the Chippewa reservations to the cities has been enormous over the years. Migration to the cities has meant an emphasis on land sales, little development of existing resources, and abandonment of tribal traditions. Only among the Red Lake Chippewa has much progress been made. And Red Lake is probably the most traditional of the Chippewa tribes.

The Sioux, my own people, have a great tradition of conflict. We were the only nation ever to annihilate the United States Cavalry three times in succession. And when we find no one else to quarrel with, we often fight each other. The Sioux problem is excessive leadership. During one twenty-year period in the last century the Sioux fought over an area from LaCrosse, Wisconsin, to Sheridan, Wyoming, against the Crow, Arapaho, Cheyenne, Mandan, Arikara, Hidatsa, Ponca, Iowa, Pawnee, Otoe, Omaha, Winnebago, Chippewa, Cree, Assiniboine, Sac and Fox, Potawatomi, Ute, and Gros Ventre. This was, of course, in addition to fighting the U.S. Cavalry continually throughout that period. The United States government had to call a special treaty session merely to settle the argument among the tribes in the eastern half of that vast territory. It was the only treaty between tribes supervised by the federal government.

But the Sioux never quit fighting. Reservation programs are continually disrupted by bickering within the reservations. Each election on a Sioux reservation is generally a fight to the finish. A ten-vote margin of some 1,500 votes cast is a landslide victory in Sioux country. Fortunately strong chairmen have come to have a long tenure on several Sioux reservations and some of the tribes have made a great deal of progress. But the tendency is always present to slug it out at a moment's notice.

The northwestern tribes also have their fierce and gentle

side. Over the past two decades there has been continual conflict between the western tribes and the Fish and Game commissions in Oregon and Washington. Violations of treaty fishing rights by the state can bring Yakimas to the riverbanks with guns so quick as to frighten an unsuspecting bystander.

Before anyone conceived of statehood for either state, Isaac Stevens, on behalf of the United States, traveled up the coast signing treaties with all of the Pacific tribes. These treaties promised perpetual hunting and fishing rights for the tribes if they would agree to remain on restricted reservations. After World War II, when the sportsmen began to have leisure time, the states sought to abrogate the treaties. But in the case of Washington there was a specific disclaimer clause in the act admitting Washington into the Union by which the state promised never to disturb the Indian tribes within its borders.

In recent years there have been a number of "fish-ins" by the smaller tribes in Washington in sporadic attempts to raise the fishing-rights issue. Unfortunately the larger tribes have not supported these people. The larger tribes cannot seem to understand that a precedent of law set against a small tribe means one for the larger tribes as well. It may well be that all Indian fishing will eventually be regulated by the states of the Northwest. This would be quite tragic as there is a fundamental difference between Indian and sports fishing. Indian people are fishing for food for their families. Sportsmen are fishing for relaxation and recreation. Indians may have to starve so that whites can have a good time on the weekends if present trends continue.

But the northwestern tribes have taken the lead in pursuing their rights in court in this century. In the last century the Cherokees went to the Supreme Court over and over again and set forth most of Indian law in its developing years. Similarly in this century the tribes of Oregon, Washington, and Idaho have won the more significant cases which have been taken to court. Such landmark cases as *Squire v. Capoeman,* a taxation case which spelled out exemption of individual allotments from income tax, *United States v. Winans,* which defined water rights and fishing rights, *Mason v. Sams,* another fishing-rights case, and *Seymour v. Superintendent,* a jurisdiction case which gave the modern definition of "Indian country"—a concept important for preservation of treaty rights—were all cases initiated by tribes of that area.

In 1967 ABC television began its ill-fated series on Custer. The Tribal Indians Land Rights Association began the national fight to get the series banned. Eventually the NCAI and other groups protested to ABC over the series and a great Indian war was on. Custer, who had never been a very bright character, was tabbed by the NCAI as the "Adolph Eichmann" of the nineteenth century. But no one could figure out the correct strategy by which ABC could be forced to negotiate.

Finally the Yakima tribal lawyer, James Hovis, devised the tactic of getting every tribe to file for equal time against ABC's local affiliate (ABC itself was not subject to FCC regulations). As tribes in the different areas began to move, ABC through its affiliate board, arranged a trip to California to discuss the program with the NCAI. Several tribes filed against the local affiliates of ABC and did receive some air time to present the Indian side of the Custer story during the brief run of the show. Later we heard that it would have cost ABC some three thousand dollars per complaint if every tribe had gone ahead and demanded FCC hearings on the controversy. Whether this was true or not we never learned, but once again the northwestern Indians had devised a legal strategy by which Indians as a national ethnic group could air their complaints. The series was canceled after nine episodes.

The greatest potential, as yet untapped, lies in Nevada. With a small total population concentrated in Las Vegas and Reno, Nevada is presently on the threshold of development. Some twenty-six tribes, mainly Paiutes and Shoshones, live in Nevada. If these tribes were ever to form a strong political or economic alliance, they would exert tremendous influence within the state. The Nevadan Indian population is fairly young and the possibility of its developing a strong Indian swing vote as it comes of age is excellent.

Perhaps even more spectacular is the pattern by which Indian land is held in that state. In the closing years of the last century there were no large reservations set up in Nevada. Instead, because the groups were so small and scattered, Indians were given public-domain allotments adjoining the larger towns and cities in Nevada. These groups were called colonies and they were simply unorganized groups of Indians living, like the Lone Ranger and Tonto used to do, "not far from town." Today the Nevada tribes have extremely valuable land in areas where development will have to move if the towns in Nevada are going to continue to grow. With few exceptions old desert lands of the last century are now prime prospects for industrial parks and residential subdivisions. If the Nevada tribes were to pursue a careful policy of land exchange, they would soon own great amounts of land and have a respectable bank account as well.

Indian tribes are rapidly becoming accustomed to the manner in which the modern world works. A generation ago most Indians would not have known which way Washington, D.C., lay. Today it is a rare tribe that does not make a visit once a year to talk with its Congressional delegation, tour the government agencies, and bring home a new program or project from the many existing programs being funded by the federal government. Many tribes receive the Congressional Record and a number subscribe to leading national publications such as *The Wall Street Journal*, *Life*, *Time*, and *Newsweek*. Few events of much importance pass the eyes of watchful tribal groups without comment.

Tribes are also becoming very skilled at grantsmanship. Among the larger, more experienced tribes, million-dollar programs are commonplace. Some tribes sharpened their teeth on the old Area Redevelopment Administration of the early sixties. When the Office of Economic Opportunity was created they jumped into the competition with incredibly complex programs and got them funded. One housing program on the Rosebud Sioux reservation is a combination of programs offered by some five different government agencies. The Sioux there have melded a winning hand by making each government agency fund a component of the total housing program for the reservation.

Some tribes take home upward of ten million dollars a

year in government programs and private grants for their reservation people. Many tribes, combining a variety of sources, have their own development officer to plan and project future programs. The White Mountain Apaches are the first tribe to have their own public relations firm to keep tribal relations with the surrounding towns and cities on an even keel.

With a change in Congressional policy away from termination toward support of tribal self-sufficiency, it is conceivable that Indian tribes will be able to become economically independent of the federal government in the next generation. Most tribes operate under the provisions of their Indian Reorganization Act constitutions and are probably better operated than most towns, certainly more honestly operated than the larger cities.

Tribes lost some ten years during the 1950's when all progress was halted by the drive toward termination. Arbitrary and unreasonable harassment of tribal programs, denial of credit funds for program development, and pressure on tribes to liquidate assets all contributed to waste a decade during which tribes could have continued to develop their resources.

Today the Indian people are in a good position to demonstrate to the nation what can be done in community development in the rural areas. With the overcrowding of the urban areas, rural development should be the coming thing and understanding of tribal programs could indicate methods of resettling the vast spaces of rural America.

With so much happening on reservations and the possibility of a brighter future in store, Indians have started to become livid when they realize the contagious trap the mythology of white America has caught them in. The descendant of Pocahontas is a remote and incomprehensible mystery to us. We are no longer a wild species of animal loping freely across the prairie. We have little in common with the last of the Mohicans. We are TASK FORCED to death.

Some years ago at a Congressional hearing someone asked Alex Chasing Hawk, a council member of the Cheyenne River Sioux for thirty years, "Just what do you Indians want?" Alex replied, "A leave-us-alone law!!"

The primary goal and need of Indians today is not for

someone to feel sorry for us and claim descent from Pocahontas to make us feel better. Nor do we need to be classified as semi-white and have programs and policies made to bleach us further. Nor do we need further studies to see if we are feasible. We need a new policy by Congress acknowledging our right to live in peace, free from arbitrary harassment. We need the public at large to drop the myths in which it has clothed us for so long. We need fewer and fewer "experts" on Indians.

What we need is a cultural leave-us-alone agreement in spirit and in fact.

2 ❖ LAWS
AND TREATIES

AFTER LYNDON B. JOHNSON had been elected he came before the American people with his message on Vietnam. The import of the message was that America had to keep her commitments in southeast Asia or the world would lose faith in the promises of our country.

Some years back Richard Nixon warned the American people that Russia was bad because she had not kept any treaty or agreement signed with her. You can trust the Communists, the saying went, to be Communists.

Indian people laugh themselves sick when they hear these statements. America has yet to keep one Indian treaty or agreement despite the fact that the United States government signed over four hundred such treaties and agreements with Indian tribes. It would take Russia another century to make and break as many treaties as the United States has already violated.

Since it is doubtful that any nation will ever exceed the record of the United States for perfidy, it is significant that statesmen such as Johnson and Nixon, both professional politicians and opportunists of the first magnitude, have made such a fuss about the necessity of keeping one's commitments. History may well record that while the United States was squandering some one hundred billion dollars in Vietnam while justifying this bloody orgy as

35

commitment-keeping, it was also busy breaking the oldest Indian treaty, that between the United States and the Seneca tribe of the Iroquois Nation, the Pickering Treaty of 1794.

After the Revolution it appeared necessary to the colonies, now states in the new confederation, that in order to have peace on the frontier a treaty would have to be signed with the Iroquois of New York. George Washington sent a delegation to Iroquois country headed by Timothy Pickering. In return for peace and friendship the United States promised to respect the lands and boundaries which the Iroquois had set for themselves and never to disturb the Indians in the use of their land. The United States also affirmed its promise that it would never claim the Indian lands.

In the early 1960's, however, a dam was built which flooded the major part of the Seneca reservation. Although the tribe hired their own engineer and offered an alternative site on which the dam would have been less expensive to construct and more efficient, the government went ahead and broke the treaty, taking the land they had decided on for the dam.

It has been alleged by people who had reason to know that this dam was part of the price of keeping Pennsylvania in line for John F. Kennedy at the 1960 Democratic convention.

Article III of the Pickering Treaty read:

> Now the United States acknowledge all the land within the aforementioned boundaries to be the property of the Seneka nation; and the United States will never claim the same, nor disturb the Seneka nation, nor any of the Six Nations, or of their Indian friends residing thereon and united with them in the free use and enjoyment thereof; but it shall remain theirs, until they choose to sell the same to the people of the United States, who have the right to purchase.

Rather than having a choice as to whether or not to sell to the United States, the Senecas were simply forced to sell. It was a buyer's market.

Hucksterism and land theft have gone hand in hand in American history. The tragedy of the past is that it set precedents for land theft today when there is no longer any real need to steal such vast areas. But more damage is being done to Indian people today by the United States government than was done in the last century. Water rights are being trampled on. Land is being condemned for irrigation and reclamation projects. Indian rights are being ground into the dirt.

It is fairly easy to trace the principal factors leading to the great land steals. The ideological basis for taking Indian land was pronounced by the Christian churches shortly after the discovery of the New World, when the doctrine of discovery was announced.

Discovery negated the rights of the Indian tribes to sovereignty and equality among the nations of the world. It took away their title to their land and gave them the right only to sell. And they had to sell it to the European nation that had *discovered* their land.

Consequently the European nation—whether England, France, Spain, or Holland—that claimed to have discovered a piece of land had the right to that land regardless of the people living there at the time. This was the doctrine of the Western world which was applied to the New World and endorsed as the will of God by the Christian churches of western Europe.

As early as 1496 the King of England, head of the English church, commissioned John Cabot to discover countries then unknown to Christian peoples and to take possession of them in the name of the English king. In Cabot's commission was the provision that should any prior Christian title to the land be discovered it should be recognized. Christianity thus endorsed and advocated the rape of the North American continent, and her representaives have done their utmost to contribute to this process ever since.

After the Revolution the new United States adopted the doctrine of discovery and continued the process of land acquisition. The official white attitude toward Indian lands was that discovery gave the United States exclusive right to extinguish Indian title of occupancy either by purchase or conquest.

It turned out that the United States acquired the land neither by purchase nor by conquest, but by a more sophisticated technique known as trusteeship. Accordingly few tribes were defeated in war by the United States, fewer still sold their land to the United States, but most sold some land and allowed the United States to hold the remainder in trust for them. In turn, the tribes acknowledged the sovereignty of the United States in preference to other possible sovereigns, such as England, France, and Spain. From this humble beginning the federal government stole some two billion acres of land and continues to take what it can without arousing the ire of the ignorant public.

This fight for land has caused much bitterness against the white man. It is this blatant violation of the treaties that creates such frustration among the Indian people. Many wonder exactly what their rights are, for no matter where they turn treaties are disregarded and laws are used to deprive them of what little land remains to them.

The original import of the treaties was allegedly to guarantee peace on the frontier. And the tribes generally held to their promises, discontinued the fighting, and accepted the protection of the United States over their remaining lands. Yet submission became merely the first step from freedom to classification as incompetents whose every move had to be approved by government bureaucrats.

Incompetency was a doctrine devised to explain the distinction between people who held their land free from trust restrictions and those who still had their land in trust. But it soon mushroomed out of proportion. Eventually any decision made by an Indian was casually overlooked because the Indian was, by definition, incompetent.

Indians often consider the history of the Jews in Egypt. For four hundred years these people were subjected to cultural and economic oppression. They were treated as slaves without rights and property although the original promise of the Pharaoh to Joseph, like the Indian treaties, spelled out Hebrew rights. Like the Great White Father, the Pharaoh turned his back on his former allies and began official oppression and destruction of rights. Yet the Hebrews survived.

America's four-hundred-year period is nearly up.

Many Indians see the necessity of a tribal regrouping comparable to the Hebrew revival of old.

What were the treaties and agreements that the United States violated? For the most part they were contracts signed with tribes living in areas into which the whites moved during the last century. Nearly a third were treaties of peace; the rest were treaties for land cession.

Some tribes signed a number of treaties which were basically land-cession treaties. The Sioux signed a great many treaties, primarily peace treaties. In the Far West many treaties were made, but never ratified by Congress, leaving them in a legalistic limbo.

A glance at some of the obscure provisions of the treaties indicates that there must have been no intention on the part of the United States to keep them. The United States was obviously promising things it could not, at least politically speaking, deliver. And the curious thing about court cases which have occurred since treaty days is that legal interpretation has been traditionally pro-Indian. Treaties must be intepreted as the Indians would have understood them, the courts have ruled. Unfortunately in many cases the tribes can't even get into court because of the ambiguous and inconsistent interpretation of their legal status.

The concept of dependency, a favorite topic in government agencies and Congress, originally came from the Delaware Treaty of September 17, 1778. Dependency, as the term is used today, implies a group of lazy, dirty Indians loafing the day away at the agency. Indeed, this is the precise connotation which people love to give. But the actual provision in the Delaware Treaty is not a social or philosophical or even political theory of man. Rather it is a narrowly economic provision of dependency, as seen in Article V:

> Whereas the confederation entered into by the Delaware Nation and the United States renders the first dependent on the latter for all the articles of cloathing, utensils and implements of war, and it is judged not only reasonable, but indispensably necessary, that the aforesaid Nation be supplied with such articles from time to time, as far as the United States may have it in their power, by a well regulated trade . . .

Dependency, as one can easily tell from the article, was simply a trade dependency. Nowhere was there any inkling that the tribe would eventually be classified as *incompetent*. Indeed, the very next article, Article VI, implies that the United States considered the Delawares as competent as any people on earth:

> . . . the United States do engage to guarantee to the aforesaid nation of Delawares, and their heirs, all their territorial rights in the fullest and most ample manner as it hath been bound by former treaties, as long as they the said Delaware nation shall abide by and hold fast the chain of friendship now entered into. And it is further agreed on between the contracting parties should it for the future be found conducive for the mutual interest of both parties to invite any other tribes who have been friends to the interest of the United States, to join the present confederation, and to form a state whereof the Delaware nation shall be the head, and have a representation in Congress: Provided, nothing contained in this article to be considered as conclusive until it meets with the approbation of Congress.

During the darkest days of the Revolution, in order to keep the Indians from siding with the British and completely crushing the new little nation, the United States held out equality and statehood to the Delawares and any other tribes they could muster to support the United States. But when the shooting was all over the Delawares were forgotten in the rush to steal their land.

This promise was not only made to the Delawares. In Article XII of the Hopewell Treaty of November 28, 1785 the United States promised the Cherokee Nation:

> That the Indians may have full confidence in the justice of the United States, respecting their interest, they shall have the right to send a deputy of their choice, whenever they think fit, to Congress.

The early dream of the Indian nations to achieve some type of peaceful compromise and enter the United States as an equal was brutally betrayed a generation later when, after winning the Supreme Court case *Worcester v. Geor-*

gia, the President of the United States refused to enforce federal law and allowed the state of Georgia to overrun the Cherokee Nation. But in those days it was not uncommon for commissioners to promise the most enticing things in treaties, knowing full well that the United States would never honor them.

Treaties initially marked off the boundaries between the lands of the Indian nations and the United States. Early treaties allowed the tribes to punish white men violating their laws and borders, but since any attempt by the tribes to exercise this right was used as an incident to provoke war, that right was soon taken away "for the Indians' own protection."

Besides marking boundaries, treaties defined alliances between the United States and tribes in the eighteenth century. England and France were still very much involved in the acquisition of land and power on the continent and it was to the best advantage of the United States to have strong Indian allies to prevent a European invasion of the fledgling United States. Thus Article II of the 1791 Treaty with the Cherokees contained the provision that

> they also stipulate that the said Cherokee Nation will not hold any treaty with any foreign power, individual state, or with individuals of any state.

When Indian people remember how weak and helpless the United States once was, how much it needed the good graces of the tribes for its very existence, how the tribes shepherded the ignorant colonists through drought and blizzard, kept them alive, helped them grow—they burn with resentment at the treatment they have since received from the United States government.

It is as if a man had invited a helpless person to his home, fed and clothed him until he was strong and able to care for himself, only to have the person he had nursed wreak incredible havoc on the entire household. And all this destruction in the name of help. It is too much to bear.

Treaties were originally viewed as contracts. Many treaties contain the phrase "contracting parties" and specify that each party must agree to the terms of the treaty for it to be valid. It would have seemed that, if treaties were contracts, the United States was required under the impairment of contracts or due process clause to protect the rights of the Indian tribes. Or at least it so seemed to the Cherokees, Choctaws, and other tribes who continually went to court to establish their property rights. But, although on one occasion, New Jersey was not allowed to break a contract with a band of the Delawares, the federal government has not traditionally recognized treaties as contracts. So tribes had no recourse in the federal courts although many treaties had provided that tribes should have rights and that the United States would stand behind the treaty provisions as guarantor.

Often when discussing treaty rights with whites, Indians find themselves being told that "We gave you the land and you haven't done anything with it." Or some commentator, opposed to the welfare state remarks, "We gave the Indians a small piece of land and then put them on the dole and they are unable to take care of themselves."

The truth is that practically the only thing the white men ever gave the Indian was disease and poverty. To imply that Indians were given land is to completely reverse the facts of history.

Treaties settled disputes over boundaries and land cessions. Never did the United States give any Indian tribe any land at all. Rather, the Indian tribe gave the United States land in consideration for having Indian title to the remaining land confirmed.

The August 13, 1802 Treaty with the Kaskaskias is one of the clearest examples of this concept. When settlement was made, it was stated in Article I that the Kaskaskias were "reserving to themselves" certain lands. Often the phrase "to live and hunt upon, and otherwise occupy as they shall see fit" was used to indicate the extent of right and lands reserved (Treaty with the Wiandot, Delaware, Ottawa, Pattawatima. and Sac, January 9, 1789). Or a passage might state that "the United States [will] never interrupt the said tribes in the possession of the lands which they rightfully claim, but will on the contrary protect them in the quiet enjoyment of the same. . ." (Treaty with the United Tribes of Sac and Fox, November 3, 1804).

Indian rights to lands reserved by them are clearly stated in the treaties. Article II of the Treaty with the Wiandot, Delaware, Ottawa, Pattawatima, and Sac of January 9, 1789, states that

> (the United States) do by these presents renew and confirm the said boundary line; to the end that the same may remain as a division line between the lands of the United States of America, and the lands of said nations, forever.

And Article III of the same treaty elaborates on the Indian title to lands reserved:

> The United States of America do by these presents relinquish and quit claim to the said nations respectively, all the lands lying between the limits above described, for them the said Indians to live and hunt upon, and otherwise to occupy as they shall see fit.

Similarly Article II of the Treaty with the Weas, October 2, 1818, stated:

> The said Wea tribe of Indians reserve to themselves the following described tract of land . . .

The United States pledged over and over again that it would guarantee to the tribes the peaceful enjoyment of their lands. Initially tribes were allowed to punish whites entering their lands in violation of treaty provisions. Then the Army was given the task of punishing the intruders. Finally the government gave up all pretense of enforcing the treaty provisions. But it was many years before the tribes were shocked into awareness that the United States had silently taken absolute power over their lands and lives.

It was not only a shock, but a breach of common decency when Congress decided that it had absolute power over the once-powerful tribes. When the Supreme Court also decided that such should be the policy in *Lone Wolf v. Hitchcock,* the silent conquest of unsuspecting tribes was complete.

At the turn of the century an agreement was reached with the Kiowa, Comanche, and Apache tribes of Oklahoma in regard to their lands. When an act ratifying the agreement was presented before Congress in the form of a bill, a rider was placed on it which had the effect of providing for the allotment of lands in severalty to the members of the tribes and opening the remainder of their reservation to white settlement.

The law was totally unrelated to the previous agreement with the tribes. When the controversy reached the Supreme Court—in the case of Lone Wolf, a Kiowa leader, versus Hitchcock, then Secretary of the Interior—to enjoin the Interior Department from carrying out the allotment, the Supreme Court ruled against the tribes. It laid down the principle that the tribes had no title to the land at all. Rather the land was held by the United States and the tribes had mere occupancy rights. Therefore the power of Congress to dictate conditions of life and possession on the reservations was limited only by its own sense of justice.

That decision slammed the door on the question of morality and justice. It was like appointing a fox to guard the chicken coop. Under the theory expounded in *Lone Wolf* the Indians had no chance whatsoever to acquire title or rights to lands which had been theirs for centuries. And without the power to acquire rights, they were cut loose from all power to enforce agreements that were generations old.

It had not been much over a century from the time when the United States had begged for its very existence to the time when it had broken every treaty—except the Pickering Treaty—and made the tribes beggars on their ancestral lands. Lands of which the United States had guaranteed to the tribes a free and undisturbed use became pawns in the old game of cowboys and Indians. And everywhere Indians appealed for help there stood a man in chaps with a big black hat.

The subject of tax exemption of Indian lands is often raised. Most Indian tribes feel that they paid taxes for all time when they gave up some two billion acres of land to the United States. This, they claim, paid the bill quite a few centuries in advance. For certainly any bargain of a contract nature would have had to include the exemption of lands reserved and retained by the tribes for their own use or it would have been unreasonable to have assumed that tribes would have signed treaties.

Furthermore, there is a real question about the right of the United States to tax Indians at all. Taxing authority and power are a function of the exercise of sovereignty. The United States never had original sovereignty over the Indian people, merely a right to extinguish the Indian title to land. Where, argue Indian people when questioned, did sovereignty come from?

Certainly the treaties do not support the contentions of the government with respect to sovereignty. The Treaty of the United Sac and the Fox tribe November 3, 1804, is a case in point. Article I states:

> The United States receive the united Sac and Fox tribes into their friendship and protection, and the said tribes agree to consider themselves under the protection of the United States, and of no other power whatsoever.

Here, certainly is not affirmation of sovereignty. At most it is a defense pact to protect the tribes and guarantee peace for the United States.

Early statutes in the colonies exempted Indians from taxation in Massachusetts, Connecticut, and Virginia and some of these still exist today. Each Thanksgiving the Virginia Indians still take a turkey, deer, clams, and other treaty payments to the Governor's mansion to fulfill their part of the treaty. The state of Virginia, at least, has kept its part of the treaty with the Virginia Indians.

Perhaps the clearest expression of exemption from taxation is contained in the Treaty of September 29, 1817, with the Wyandot, Seneca, Delaware, Shawanese, Potawatomees, Ottawas, and Chippeway. This treaty states in Article XV that

> The tracts of land herein granted to the chiefs for the use of the Wyandot, Shawnese, Seneca and Delaware Indians, and the reserve for the Ottawa Indians, shall

not be liable to taxes of any kind so long as such land continues the property of the said Indians.

Succeeding treaties generally provided for lands to be held "as Indian lands are held." From this practice tribes have felt that their lands were tax free and the federal government has upheld the taxation theory of the tribes, although with an added twist. Current federal theory indicates the federal government supports tax exemption on the basis of its trusteeship rather than on the basis of its long-standing treaty promises.

Courts have generally upheld tribal claims to tax exemption. In *The Kansas Indians,* a Supreme Court case of the last century, Kansas was prohibited from taxing the lands of the Shawnees because they still kept their tribal entity intact and maintained their relationship with the federal government.

Such a decision would seem to indicate that tax exemption is a general right of Indian tribes based upon their cessions of land in the last century. Later courts have found reasons for tax exemption all the way from such exotic theories as Indians being a *federal activity* to a vague and generalized purpose of *rehabilitation* of the individual Indian, whose progress would be impeded by taxation.

Because taxation is such a nebulous and misunderstood concept, the general public usually believes that Indians *get away with* millions of dollars of tax-free money. In fact, as has been pointed out many times, the income from taxing the entire Navajo reservation, some sixteen million acres, would be less than the income from taxing a large bank building in downtown Phoenix.

Another primary concern of the Indian people through the years has been the protection of their hunting and fishing rights. In the early days Indians preferred to feed themselves by hunting and fishing, and some tribes refused to move or change reservations until they were assured that there would be plenty of game available to feed their people.

The first few years after the Revolution saw a great movement of settlers westward, and although Indians ceded land, they rarely gave up their hunting rights on the land sold. The Treaty of August 3, 1795, with the Wyan-

dots, Delawares, Shawanoes, Ottawas, Chippewa, Puta-
wantimes, Miamis, Eel-River, Weea's, Kickapoos, Pianka-
shaws, and Kaskaskias states in

Article VII: The said tribes of Indians, parties to this
treaty, shall be at liberty to hunt within the territory
and lands which they have now ceded to the United
States, without hinderance of molestation, so long as
they demean themselves peaceably, and offer no in-
jury to the people of the United States.

Recent conflicts between Indian people and the states of
Idaho, Washington, and Oregon have stemmed from treaty
provisions such as these by which Indian people reserved
for themselves an easement on lands they ceded for hunting and fishing purposes. Today hunting and fishing are an
important source of food of poverty-stricken Indian peoples, but they are merely a sport for white men in the
western Pacific states. Yet the states insist upon harassment of Indian people in continual attempts to take by
force what they promised a century earlier would be reserved for Indians forever.

It is the actions of scattered, yet powerful groups of
white men breaking the treaties that cause nearly all of the
red-white tensions today. Foremost of the whites violating
Indian treaties have been the fish and game departments in
Washington, Oregon, Wisconsin, and Nevada and the
Corps of Army Engineers.

Recently the Supreme Court once again had an Indian
fishing case before it and the decision was so vague and
indecisive that neither Indians nor the state could determine the next course of action.

The fishing controversy can be stated simply. Indians
have reserved the right to hunt and fish off the reservation
because there was not sufficient game on the reservations
to feed their families. In the meantime, powerful sportsmen's clubs of overweight urbanites who go into the
woods to shoot at each other each fall, have sought to
override Indian rights, claiming conservation as their motive.

Meanwhile the general public has sat back, shed tears
over the treatment of Indians a century ago, and be-

moaned the plight of the Indian. In many instances, when the tribes have attempted to bring their case before the public, it has turned a deaf ear, claiming that the treaties are some historical fancy dreamed up by the Indian to justify his irresponsibility.

This despite the fact that during the period before the War of 1812 the United States government hurriedly sent emissaries to the western tribes and tried to force them to choose sides against Great Britain. Again when the life of the small nation was hanging in the balance, the United States was eager to have the support of the Indian tribes.

Article II of the Treaty with the Wyandots, Delawares, Shawanese, Senecas, and Miamies of July 22, 1814, provided that:

> The tribes and bands abovementioned, engage to give their aid to the United States in prosecuting the war against Great Britain, and such of the Indian tribes as still continue hostile; and to make no peace with either without the consent of the United States the assistance herein stipulated for, is to consist of such a number of their warriors from each tribe, as the president of the United States, or any officer having his authority therefore, may require.

Within a generation these same tribes that fought and died for the United States against Great Britain were to be marched to the dusty plains of Oklahoma, dropped in an alien and disease-ridden land, and left to disappear. Hardly had the war been concluded when the first of a series of removal treaties began to force the tribes west across the Mississippi, first to Missouri and Arkansas, then on to Oklahoma. By 1834 the United States had pretty well cleared the eastern states of the former Indian allies.

On reviewing the record of the United States in its Indian treaties, it seems humorous to Indian people to hear the outraged cries against Communist domination and infidelity. Indeed, Czechoslovakia and Hungary got off easier with Russia than did America's allies in the War of 1812. And few Communist satellites have been treated as have the Five Civilized Tribes whose treaty rights were declared in the Supreme Court and yet who were powerless against the perfidy of Andrew Jackson.

Perhaps the greatest betrayal of Indian people was the treatment accorded the Choctaws. Treaty after treaty was signed with the Choctaws, one of the so-called Five Civilized Tribes (because they were so like white men), until the final treaty of Dancing Rabbit Creek forced them across the Mississippi to the parched plains of Oklahoma. The Choctaws stubbornly resisted each encroachment but were finally forced to make the long trek westward.

In an earlier treaty, ten years prior to Dancing Rabbit Creek, the Choctaws had asked for a provision guaranteeing that the United States would never apportion the lands of the tribe, as they preferred to hold their lands in common. So in the Treaty of January 20, 1825, Article VII, the United States provided that "the Congress of the United States shall not exercise the power of apportioning the lands."

Just prior to the admission of Oklahoma as a state, the lands of the Choctaw were allotted, although a minority opinion in the report on the Dawes Allotment Act stated that perhaps the Choctaw method of holding land in common was superior to that of the white man because there was so little poverty among the members of the Five Civilized Tribes.

Today the Choctaws and people of the other "Civilized" Tribes are among the poorest people in America. Their little allotments have been subdivided and grown smaller. As they are sold the people move into friends' and neighbors' allotments, huddling there in absolute destitution.

During the drive to sever federal services in the 1950's the Choctaws were talked into agreeing to terminate the federal responsibilities. Over the last ten years they have waged a continual fight to postpone the time when they must surrender all lands, rights, and services. The condition of the people is so bad that only a massive crash program of development can save the tribe from its poverty. Yet in the ten years since termination was proposed the tribe and its members have even been denied the use of loan funds from the Interior Department which could be used to develop projects that would employ Choctaws.

There has been another side to the machinations of the United States government against the Indian tribes, however, and that was the unilateral action of the Congress.

Paralleling treaty negotiations, throughout history statues were continually passed by Congress to regulate Indian Affairs. Although a treaty would promise one thing, subsequent legislation, designed to expand the treaty provisions, often changed the agreements between tribe and federal government completely.

Continual infringement on treaty rights by statute rarely reached the ears of the tribesmen in time to remedy the situation either by further agreements or appeals to conscience. Some actions were outright thefts of land, such as the wholesale giveaway to railroads for construction purposes. Other detrimental laws were overtly philanthropic and seemed to reflect just dealings between the Congress and the tribes. But in all respects, the beneficial aspects of Congressional actions affecting Indian tribes have been so minute that they are irrelevant.

Congress has passed a number of important pieces of legislation which pertain to the relationships between the United States government and the various Indian tribes. Some of these stand out over the years as landmarks in the ever-changing federal policy.

Even prior to the Constitution, the Northwest Ordinance, passed by the Congress of the Articles of Confederation, outlined a lofty attitude and policy for dealing with Indian people:

> The utmost good faith shall always be observed towards the Indians; their land and property shall never be taken from them without their consent; and in the property, rights, and liberty, they never shall be invaded or disturbed, unless in just and lawful wars authorized by Congress; but laws founded in justice and humanity shall from time to time be made for preventing wrongs being done to them, and for preserving peace and friendship with them

It was just a short time later that the Treaty with the Delawares, discussed above, was signed and the big push westward over the prostrate bodies of slaughtered Indians was begun.

Subsequent policies have generally referred to the policy of humanity and justice initially outlined by the Northwest

Ordinance. Many a land steal has been covered up with the generalities of the Northwest Ordinance.

Certain influential white men knew quite early that the shores of the Great Lakes, particularly Lake Superior, contained immense deposits of copper and other minerals. And there was a desperate need for copper in early America. On April 16, 1800, a Joint Resolution was passed in Congress authorizing the President to determine whether Indian title to copper lands adjacent to Lake Superior was still valid and, if so, the terms on which Indian title could be extinguished.

In the Treaty of August 5, 1826, almost as if it were an afterthought, an article (III) stated:

> The Chippewa tribe grant to the government of the United States the right to search for, and carry away, any metals or minerals from any part of their country. But this grant is not to affect the title of the land, nor the existing jurisdiction over it.

The Chippewas, in the dark as to the importance of their mineral wealth, signed the treaty. This was the first clearcut case of fraudulent dealings on the part of Congress. Certainly no one could have accused the Congress of "utmost good faith."

Close examination of subsequent Congressional dealings shows a record of continued fraud covered over by pious statements of concern for their *wards*.

The basis for Congressional interference into the realm of Indian activities was originally the third clause in section 8 of Article I of the Constitution, which declared that Congress had the "power to regulate Commerce . . . with the Indian tribes. . . ." From this obscure phrase—which if we reread the early Delaware treaty was to provide the Delaware with modern utensils they needed—came the full-blown theory of the incompetency of the Indian, his wardship, and the plenary power of Congress to exercise its whim over Indian people.

The next important statute referring to the Indian people was the Act of March 3, 1819 (3 Stat 679), which was entitled "An act making provision for the civilization of the Indian tribes adjoining the frontier settlements." This act stipulated that:

. . . for the purpose of providing against the further decline and final extinction of the Indian tribes adjoining the frontier settlements of the United States, and for introducing among them the habits and arts of civilization, the President of the United States shall be, and he is hereby authorized, in every case where he shall judge improvement in the habits and condition of such Indians practicable, and that the means of instruction can be introduced with their own consent, to employ capable persons of good moral character, to instruct them in the mode of agriculture suited to their situation . . .

In essence, although the treaties read that the United States would *never disturb* the tribes on the land they had reserved to themselves, Congress determined that it had the right to make Indians conform to their idea of civilization and outlined the great legislative attempt to make them into farmers.

Practically all subsequent legislation has revolved around the Congressional desire to make Indians into white farmers. Most laws passed to administer Indian lands and property have reflected the attitude that, since Indians have not become successful white farmers, it is perfectly correct to take their land away and give it to another who will conform to Congressional wishes.

One of the two most important laws passed in the last century was the Indian Trade and Intercourse Act of June 30, 1834 (4 Stat 729). This act concentrated mainly on the trade aspect of Indian Affairs and was supplemented by a companion act outlining the Bureau of Indian Affairs and its duties. From these two acts came the immense power of the Department of the Interior over the lives and property of the Indian people.

The other important law of the last century was the General Allotment Act, or the Dawes Act, passed in 1887 and amended in 1891, 1906, and 1910 until it included nearly every tribe in the country. The basic idea of the Allotment Act was to make the Indian conform to the social and economic structure of rural America by vesting him with private property.

If, it was thought, the Indian had his own piece of land, he would forsake his tribal ways and become just like the white homesteaders who were then flooding the unsettled areas of the western United States. Implicit in the ideology behind the law was the idea of the basic sameness of humanity. Just leaving tribal society was, to the originators of the law, comparable to achieving an equal status with whites.

But there was more behind the act than the simple desire to help the individual Indian. White settlers had been clamoring for Indian land. The Indian tribes controlled nearly 135 million acres. If, the argument went, that land were divided on a per capita basis of 160 acres per Indian, the Indians would have sufficient land to farm and the *surplus* would be available to white settlement.

So the Allotment Act was passed and the Indians were allowed to sell their land after a period of twenty-five years during which they were to acquire the management skills to handle the land. However, nothing was done to encourage them to acquire these skills and consequently much land was immediately leased to non-Indians who swarmed into the former reservation areas.

By 1934 Indians had lost nearly 90 million acres through land sales, many of them fraudulent. The basic device for holding individual lands was the trust, under which an Indian was declared to be incompetent. Indians were encouraged to ask for their papers of competency, after which land was sold for a song by the untutored Indian who had never heard of buying and selling land by means of a paper.

Many Indians sold their land for a mere fraction of its value. Others received title to their land and lost it through tax sales. In general the policy was to encourage the sale of Indian lands, as it was believed that this process would hasten the integration of Indians into American society.

The churches strongly supported the Dawes Allotment Act as the best means available of Christianizing the tribes. Religion and private property were equated in the eyes of many churchmen. After all, these were the days when J. P. Morgan used to take entire trainloads to the Episcopal conventions and John D. Rockefeller had his Baptist advisor helping him distribute his wealth. Wealth was an index of sainthood.

Bishop William H. Hare, noted missionary bishop of the Episcopal Church, is said to have remarked that the Allotment Act would show whether the world or the church was more alert to its opportunity. In other words, it was to be a race between the stealers of men's land and the stealers of men's souls for two unrelated goals—90 million acres of land and the Christianizing of some of the feathered friends who lived on those lands.

It was, of course, no contest. The church came in a dead last. Indians were not magically turned into white, churchgoing farmers by their little plot of ground. Sharper white men than the missionaries, representing the Christians' traditional opponent, easily won the contest. And the American Indians were the losers. But at least they had the comfort of hearing the missionaries' sermons against greed.

Gone apparently was any concern to fulfill the articles of hundreds of treaties guaranteeing the tribes free and undisturbed use of their remaining lands. Some of the treaties had been assured by the missionaries. The Indians had not, however, been given lifetime guarantees.

Perhaps the only bright spot in all of Indian-Congressional relations came at the beginning of the New Deal. Backed by a sympathetic President and drawn up by scholar John Collier—probably the greatest of all Indian commissioners—the Indian Reorganization Act was passed in 1934.

This act, known popularly as the Wheeler-Howard Act, provided for self-government of the reservations by the Indian residents. Written into the law was a prohibition on further allotment of Indian lands and provisions for land consolidation programs to be undertaken by the tribal councils in order to rebuild an adequate land base.

In many cases the Indian Bureau was authorized to buy land for landless Indians and to organize them as recognized tribal groups eligible for governmental services. Programs for rehabilitation were begun, Indians were given preference in hiring within the Bureau of Indian Affairs, and a revolving loan fund for economic development was created. Overall the IRA was a comprehensive piece of legislation which went far beyond previous efforts to develop tribal initiative and responsibility, but one provision was unfortunate. Once having voted down the acceptance of the provisions of the act, a reservation was forbidden from considering it again.

Unfortunately, Indian tribes were given only a short ten years under this act to bring themselves to an economic and social standard equal with their white neighbors. Following World War II the Congressional policy toward Indian self-government was to change radically. But that story deserves a special chapter in this book.

In looking back at the centuries of broken treaties, it is clear that the United States never intended to keep any of its promises. Like other areas of life, the federal government adapted its policies to the expediency of the moment. When the crisis had passed, it promptly proceeded on its way without a backward glance at its treachery.

Indian people have become extremely wary of promises made by the federal government. The past has shown them that even the most innocent-looking proposal is often fraught with implications the sum total of which is loss of land.

Too often the attitude of the white man was, "Tell the Indians anything to keep them quiet. After they are settled down we can do what we want to do." Alvin Josephy brings this attitude out magnificently in his book *The Nez Perce Indians and the Opening of the Northwest.*

"What," people often ask, "did you expect to happen? After all, the continent had to be settled, didn't it?"

We always reply, "Did it?" And continue, "If it did, did it have to be settled in that way?" For if you consider it, the continent is now settled and yet uninhabitable in many places today.

There were many avenues open for the government besides wholesale theft. In Canada, for example, there are Indian reservations in every province. Indians have not had their basic governmental forms disturbed. They still operate with chiefs and general councils. Nor were they forced to remove themselves whenever and wherever the white man came. Nor did they have their lands allotted and then stolen piece by piece from under them.

It would have been fairly simple for the federal government to have provided a special legal status whereby Indian rights would have vested while keeping their original sovereignty and entitlements of self-government. There was no need for the government to abruptly change from treaty negotiations to a program of cultural destruction, as it did in 1819 with its Indian assimilation bill. And when the Five Civilized Tribes had adapted to a semi-white political structure the government could have supported the great experiment of the Cherokees instead of removing them to Oklahoma.

Even in the closing years of the last century, when the tribes had by and large adapted from hunters to ranchers, the government could have kept its promises and left the tribes alone. There was no reason for it to allot the lands of the Choctaw. The United States had promised never to do so. Yet, in large measure, if there is Indian poverty today—and Indians rank lowest of any group in every conceivable statistic used to measure poverty—it is the fault of the United States government.

The betrayal of treaty promises has in this generation created a greater feeling of unity among Indian people than any other subject. There is not a single tribe that does not burn with resentment over the treatment it has received at the hands of an avowedly *Christian* nation. New incidents involving treaty rights daily remind Indian people that they were betrayed by a government which insists on keeping up the façade of maintaining its commitments in Vietnam.

The complicity of the churches too is just beginning to be recognized. After several hundred years of behind-the-scenes machinations, the attempt of the churches to appear relevant to the social needs of the 1960's is regarded as utter hypocrisy by many Indian people. If, they argue, the churches actually wanted justice, why haven't they said or done anything about Indian rights? Why do they continue to appear in bib-overalls at the Poor People's March? Why do they wait until a problem is nearly solved and then piously proclaim from the pulpits that they have discovered that the movement is really God's will?

Even today Indian rights are stuck in a legalistic limbo from which there is apparently no escape. When a tribe tries to get its rights defined it is politely shunted aside. Some tribes have gone to the Supreme Court to seek relief against the United States by claiming a violation of their rights as wards. They have been told in return that they are not wards but "dependent domestic nations." And when other tribes have sought relief claiming that they are dependent domestic nations, they have been told they are "wards of the government."

Under the laws and courts of the present there is no way for Indian people to get the federal government to admit they have rights. The executive branch of the government crudely uses Indian lands as pawns in the great race to provide pork-barrel agencies with sufficient dam-building projects to keep them busy.

Until America begins to build a moral record in her dealings with the Indian people she should not try to fool the rest of the world about her intentions on other continents. America has always been a militantly imperialistic world power eagerly grasping for economic control over weaker nations.

The Indian wars of the past should rightly be regarded as the first foreign wars of American history. As the United States marched across this continent, it was creating an empire by wars of foreign conquest just as England and France were doing in India and Africa. Certainly the war with Mexico was imperialistic, no more or less than the wars against the Sioux, Apache, Utes, and Yakimas. In every case the goal was identical: land.

When the frontier was declared officially closed in 1890 it was only a short time before American imperialistic impulses drove this country into the Spanish-American War and the acquisition of America's Pacific island empire began. The tendency to continue imperialistic trends remained constant between the two world wars as this nation was involved in numerous banana wars in Central and South America.

There has not been a time since the founding of the republic when the motives of this country were innocent. Is it any wonder that other nations are extremely skeptical about its real motives in the world today?

When one considers American history in its imperialistic light, it becomes apparent that if morality is to be achieved in this country's relations with other nations a return to basic principles is in order. Definite commitments to fulfill extant treaty obligations to Indian tribes would be the first step toward introducing morality into American foreign policy.

Many things can immediately be done to begin to make amends for past transgressions. Passage of federal legislation acknowledging the rights of the Indian people as contained in the treaties can make the hunting and fishing rights of the Indians a reality.

Where land has been wrongfully taken—and there are few places where it has not been wrongfully taken—it can be restored by transferring land now held by the various governmental departments within reservation boundaries to the tribes involved. Additional land in the public domain can be added to smaller reservations, providing a viable land base for those Indian communities needing more land.

Eastern tribes not now receiving federal services can be recognized in a blanket law affirming their rights as existing communities and organized under the Indian Reorganization Act. Services can be made available to these communities on a contract basis and the tribes can be made self-sufficient.

Mythical generalities of what built this country and made it great must now give way to consideration of keeping contractual obligations due to the Indian people. Morality must begin where immorality began. Karl Mundt, in commenting on the passage of the Indian Claims Commission Bill in 1946, stated:

> . . . if any Indian tribe can prove that it has been unfairly and dishonorably dealt with by the United States it is entitled to recover. This ought to be an example for all the world to follow in its treatment of minorities.

The Indian Claims Commission opened a special commission for tribes that had been swindled in land transactions in the last century. But a great many cases have not been heard and a great many others which have been heard produced exceedingly harsh decisions against the tribes. In addition, eastern tribes were not allowed to press claims at all. And since the termination policy has been in effect, additional moral claims of tribes who were severely hurt by that policy have arisen.

The Indian Claims Commission is, or should be, merely the first step in a general policy of restitution for past betrayals. Present policy objectives should be oriented toward restitution of Indian communities with rights they enjoyed for centuries before the coming of the white man.

The world is indeed watching the behavior of the United States. Vietnam is merely a symptom of the basic lack of integrity of the government, a side issue in comparison with the great domestic issues which must be faced—and justly faced—before this society destroys itself.

Cultural and economic imperialism must be relinquished. A new sense of moral values must be inculcated into the American blood stream. American society and the policies of government must realistically face the moral problems created by the roughshod treatment of various segments of that society. The poverty program only begins to speak of this necessity, the Employment Act of 1946 only hinted in this direction. It is now time to jump fully into the problem and solve it once and for all.

3 ❖ THE DISASTROUS POLICY OF TERMINATION

PEOPLE OFTEN FEEL guilty about their ancestors killing all those Indians years ago. But they shouldn't feel guilty about the distant past. Just the last two decades have seen a more devious but hardly less successful war waged against Indian communities. In the old days blankets infected with smallpox were given to the tribes in an effort to decimate them. In the past they were systematically hunted down and destroyed. Were an individual citizen to do this it would be classified as cold-blooded murder. When it was done by the U.S. Army it was an "Indian war." But during the past twenty years federal medical services have been denied various tribes, resulting in tremendous increase in disease.

The Congressional policy of termination, advanced in 1954 and pushed vigorously for nearly a decade, was a combination of the old systematic hunt and the deprivation of services. Yet this policy was not conceived as a policy of murder. Rather it was thought that it would provide that elusive "answer" to the Indian problem. And when it proved to be no answer at all, Congress continued its policy, having found a new weapon in the ancient battle for Indian land.

The roots of termination extend backward in time to the early years of the Roosevelt administration. The New Deal ushered in a new program for the Indian people. The Meriam Report of 1928 had shown that Indian tribes were in a desperate situation. There had been no progress of any kind on the reservations since they were set up. The people were in the final stages of demise.

Pressures for reform coincided with the election of Roosevelt, who appointed John Collier as Commissioner of Indian Affairs. Collier was a well-known anthropologist of liberal persuasion. He quickly pushed the Wheeler-Howard Act through Congress in 1934 and gave the reservations their first taste of self-government in nearly half a century.

The Senate Interior Committee that handled Indian legislation kept alive its investigative powers over Indian Affairs by periodically renewing the original Congressional resolution which authorized it to initiate the Meriam Report investigation. The committee intended to ride herd on the programs of the New Deal lest any "foreign" influences should develop. It could not conceive of returning self-government to a people who should have disappeared long ago.

By 1943 the Senate Interior Committee was convinced that the Indian Bureau should be abolished. But the sentiment did not take hold in any discernible policy determinations because of the war.

The House Interior Committee, not to be outdone by its colleagues in the other chamber, authorized an investigation of Indian Affairs by a special subcommittee headed by Karl Mundt, Republican of South Dakota. The committee reported that the Wheeler-Howard Act was not accomplishing its task of bringing the Indian people up to the level of their white neighbors.

In 1947 the Senate Civil Service Committee held hearings on ways that government payrolls could be cut and expenditures reduced. The Republicans had captured Congress that autumn and they were looking for defenseless New Deal programs to trim. They found a natural in the Bureau of Indian Affairs.

William Zimmerman, Acting Commissioner of Indian Affairs, was asked to give testimony on the possibility of reducing personnel in the bureau by releasing some of the tribes from federal supervision. The committee was primarily interested in a consolidation of functions and the subsequent savings of federal funds.

Zimmerman was anxious to remain a neutral party and so presented the committee with a series of recommendations, none of which would have resulted in substantial savings.

He classified the existing tribes into three categories. The first class was composed of tribes that could immediately be terminated from federal services, providing certain protections were given them. The second class consisted of tribes that might possibly achieve self-sufficiency within ten years following an intensified program of development. The last class had an indefinite time period in which federal services were needed.

In view of the three categories it is clear that Zimmerman had assumed the tribes would make substantial progress under already existing programs and take on increasing responsibilities for those programs. He also assumed that Congress would adopt a rational and understanding approach to the subject.

So Zimmerman laid out the criteria by which he had classified the tribes:

. . . in making up these three groups of tribes, I took four factors into account.

The first one is the degree of acculturation of the particular tribe. That includes such factors as the admixture of white blood, the percentage of illiteracy, the business ability of the tribe, their acceptance of white institutions and their acceptance by whites in the community.

The second factor is the economic condition of the tribe, principally the availability of resources to enable either the tribe or the individuals, out of their tribal or individual assets, to make a reasonably decent living.

The third factor is the willingness of the tribe and its members to dispense with federal aid.

The last criterion is the willingness and ability of the State in which the tribe is located to assume the responsibilities.

There was no doubt that Zimmerman regarded Indian consent and understanding among the important factors to be considered in any alteration of the existing relationship. But there was also an emphasis on the willingness of the state to assume responsibility for the tribe and its members.

Zimmerman had prepared sample withdrawal plans, which he shared with the committee members:

> I have prepared separate bills for the Klamath, Osage and Menominee tribes.
>
> I took those as examples, as specimens, because each of them has substantial assets, each of them has a small degree of tribal control, and each of them has indicated that it wants to assume more control, if not full control, of its tribal assets and its tribal operations.
>
> Each of those tribes further has prior legislation under which the Department supervises the operations. For that reason it seems to me best to suggest, *as types at least*, these three different tribes. [emphasis added]

The Acting Commissioner suggested three special plans by which the bureau might consider it possible to end federal supervision and enable the tribe to have some chance of success. For the Klamath, a rich timber tribe located near Crater Lake, Oregon, it was envisioned that all funds would remain subject to Congressional appropriation so that the tribal council would not be subjected to undue pressure for distribution by the reservation people.

A corporation to operate the massive Klamath forest by sustained-yield methods would be organized by the tribe. Officials would be subject to federal laws and courts for acts of malfeasance, to guarantee proper administration of the corporation. Because of treaty rights of tax exemption the forest would remain untaxable until Contress provided otherwise in consultation with the tribe.

The plan advanced for the Menominee tribe of Wisconin was similar. Earlier it had been awarded $1.5 million in a claim against the United States and took its judgment in land, consolidating its reservation into one large tract. The Menominees had previously successfully resisted the Allotment Act and issued use rights to members of the tribe instead of allotments. In that sense only were they different from the Klamaths, who had an allotted reservation.

The Menominees had a sawmill with a dual purpose—to provide jobs for tribal members and income for the tribe. Zimmerman foresaw a fifty-year period of tax exemption on the Menominee forest as the most feasible proposal.

The Osages had already distributed shares of their tribal estate in "headrights," allotted the land, and retained the subsurface mineral rights, which provided oil royalties to holders of headrights. The sample bill for the Osage provided that all funds administered by the Interior Department would henceforth be administered by the tribe, subject to audit at any time by Interior officials.

Proposals were also made that California and North Dakota take over the affairs of the tribes within their boundaries. The federal government would provide a subsidy to the states equal to what it had been spending on the Indians in the two states, to ensure that no programs be cut back. After a ten-year trial period the arrangement would be made permanent, unless Congress made other provisions. Part of the California proposal included the requirement that the state match a five-million-dollar development program for Indian families.

Every plan put forward by Zimmerman required that the tax immunity remain in Indian lands until the tribal enterprise was financially secure in its new method of operation. Plans also included provisions for approval by a clear majority of the adult members of the tribes before they were to go into effect, and some proposals were not to be initiated by the bureau but had to come from the tribal governing body at its own request.

The suggestions were basically sound. They incorporated plans that had been discussed in the past between the bureau and the tribes. If carried out according to the original design, the program would have created a maximum of self-government and a minimum of risk until the tribes had confidence and experience in the program.

Unfortunately, the committee dropped Zimmerman's suggestions when it was discovered that the termination of even fifty thousand Indians would have had little effect on the Interior budget. Using the criteria of the committee— the reduction of federal expenditures—termination of Indian tribes was not a significant program. But discussion of the proposal provided the ammunition that would later be used to sink tribal ships of state.

Three years after the Senate hearings the House Interior Committee began a massive study of Indian Affairs. Unbeliveably, it recommended using the philosophy of René Descartes, French rationalist of the 1600's, as a method of research:

As a multitude of laws often only hampers justice, so that a State is best governed when, with few laws, these are rigidly administered; in like manner, instead of the great number of precepts of which Logic is composed, I believed that the four following would prove perfectly sufficient for me, providing I took the firm and unwavering resolution never in a single instance to fail in observing them.

The first was never to accept anything for true which I did not clearly know to be such; that is to say, carefully to avoid precipitancy and prejudice, and to comprise nothing more in my judgment than what was presented to my mind so clearly and distinctly as to exclude all ground of doubt.

The second, to divide each of the difficulties under examination into as many parts as possible, and as might be necessary for its adequate solution.

The third, to conduct my thoughts in such order that, by commencing with objects the simplest and easiest to know, I might ascend little by little, and as it were step by step, to the knowledge of the more complex; assigning in thought a certain order even to those objects which in their own nature do not stand in relation of antecedence and sequence.

And last, in every case to make enumerations so complete, and reviews so general, that it might be assured that nothing was omitted.

In sum, the committee declared: "If we can order our treatment of materials in Indian Affairs after this fashion it should be possible to grasp firmly the essentials or the problems involved and to cope with them correspondingly well."

This insight was not the least of the committee's recommendations, however, as committee members fancied themselves to be powers of great historical importance. Thus they further proposed to use the Domesday survey of 1086 as the model for a twentieth-century investigation of Indian problems:

This extensive report on an entire nation should serve as a model for the administration of Indian Affairs today. There is a need for an exact, highly localized and thorough accounting of all Indian properties and Indian tribes as a complete allotment and dissolution of separate Indian tribal economic and political organization is contemplated. A survey along the lines of the Domesday project would furnish an inventory of all the basic facts needed to complete Indian assimilation. The Congress and Federal Government exercise the function of sovereignty over the Indians in the same manner as that by the King of England over his domains. The title to Indian lands and federal public domain lands would be clearly and precisely stated for every locality. Present day information on Indian property and population is generally piecemeal, confused, and probably unreliable. There is a real need for a Domesday Survey of Indian Affairs.

Little did the general public or the Indian tribes realize the bizarre theories underlying Congressional thinking on termination.

If any other group had been subjected to research techniques of the era of William the Conqueror the nation would have risen in indignation and called for an investigation. But in the whimsical world of the Interior committees, Indians were such an unknown commodity that the ridiculous made sense, the absurd was normal.

With this contemptuous announcement of royal power of Congressional committees, the stage was set for the disastrous era of the Eighty-third and ensuing congresses and the termination period in Indian Affairs.

The way had been prepared for this era by the attitude of Dillon Myer, a Truman appointee as Commissioner of Indian Affairs, who started the bureau on the termination trail when he had assumed office in 1950. Myer had been in charge of the Japanese internment camps during World War II and "knew" how to deal with minority rights.

He embarked on a withdrawal program in August of 1952, before Congress had even authorized its great Domesday study. "At this point," Myer wrote to his bureau employees, "I want to emphasize that withdrawal program formulation and effectuation is to be a cooperative effort of Indian and community groups affected, side by side, with Bureau personnel. We must lend every encouragement to Indian initiative and leadership. I realize that it will not be possible always to obtain Indian cooperation."

"Full understanding," Myer went on, "by the tribal membership should be attained in any event, and agreement with affected Indian groups must be attained if possible. In the absence of such agreement, however, I want our differences to be clearly defined and understood by both the Indians and ourselves. We must proceed, even though Indian cooperation may be lacking in certain cases."

The policy from Commissioner to field clerk was to get rid of Indians as quickly as possible, treaties or no. When the termination hearings were later held, the bureau had much to say. It gave every possible excuse to get rid of the particular tribe which was under consideration by the committee.

The Republicans entered the White House in the 1952 election and assumed control of Congress for the second time in two decades. Two conservatives were named to head the Indian subcommittees in the Senate and House: Arthur Watkins, a Mormon from Utah, headed the Indian Subcommittee of the Senate Interior committee and E. Y. Berry from South Dakota headed the House counterpart. Both Watkins and Berry were determined to bring Indian

Affairs to a swift conclusion. They had sat too long as junior members of the subcommittees not to relish the opportunity which now presented itself. They wanted to take the helm and make policy. Together they decided to hold joint hearings on all Indian bills so that there would be no conflicts between the Senate and House versions of legislation. A decision by the Joint Subcommittee could pass both houses of Congress simultaneously, and opposition as well as public awareness could be held to a minimum.

On June 9, 1953, the first shot of the great twentieth century Indian war was fired when Representative William Henry Harrison, a descendant of an old Indian fighter of the last century, introduced House Concurrent Resolution 108 in the Eighty-third Congress. HCR 108 declared the intention of Congress to terminate federal supervision at the "earliest possible time." Green light for Watkins and Berry. They waited only until the following February before launching their attack. And supervision, as it turned out, meant services only.

February, 1954, saw the beginning of a systematic attack on every tribe in the nation. Gone were the four factors which Zimmerman had used in 1947 to classify tribal readiness for termination. Watkins' idea was to get rid of as many tribes as possible before the 1956 elections. He feared that if the Great Gollfer were not re-elected the movement would be stopped by a President who might pay attention to what was happening in the world around him.

The first termination case—concerning small bands of Paiutes in Utah—set the precedent for the Senate Interior Committee, from Arthur Watkins, conservative Republican from Utah in 1954, to Henry Jackson, pseudo-liberal Democrat from Washington in 1968. The basic approach of the Senate committee never varied for fourteen years. Unbearable pressures, lies, promises, and threats of termination were made whenever a tribe won funds from the United States because of past swindles by the federal government. Whenever a tribe needed special legislation to develop its resources, termination was often the price asked for the attention of the committee. And if a tribe compromised with the Senate Committee it was on the road to termination. Quarter was asked but none given.

In this first case, Watkins made sure that some of his Utah Indians were the first to go in order to prove he was not picking on Indians of other states. It did not matter that the Paiutes had not been mentioned either by Zimmerman or in HCR 108. Watkins was determined to demonstrate fairness, as if once he had irrationally harmed Indians from his own state he would be free to do whatever he wanted with all those elsewhere.

He forced consent, if it can be called that, of these small bands of southern Utah by promising them recognition by the federal government of their tribal marriages. But when the legislation came out there was no mention of tribal marriages, only of removal of federal services. The Paiutes had been too poor to come to Washington for the hearings, and when the found out what Watkins had done it was too late. They were placed under a private trustee who rarely communicated with them, and in a more restrictive trusteeship than they had known when under federal supervision. Thus did Watkins "free" his Indians.

In another case, the Klamaths had received a judgment against the United States for $2.6 million. But they needed enabling legislation to spend it. Watkins withheld approval of the Joint Subcommittee until the Klamaths agreed to his termination bill. The state of Oregon was hardly consulted at all. Thus two basic factors of the four presented by Zimmerman for ending federal supervision were lacking from the very beginning. Termination of the Klamaths had neither tribal nor state willingness.

The Klamath bill had been so hastily written that it had to be amended to prevent a wholesale collapse of the lumber industry on the West Coast. Since it had originally called for immediate clear-cutting of eighty-million-dollars' worth of timber, the market appeared headed for total disaster because of the great quantity of wood that would suddenly depress the market. Strangely, there was no conspiracy to cheat the Klamaths, the legislation was simply so sloppily written that no one on the Senate or House committee realized what clear-cutting a massive forest meant. The committee members' only desire was to get the termination of the tribe over with as quickly as possible. If that meant cutting every tree in Oregon, they would have so authorized, simply to get on to another tribe.

In another example, the Kansas Potawatomi tribe was considered to be in such a low economic status that to assist it was felt to be too expensive. Better, the bureau said, to let the Potawatomis expire as private citizens than to have anyone find out how badly the federal government had shirked its responsibilities. Somehow they escaped the blow, although bureau assistance to them since 1954 has been nil.

In yet another example, the Alabama-Coushattas had a small reservation in Texas. They had been spared during the Texas Ranger sweep a century earlier because they had hidden Sam Houston when the Mexican government was after him during Texas' war with Mexico.

The bureau, meeting with the tribal council, told them the termination bill was concerned with forest management. They stated that any more cutting of timber on tribal lands would not be allowed unless the tribe agreed to the proposal. The tribe agreed, the law was quickly passed with little consultation with the state of Texas, and the tribe was placed under state trusteeship. There is still a question whether or not the constitution of Texas was violated.

Frantically the Joint Subcommittee searched for vulnerable and unsuspecting tribes for their termination program. Poor tribes with no means to come to Washington and protest against proposals were in greatest danger. Absolute terror spread though Indian country as the power of the committee was arbitrarily used against the helpless Indian communities.

The Flatheads of Montana were saved only by the direct intervention of Mike Mansfield, who reminded the committee of the treaty rights of the tribe. The Florida Seminoles, 80 percent illiterate, were saved only through the intervention of the DAR's of that state.

Total relocation of the seven thousand Mountain Chippewas of North Dakota was considered. Watkins' plan was simply to relocate the Indians in a large city and forget about them. But the plan was blocked when North Dakota, in a fit of Christian charity, refused to provide any services whatsoever for the Chippewas should they be terminated.

The tragedy of the Menominee tribe of Wisconsin illustrates the extent of termination's failure. The tribe was one of the few paying for all its own services. The sum of $520,714.00 was budgeted by the tribe for the reservation the year before termination. The tribe invested $285,000 in construction projects, $56,745.00 for education, $47,021 for welfare, and $130,000 for health. It set aside $42,615 for law and order activities. The federal government, which was obligated to provide all of these services, actually spent only $95,000 for roads and $49,000 for education, on a matching basis with the state and tribe. The total federal cost per year for the Menominees was $144,000 or $50.85 per Indian. There was, consequently, not much to be saved by terminating them.

But they had won a $8.5 million judgment against the United States in the Court of Claims and needed legislation to distribute it. In 1908 federal legislation was passed which had given the Forest Service responsibility for administering the Menominee resources on a sustained-yield basis. In violation of this law, local government foresters had decided to clear-cut the forest, and the income which should have come to the Menominees through the years on a sustained-yield basis was deprived them. Finally, in 1951 they had won their judgment against the United States, and the money was deposited to the tribe's account in the U.S. Treasury.

The Joint Subcommittee, particularly in the person of Watkins, was outraged that the tribe had been vindicated. They were determined to silence the Menominees once and for all. When a bill passed the House Interior Committee, which authorized the distribution of the judgment money, Watkins attached a provision to the bill in the Senate, requiring the tribe to submit to termination in order to get the money. The Menominees objected to the provision and Watkins held the bill until the end of the year.

There are varying reports on the sequence of developments after that. In 1960, when the Menominees went to Congress to get an extension on the date set for final termination of federal responsibilities, Senator Frank Church, then chairman of the Indian Subcommittee of the Senate, inquired of Mr. Lee of the Bureau of Indian Affairs just how the Menominee termination had come about. The record, as of 1960, is enlightening:

SENATOR CHURCH: Mr. Lee [from Interior] will you take me back a few years and tell me how this business got started? It is my understanding that originally the Menominee Tribe recovered a judgment against the Government which required legislation to distribute to the members of that tribe.

MR. LEE: That is correct.

SENATOR CHURCH: Legislation was proposed to effect a per capita distribution of this judgment fund.

MR. LEE: That is correct, $1,500.

SENATOR CHURCH: When it came to the Senate, the Senate amended the bill to provide that termination should take place in conjunction with the distribution of this money.

MR. LEE: That is correct. It was an interim step. In the meantime, Congress passed Senate Joint Resolution 108, which provided for the termination of certain tribes. I believe there were 10 tribes. Specifically——

SENATOR CHURCH: Was the Menominee Tribe one of the 10 tribes?

MR. LEE: The Menominee Tribe was one of the tribes. As you have indicated, when H.R. 2828 was introduced in the 83rd Congress, it was passed by the House as a separate per capita bill of $1,500 per individual.

The Senate amended it and tacked termination on it and sent it back to the House. There were a number of conferences on it and finally, they worked out a compromise. This gets into the second question as to whether or not there was approval by the Indians.

SENATOR CHURCH: That is my second question. Did the Menominee Tribe, after this legislation was passed, then approve of termination by referendum of any kind?

MR. LEE: No, sir. As I recall, there was no referendum. The tribal delegates can correct me on this. They had a group that was negotiating with the conferees here in Washington and they stood up in the committees and agreed to this termination, I think, on the basis that the termination was coming regardless because of the resolution requiring termination.

SENATOR CHURCH: For this particular tribe?

MR. LEE: For this particular tribe.

SENATOR CHURCH: The question of termination was never taken to the Indians and put to a vote?

MR. LEE: As near as I know, there was never a general vote on termination in the tribe. Am I correct in that?

MR. WILKINSON: I can add one clarifying point to that. The chairman of the Indian Subcommittee of the Senate went to the reservation and met with the general council.

SENATOR ANDERSON: Senator Watkins.

MR. WILKINSON: That is right. There were approximately 150 people present. They voted that day to accept termination. There is one item which I thinks bears on it, which I think influenced the tribe to vote that way.

They were told that they could not have a per capita payment unless they accepted termination. Based on that, I felt they accepted it.

SENATOR ANDERSON: Senator Wakins did go there, he did present the matter, he did discuss it, he came back and reported to us that the tribe was enthusiastic for termination.

Of course, the answer was they were enthusiastic for the $1,500.

Senator Watkins had indeed gone to the Menominees and threatened the Indians. Recalling his visit, Watkins stated:

It was a very interesting experience. I appreciated your help in introducing me to those people and giving me the opportunity to see how they lived, how they felt about it. That was one of the most interesting experiences of the whole trip.

MR. WAUPOCHICK (a Menominee): We wish you could have stayed longer.

SENATOR WATKINS: I had the same experience visiting Europe, *the refugee camps of the Near East.* (emphasis added)

The Menominees had been so poor in comparison to other Americans that the only experience Watkins could relate his reservation visit with was his visit to refugee camps of the Near East after World War II.

The initial plan was for the Menominee forest to be turned over to the tribe for management. This plan was predicated on the fact that the Menominee tribe had over ten million dollars in the federal treasury. But the Menominees had to agree to termination in order to get a per capita distribution of that money authorized. Therefore the termination plan was based upon money that no longer existed.

Wisconsin strongly opposed the Menominees' termination. It was worried about the eventual effect of the plan on the community and the state. Mr. Harder, an official representing the Wisconsin Tax Commission, expressed the attitude of the state most concisely:

> . . . I am concerned about that; because if they have to go to heavy taxation of their timberlands, that means they will have to cut on some other basis than their present sustained-yield method. And as soon as that happens, the forests will eventually deplete, and we may have a substantial welfare problem. That is a problem the State of Wisconsin now has with the Indians in the Bad River Reservation, where the lands were allotted, and the Indians sold their lands, and now they are on relief, in prosperous times as well as poor times. It is a continuing problem. And the State doesn't want anything like that to happen in this instance.

But Watkins, ideologically bound to traditional Republican myths, insisted that the state was more efficient than the federal government per se:

> Of course it is admitted the Federal Government moves slower than anybody else. The State government would be far more efficient. That is one reason we think federal supervision should be terminated, one among many reasons, because we can't move as fast as we should.

The tribal attorney, Mr. Wilkinson, appealed to the record of the Senate Civil Service Committee in which the original Zimmerman testimony was presented. Watkins callously informed him:

> If you want to comment on what he said, all right, but as far as I am personally concerned, and I think the rest of the committee, it is not going to make a lot of difference one way or another, except indicating that that far back this matter was discussed. So that there won't be any implication that certain parts of it haven't been brought up, I think that all of it should be included in this report and that will be the Chair's ruling.

So a reference to the Zimmerman recommendations which included the fifty-year tax exemption for the forest proved fruitless by the defenseless Menominees.

Their last argument was voiced by Antoine Waupochick, Chairman of the Menominee Advisory Council:

> History records that the Menominees have been loyal to this Government and have stood by their bargains when they have relinquished land to the United States. We think that your action should be governed by a desire to see that history will record that Congress was loyal to the Menominee people.

There was, however, no appeal for the tribe, either to historic commitments made by the federal government or to common sense of the present. Even after liberal Democrats took over the subcommittee after the 1958 sweep and firmly controlled the Senate in 1960, the attitude remained the same—dogmatic and idealistic:

> MR. GRIGNON [a Menominee]: . . . I believe if we are to terminate December 31, (the tribe was seeking an extension) with our economy so low where we cannot afford this county which is the cheapest for us to take, we will go until our money runs out. It is a question of what reserve we have in the fund.
>
> SENATOR CHURCH: I think what Senator Anderson said was pretty wise. He suggested if you went on your own initiative, responsibility and resources, you might find a little resurgency of energy in the operation of the mill and things of that nature that might carry you along. It is the constant spoon

feeding from the Federal Government that has held you back, is it not? You were getting ready for termination in 1954. Some tribes have terminated, you know, and they are getting along pretty well. But not the Menominees.

MR. GRIGNON: I believe one thing, Senator. If we were still making the kind of money as in 1958, I believe we certainly could terminate December 31, and be successful. If the economy was up, there would be no question in my mind.

Instead of providing assistance or admitting that a horrendous mistake had been made years ago, Frank Church admonished the Menominees to be more energetic.

But even Church, boy liberal from Idaho, had his moments of lucidity:

This is the thing that disturbs me. We have come to the nub of this morning. All of the reasons that are put forth in support of extending the termination date make it plain that a 6 month extension is patently insufficient. This is evident on the face of the statement you have made. You support the extension because you say you have a marginal economy. You are going to have a marginal economy at the end of 6 months because to make it any other kind of economy is going to be an effort that will extend over many years.

The first War on Poverty by the Democrats was conducted in 1960 against a defenseless Indian tribe that asked only for justice. These same Senators who cold-bloodedly created a pocket of poverty in Wisconsin would later vote for the War on Poverty with good conscience.

With termination came the closing of the Menominee hospital. The tribe was unable, with the additional burden of taxation, to keep up its health program. Deprived of medical services and with poor housing, the infant death rate continued to rise. By July 1964, 14 percent of the county, which was the former reservation area, was receiving welfare payments. The State Department of Public Welfare estimated that Menominee county needed a transfusion of ten to twenty million dollars to bring it up to par with other Wisconsin counties.

How much did the Menominee termination save the federal government? By 1960 the costs simply to plan for termination had become tremendous:

> MR. LEE: First, about how much money has been appropriated; there has been $500,000 appropriated to reimburse the tribe for their termination expenses. We have spent, including the reimbursement termination expenses $700,000 for special road construction, $644,000 I mentioned on special adult education program. We have already reimbursed $195,500 to the tribe for their termination expenses. We anticipate between now and the termination, if the termination does not drag on, another $161,000. HEW, as I understand it, has committed $510,000 for school construction. We have spent $136,000 in addition to agency expenses which were previously carried by the tribe. We are in the process of completing a survey for about $35,000. We have just made another assignment of a Bureau staff member mentioned this morning, of $6,000. This will bring a total we anticipate of $2,357,039 by December 31 (1960).

In addition to the $2,357,039, however, in 1961 the federal government had to give the Menominees $1,098,000 over a period of five years, to cover education and health subsidies for problems caused by termination. In 1966, because the county was rapidly going downhill, another law was passed giving the tribe another $1.5 million over a three-year period. By 1964 the state of Wisconsin had granted the tribe some $52,363 in special contributions to welfare costs. But by then the situation was so desperate that the state was forced to make a special grant of $1 million to individuals in the county to keep their shares in the Menominee Enterprises from going out of Menominee hands and disenfranchising the tribe from its forest.

Clearly, with some $5 million of special federal aid, over $1 million in state aid, and a rapidly sinking economy combined with increasing health and education problems and a skyrocketing tuberculosis rate, termination has not been a success for the Menominees. It has been a rationally planned and officially blessed disaster of the United States Congress.

Whenever a tribe has been terminated all federal assistance stops. The number of Indian people who have died because health services were unavailable is difficult to define, but must certainly run into a significant number.

With the advent of the War on Poverty the push for termination has slowed, but certainly not stopped. Chief advocate of termination is James Gamble, staff member of the Senate Interior Committee, which is the parent committee of the Indian Subcommittee. Gamble has remained in the background while Henry Jackson, Chairman of the committee, has had to accept public responsibility for Gamble's moves against the tribes.

Rarely does a judgment bill come before the committee but what Gamble tries to have a termination rider attached. So powerful is Gamble that Jackson might be characterized as his front man. But Jackson is busy with his work on the Foreign Relations and other important committees and so he accepts Gamble's recommendations without much consideration of alternatives.

The chief termination problem in recent years has been that of the Colville tribe of Eastern Washington, Jackson's home state. In the closing years of the 1950's the Colvilles received some land back. This land had been part of the reservation and was opened for homestead. However, when some of it remained unused, the tribe asked for its return. Termination was the price the Colvilles were asked to pay for their own land.

Analysis of the Colville termination bill as it is now proposed reveals Gamble's method of operation. The bill provides that the act will become effective after a referendum of the adult members of the tribe. No provision is included to require that a majority of the enrolled adult members vote in the referendum. Thus a majority of fifty voters out of the five thousand plus tribal members would be sufficient to terminate the tribe. Zimmerman's original proposal, which incidentally contained no reference to the Colvilles, provided for a majority of the enrolled adults to *initiate* any movement toward termination of supervision. The bill is comparable to a corporation being required to liquidate on the vote of those present at a stockholders' meeting, with no majority of stock being sufficient to carry the motion.

After the referendum is taken, the members will find out what they voted for. The reservation will then be appraised by three independent professionals and the three figures averaged. The average value is the price the United States will pay the tribe for its reservation. Any other group of American citizens would not dream of selling their property without knowing what the price was. Yet, since Congress is presumed to act with good faith toward the Indian people, this bill is considered to be sufficient justice for them. Can you imagine Henry Jackson, sponsor of the bill, walking into the offices of white businessmen in Everett, Washington, and asking them to sell him their property, with values to be determined six months after the sale? Jackson expects, and intends to write into law, a provision for Indians to do exactly this.

Section 15 of the bill is a typical Gamble gambit. There is a provision that while the money is being distributed, the Secretary of the Interior can determine whether any member of the tribe is incompetent and appoint a guardian for him. Incompetency is never mentioned as a requirement for voting in the first part of the bill. But hidden in the middle is a provision giving the Secretary of the Interior unlimited discretionary power over Indian people. Theoretically the Secretary could declare all of the Colvilles incompetent and place them under a private trustee. They would then be judged too incompetent to handle their own money, but competent enough to vote to sell their reservation. Is it any wonder that Indians distrust white men?

The major tribes of the nation have waged a furious battle against the Colville termination bill. Fortunately the House Interior Committee has been sympathetic to Indian pleas and has to date not passed the bill. Another mood, however, can come over the House committee and sentiment may turn toward termination. This uncertainty creates fear and resentment among Indian people.

Under consideration at the present time is another termination bill. In 1964 the Seneca Nation of New York finally received its compensation for the land taken for the Kinzua Dam. Kinzua, as you will recall, was built by breaking the Pickering Treaty of 1794, which had pledged that the Senecas would remain undisturbed in the use of their land.

But before the Senecas could get the Senate Interior Committee to approve their judgment bill they had to agree to section 18, a termination rider, which required the Senecas to develop a plan for termination within three years. The Senate was determined to punish the tribe for having the temerity to ask for compensation for land which the United States had illegally taken.

If termination means the withdrawal of federal services in order to cut government expenditures, then the Seneca termination requirement is only ironic. The only federal assistance the Senecas received in recent years was a staff man assigned by the Bureau of Indian Affairs to assist them in problems caused the tribe by the building of Kinzua Dam.

The Seneca bill proposes to capitalize annuities payable to the Senecas under a number of treaties and pay the tribe outright. Annuities amount to very little, but the Senecas regard them as highly symbolic, as they represent the historic commitments of the tribe and the United States. They have more of a religious and historical significance than they do monetary value.

Section 9 of the bill provides that the act shall not become effective until a resolution consenting to its provisions has been approved by a majority of the eligible voters of the Seneca Nation voting in a referendum. Why the difference between the Seneca bill and the Colville bill as to voting requirements? Gamble and Jackson are responsible for the Colville bill. The Bureau of Indian Affairs drafted the Seneca bill.

Termination is the single most important problem of the American Indian people at the present time. Since 1954 the National Congress of American Indians and most inter-tribal councils of the various states have petitioned the Senate committee and the Congress every year for a change in policy. There has been no change.

Sympathetic Senators and Congressmen have introduced new policy resolutions to take the place of the old HCR 108—which, Gamble insists, is Congressional policy though such resolutions usually die at the end of each

Congress. Rarely do these new policy statements receive more than perfunctory attention. None are ever passed.

Indian people receive little if any help from their friends. Churches have been notably unsympathetic, preferring to work with the blacks, where they are assured of proper publicity. The attitude of the churches is not new. My father was fired from his post with the Episcopal Church for trying to get the church involved with the termination issue in the 1950's. Had the churches supported the Indian people in 1954, we could be tempted to believe their sincerity about Civil Rights today. But when the going is rough, churches disappear from sight, Judas, not Peter, characterizes the Apostolic succession.

The response from the American public had been gratifying at times, disappointing at other times. Public support for the Senecas was widespread but the land was still taken and a termination rider added. Interest on the Colville termination has not been great because the problem of fishing rights in the same area has received all of the publicity. In general, the public does not understand the issue of termination, and public statements of termination-minded Senators make it appear to be the proper course of action.

Too often termination has been heavily disguised as a plan to offer the Indian people full citizenship rights. Thus the Washington State legislature has been continually and deliberately misled by a few urban and termination-minded Colvilles into passing a resolution asking for the extinguishment of the Colville tribal entity and the vesting of the Colville people with "full citizenship" rights.

In fact, the Citizenship Act of 1924 gave all Indians full citizenship without affecting any of their rights as Indian people. So the argument of second-class citizenship as a justification of termination is spurious from start to finish.

In practice, termination is used as a weapon against the Indian people in a modern war of conquest. Neither the Senecas nor the Colvilles were listed in the original discussion of termination by Acting Commissioner Zimmerman in 1947. Nor were these tribes listed in House Concurrent Resolution 108, which outlined termination and mentioned tribes eligible for immediate consideration.

Both tribes have had to submit to termination provisions in legislation which had nothing to do with the termination policy as originally defined by Congress. The Senecas and the Colvilles got caught in the backlash of Congressional ire at the Bureau of Indian Affairs. The Senecas had money coming to them because of the gross violation of their rights under treaty. The Colvilles wanted land returned which was theirs and which had been unjustly taken years before.

In the case of the Colvilles the record is doubly ironic. The tribe rejected the provisions of the Indian Reorganization Act and was determined to operate under a constitution of its own choosing. At the same time, under the IRA the Secretary of the Interior has full authority to return lands to the tribe, but he does not have authority to return lands to non-IRA tribes. Thus failure years before to adopt a constitution under the Indian Reorganization Act unexpectedly backfired on the tribe.

When the Kennedys and King were assassinated people wailed and moaned over the "sick" society. Most people took the assassinations as a symptom of a deep inner rot that had suddenly set in. They needn't have been shocked. America has been sick for some time. It got sick when the first Indian treaty was broken. It has never recovered.

When a policy is used as a weapon to force cultural confrontation, then the underlying weakness of society is apparent. No society which has real and lasting values need rely on force for their propagation.

It is now up to the American people to make their will known. Can they condone the continual abuse of the American Indian by Congressmen and bureaucrats who use an unjust Congressional policy to threaten the lives and property of Indian people? Is the word of America good only to support its ventures overseas in Vietnam or does it extend to its own citizens?

If America has done to us as it wishes others to do to her, then the future will not be bright. America is running up a great debt. It may someday see the wholesale despoliation of its lands and people by a foreign nation.

4 ❖ ANTHROPOLOGISTS
AND OTHER FRIENDS

INTO EACH LIFE, it is said, some rain must fall. Some people have bad horoscopes, others take tips on the stock market. McNamara created the TFX and the Edsel. Churches possess the real world. But Indians have been cursed above all other people in history. Indians have anthropologists.

Every summer when school is out a veritable stream of immigrants heads into Indian country. Indeed the Oregon Trail was never so heavily populated as are Route 66 and Highway 18 in the summer time. From every rock and cranny in the East *they* emerge, as if responding to some primeval fertility rite, and flock to the reservations.

"They" are the anthropologists. Social anthropologists, historical anthropologists, political anthropologists, economic anthropologists, all brands of the species, embark on the great summer adventure. For purposes of this discussion we shall refer only to the generic name, anthropologists. They are the most prominent members of the scholarly community that infests the land of the free, and in the summer time, the homes of the braves.

The origin of the anthropologist is a mystery hidden in the historical mists. Indians are certain that all societies of the Near East had anthropologists at one time because all those societies are now defunct.

Indians are equally certain that Columbus brought anthropologists on his ships when he came to the New World. How else could he have made so many wrong deductions about where he was?

While their historical precedent is uncertain, anthropologists can readily be identified on the reservations. Go into any crowd of people. Pick out a tall gaunt white man wearing Bermuda shorts, a World War II Army Air Force flying jacket, an Australian bush hat, tennis shoes, and packing a large knapsack incorrectly strapped on his back. He will invariably have a thin sexy wife with stringy hair, an IQ of 191, and a vocabulary in which even the prepositions have eleven syllables.

He usually has a camera, tape recorder, telescope, hoola hoop, and life jacket all hanging from his elongated frame. He rarely has a pen, pencil, chisel, stylus, stick, paint brush, or instrument to record his observations.

This creature is an anthropologist.

An anthropologist comes out to Indian reservations to make OBSERVATIONS. During the winter these observations will become books by which future anthropologists will be trained, so that they can come out to reservations years from now and verify the observations they have studied.

After the books are writen, summaries of the books appear in the scholarly journals in the guise of articles. These articles "tell it like it is" and serve as a catalyst to inspire other anthropologists to make the great pilgrimage next summer.

The summaries are then condensed for two purposes. Some condensations are sent to government agencies as reports justifying the previous summer's research. Others are sent to foundations in an effort to finance the next summer's expedition west.

The reports are spread all around the government agencies and foundations all winter. The only problem is that no one has time to read them. So five-thousand-dollar-a-year secretaries are assigned to decode them. Since the secretaries cannot read complex theories, they reduce the reports to the best slogan possible and forget the reports.

The slogans become conference themes in the early spring, when the anthropologist expeditions are being planned. The slogans turn into battle cries of opposing groups of anthropologists who chance to meet on the reservations the following summer.

Each summer there is a new battle cry, which inspires new insights into the nature of the "Indian problem." One summer Indians will be greeted with the joyful cry of "Indians are bilingual!" The following summer this great truth will be expanded to "Indians are not only bilingual, THEY ARE BICULTURAL!"

Biculturality creates great problems for the opposing anthropological camp. For two summers they have been bested in sloganeering and their funds are running low. So the opposing school of thought breaks into the clear faster than Gale Sayers playing against the little leaguers. "Indians," the losing "anthros" cry, "are a FOLK people!" The tide of battle turns and a balance, so dearly sought by Mother Nature, is finally achieved.

Thus go the anthropological wars, testing whether this school or that school can endure longest. And the battlefields, unfortunately, are the lives of Indian people.

You may be curious as to why the anthropologist never carries a writing instrument. He never makes a mark because he ALREADY KNOWS what he is going to find. He need not record anything except his daily expenses for the audit, for the anthro found his answer in the books he read the winter before. No, the anthropologist is only out on the reservations to VERIFY what he has suspected all along—Indians are a very quaint people who bear watching.

The anthro is usually devoted to PURE RESEARCH. Pure research is a body of knowledge absolutely devoid of useful application and incapable of meaningful digestion. Pure research is an abstraction of scholarly suspicions concerning some obscure theory originally expounded in pre-Revolutionary days and systematically checked each summer since then. A 1969 thesis restating a proposition of 1773 complete with footnotes to all material published between 1773 and 1969 is pure research.

There are, however, anthropologists who are not as clever at collecting footnotes. They depend upon their field observations and write long adventurous narratives in which their personal observations are used to verify their suspicions. Their reports, books, and articles are called APPLIED RESEARCH. The difference, then, between Pure and Applied research is primarily one of footnotes. Pure has many footnotes, Applied has few footnotes. Relevancy to subject matter is not discussed in polite company.

Anthropologists came to Indian country only after the tribes had agreed to live on reservations and had given up their warlike ways. Had the tribes been given a choice of fighting the cavalry or the anthropologists, there is little doubt as to who they would have chosen. In a crisis situation men always attack the biggest threat to their existence. A warrior killed in battle could always go to the Happy Hunting Grounds. But where does an Indian laid low by an anthro go? To the library?

Behind each successful man stands a woman and behind each policy and program with which Indians are plagued, if traced completely back to its origin, stands the anthropologist.

The fundamental thesis of the anthropologist is that people are objects for observation, people are then considered objects for experimentation, for manipulation, and for eventual extinction. The anthropologist thus furnishes the justification for treating Indian people like so many chessmen available for anyone to play with.

The massive volume of useless knowledge produced by anthropologists attempting to capture real Indians in a network of theories has contributed substantially to the invisibility of Indian people today. After all, who can conceive of a food-gathering, berry-picking, semi-nomadic, fire-worshiping, high-plains-and-mountain-dwelling, horse-riding, canoe-toting, bead-using, pottery-making, ribbon-coveting, wickiup-sheltered people who began *flourishing* when Alfred Frump mentioned them in 1803 in his great work on Indians entitled *Our Feathered Friends* as real?

Not even Indians can relate themselves to this type of creature who, to anthropologists, is the "real" Indian. Indian people begin to feel that they are merely shadows of a mythical super-Indian. Many anthros spare no expense to reinforce this sense of inadequacy in order to further support their influence over Indian people.

In Washington, bureaucrats and Congressmen are outraged to discover that this "berry-picking food gatherer" has not entered the mainstream of American society. Programs begin to shift their ideological orientation to cover the missing aspect which allowed the berry picker to "flourish." Programs and the people they serve thus often have a hidden area of misunderstanding which neither administrators nor recipients realize.

Over the years anthropologists have succeeded in burying Indian communities so completely beneath the mass of irrelevant information that the total impact of the scholarly community on Indian people has become one of simple authority. Many Indians have come to parrot the ideas of anthropologists because it appears that the anthropologists know everything about Indian communities. Thus many ideas that pass for Indian thinking are in reality theories originally advanced by anthropologists and echoed by Indian people in an attempt to communicate the real situation.

Since 1955 there have been a number of workshops conducted in Indian country as a device for training "young Indian leaders." Churches, white Indian-interest groups, colleges, and finally, poverty programs have each gone the workship route as the most feasible means for introducing new ideas into younger Indians so as to create "leaders."

The tragic nature of the workshops is apparent when one examines their history. One core group of anthropologists, helpful in 1955 and succeeding years, has institutionalized the workship and the courses taught in it. Trudging valiantly from workshop to workshop, from state to state, college to college, tribe to tribe, area to area, these noble spirits have served as the catalyst for the creation of workshops which are identical in purpose and content and often in the student body itself.

The anthropological message to young Indians has not varied a jot or tittle in ten years. It is the same message these anthros learned as fuzzy-cheeked graduate students in the post-war years—Indians are a folk people, whites are an urban people, and never the twain shall meet.

Derived from this basic premise have been such sterling insights as Indians are between two cultures, Indians are bicultural, Indians have lost their identity, and Indians are warriors. These insights, propounded every year with deadening regularity and an overtone of Sinaitic authority, have come to occupy a key block in the development of young Indian people. For these slogans have come to be excuses for Indian failures. They are crutches by which young Indians have avoided the arduous task of thinking out the implications of the status of Indian people in the modern world.

Indian Affairs today suffers from an intellectual stagnation that is astounding. Creative thought is sparse. Where the younger black students were the trigger to the Civil Rights movements with sit-ins in the South, young Indians have become unwitting missionaries spreading ancient anthropological doctrines which hardly relate to either anthropology or to Indians. The young blacks invented Black Power and pushed the whole society to consider the implications of discrimination which in turn created racial nationalism. Young Indians have barely been able to parody some black slogans and have created none of their own.

If there is one single cause which has importance today for Indian people, it is tribalism. But creation of modern tribalism has been stifled by the ready acceptance of the "Indians-are-a-folk-people" premise of the anthropologists. Creative thought in Indian Affairs has not, therefore, come from younger Indians. Rather it has come from the generation of Indians supposedly brainwashed by government schools and derided as "puppets" of the Bureau of Indian Affairs.

Because other groups have been spurred on by their younger generation, Indians have come to believe that through education a new generation of leaders will arise to solve the pressing contemporary problems. Tribal leaders have been taught to accept this thesis by the scholarly community in its annual invasion of the reservations. Bureau of Indian Affairs educators harp continually on this theme. Wherever authority raises its head in Indian country, this thesis is its messsage.

The facts prove the opposite, however. Relatively untouched by anthropologists, educators, and scholars are the Apache tribes of the Southwest. The Mescalero, San Carlos, White Mountain, and Jicarilla Apaches have very few young people in college compared with other tribes. They have even fewer people in the annual workshop orgy during the summers. If ever there was a distinction between folk and urban, this group of Indians characterizes the revered anthropological gulf.

Concern among the Apaches is, however, tribal. There is little sense of a "lost identity." Apaches could not care less about the anthropological dilemmas that worry other tribes. Instead they continue to work on the massive plans for development which they themselves have created. Tribal identity is assumed, not defined, by the reservation people. Freedom to choose from a wide variety of paths of progress is a characteristic of the Apaches; they don't worry about what type of Indianism is "real." Above all, they cannot be ego-fed by abstract theories and hence unwittingly manipulated.

With many young people from other tribes the situation is quite different. Some young Indians attend workshops over and over again. Folk theories pronounced by authoritative anthropologists become opportunities to escape responsibility. If, by definition, the Indian is hopelessly caught between two cultures, why struggle? Why not blame all one's lack of success on this tremendous gulf between two opposing cultures? Workshops have become, therefore, summer retreats for non-thought rather than strategy sessions for leadership enhancement.

Herein lies the Indian sin against the anthropologist. Only those anthropologists who appear to boost Indian ego and expound theories dear to the hearts of workshop Indians are invited to teach at workshops. They become human recordings of social confusion which are played and replayed each summer to the delight of people who refuse to move on into the real world.

The workshop anthro is thus a unique creature, partially self-created and partially supported by the refusal of Indian young people to consider their problems in their own context. The normal process of maturing has been confused with cultural difference. So maturation is cast aside in favor of cult recitation of great truths which appear to explain the immaturity of young people.

While the anthro is, in a very real sense, the victim of the Indians, he should nevertheless recognize the role he has been asked to play and refuse to play it. Instead, the temptation to appear relevant to a generation of young In-

dians has clouded his sense of proportion. Workshop anthros often ask Indians of tender age to give their authoritative answers to problems which an entire generation of
Indians is just now beginning to solve. Thus, where the
answer to reservation health problems may be adequate
housing in areas where there has *never* been adequate
housing, young Indians are shaped in their thinking processes to consider vague doctrines on the nature of man
and his society.

It is very unsetling for a teen-age Indian to become an
instant authority equal in status with the Ph.D. interrogat-
ing him. Yet the very human desire is to play that game
every summer, for the status acquired in the game is
heady. And as according to current rules of the game,
answers can only be given in vocabulary created by the
Ph.D., the entire leadership-training process internalizes itself and has no outlet beyond the immediate group. Real
problems, superimposed upon the ordinary problems of
maturing, thus become insoluble burdens that crush people
of great leadership potential.

Let us take some specific examples. One workshop discussed the thesis that Indians were in a terrible crisis.
They were, in the words of friendly anthro guides, BE-
TWEEN TWO WORLDS. People between two worlds,
the students were told, DRANK. For the anthropologists,
it was a valid explanation of drinking on the reservation.
For the young Indians, it was an authoritative definition of
their role as Indians. Real Indians, they began to think,
drank and their task was to become real Indians for only
in that way could they re-create the glories of the past.

So they DRANK.

I lost some good friends who DRANK too much.

Abstract theories create abstract action. Lumping together the variety of tribal problems and seeking the demonic principle at work which is destroying Indian people
may be intellectually satisfying. But it does not change the
real situation. By concentrating on great abstractions, anthropologists have unintentionally removed many young
Indians from the world in which problems are solved to
the lands of makebelieve.

Regardless of theory, the Pyramid Lake Paiutes and the
Gila River Pima Maricopas are poor because they have

been systematically cheated out of their water rights, and on desert reservations water is the most important single factor in life. No matter how many worlds Indians straddle, the Plains Indians have an inadequate land base that continues to shrink because of land sales. Straddling worlds is irrelevant to straddling small pieces of land and trying to earn a living.

Along the Missouri River the Sioux used to live in comparative peace and harmony. Although the allotments were small, families were able to achieve a fair standard of living through a combination of gardening and livestock raising and supplemental work. Little cash income was required because the basic necessities of food, shelter, and community life were provided.

After World War II anthropologists came to call. They were horrified that the Indians didn't carry on their old customs such as dancing, feasts, and giveaways. In fact, the people did keep up a substantial number of customs. But these customs had been transposed into church gatherings, participation in the county fair, and tribal celebrations, particularly fairs and rodeos.

The people did Indian dances. BUT THEY DIDN'T DO THEM ALL THE TIME.

Suddenly the Sioux were presented with an authority figure who bemoaned the fact that whenever he visited the reservations the Sioux were not out dancing in the manner of their ancestors. In a real sense, they were not real.

Today the summers are taken up with one great orgy of dancing and celebrating as each small community of Indians sponsors a weekend pow-wow for the people in the surrounding communities. Gone are the little gardens which used to provide fresh vegetables in the summer and canned goods in the winter. Gone are the chickens which provided eggs and Sunday dinner. In the winter the situation becomes critical for families who spent the summer dancing. While the poverty programs have done much to counteract the situation, few Indians recognize that the condition was artificial from start to finish. The people were innocently led astray and even the anthropologists did not realize what had happened.

Another beautiful example of nonsensical scholarly dribble that has had a great effect on Indians' lives was an event that happened in the summer of 1968. A proposal was written to solve the desperate credit needs of reservation communities. Without a sufficient amount of capital to begin small businesses, no area can achieve economic stability. Tribes had sought a credit bill in Congress for ten years without any noticeable movement in the two Interior committees.

So a scheme was devised in a place far from Indian country to make use of existing funds in the community to generate credit within the reservation for use by the people. The basic document stated that like all undeveloped areas, Indian reservations have a great deal of HOARDED wealth. The trick, according to this group of experts, was to gain the Indians' confidence, get them to bring their hoarded wealth from hiding, and make them invest that wealth in reservation banks, mutual funds, and small businesses.

I could not believe the proposition myself. I had visited a great many reservations and seen the abject poverty, most of its cause directly attributed to the refusal by Congress to provide credit or to bureaucratic ineptness. I had served on the Board of Inquiry into Hunger and Malnutrition in the United States and had been shaken at what we had found, not only in Indian reservations, but in rural America generally. If there was hoarded wealth on those reservations, it was very well hidden!

Yet people I talked with concerning the idea were pretty much convinced that the authors of the document had hit the nail on the head. Some yearned to get the program going to see what could be done on specific reservations. One reservation suggested had had employment only once before in this century. That was during the Depression, when CCC camps were put up on the reservation and conservation was used to provide employment for the people. That era lasted about three or four years and then World War II forced cancellation of the camps.

I could not be convinced that wages earned in the CCC camps had been carefully preserved through the great blizzard of 1949, through the Korean War, through the prosperous days of the 1950's, through the Vietnam struggle, and were now gathering mildew in their hiding places beneath the dirt floors of the log cabins on the reservation.

The proposal was designed for the days of Silas Marner in merry old England, when the industrial revolution was just beginning to reach into the countryside.

Hopefully the project has been dropped. To be kindly, it was unrealistic from the very inception. But in my mind's eye I can still visualize what the scene would be as one of its proponents described it to me.

From every nook and cranny, from every butte and mesa, Indians came swarming into Pine Ridge, South Dakota. In wagons and old cars they came, afoot and astride their ponies. Into the agency they moved, a relentless stream of investors. At a table sat two accountants and a distinguished economist, recording each family's investment in a massive bank deposit book. Gradually the little leather pouches were piled higher and higher as thousands of dollars of coin of the realm once again greeted the sun.

Rare coin collectors stood off to the side, looking for large greenbacks, Spanish doubloons, and Greek drachmas, hidden since pre-Colonial times. Occasionally a Viking coin, evidence of Leif Ericson's tourist activities, came to the table, greeted by opposing scholars as authentic and counterfeit as ideology dictated. With pleased looks the economists, anthropologists, and other scholars stood observing the scene. At last, they chortled, Indians were in the mainstream of American life.

I do not place much faith in well-footnoted proposals.

One of the wildest theories, to my way of thinking, has been advocated by some very dear friends of mine. Since we cuss and discuss the theory with monotonous regularity, I feel free to outline my side of the controversy. Their side has had the benefit of publication in scholarly journals for years.

The Oglala Sioux are perhaps the most famous of the Sioux bands. Among their past leaders were Red Cloud, the only Indian who ever defeated the United States in war, and Crazy Horse, most revered of the Sioux war chiefs. The Oglala were, and perhaps still are, the meanest group of Indians ever assembled. They would take after a cavalry troop just to see if their bow strings were taut enough.

After they had settled on the reservation, the Oglalas made a fairly smooth transition to the new life. They had good herds of cattle, they settled along the numerous creeks that cross the reservation, and they created a very strong community spirit. The Episcopalians and the Roman Catholics had the missionary franchise on the reservation and the tribe was pretty evenly split between the two. In the Episcopal church, at least, the congregations were fairly self-governing and stable.

During the years since the reservation was created, members of other tribes came to visit and ended up as residents. Dull Knife's Cheyennes hid at Pine Ridge for a while and a group of them came to be permanent residents. Osages, Kaws, and other Oklahoma tribes also had scattered families living on the reservation.

Over the years the Oglala Sioux have had a number of problems. Their population has grown faster than their means of support. The government allowed white farmers to come into the eastern part of the reservation and create a county, with the best farm lands owned or operated by whites. The reservation was allotted and when ownership became too complicated, control of the land passed out of Indian hands. The government displaced a number of families during the last world war by taking a part of the reservation for use as a bombing range to train crews for combat. Only in 1968 was the land returned to tribal and individual use.

The tribe became a favorite subject for study quite early because of its romantic past. Gradually theories arose attempting to explain the apparent lack of progress of the Oglala Sioux. The real issue, white control of the reservation, was overlooked completely. Instead, every conceivable intangible cultural distinction was used to explain lack of economic, social, and educational progress of a people who were, to all intents and purposes, absentee landlords because of the government policy of leasing their lands to whites.

One study advanced the startling proposition that Indians with many cattle were, on the average, better off than Indians without cattle. Cattle Indians, apparently, had more capital and income than did non-cattle Indians. The study had innumerable charts and graphs which demonstrated this great truth beyond doubt of a reasonably prudent man.

Studies of this type were common but unexciting. They lacked that certain flair of insight so beloved by anthropologists. Then one day a famous anthropologist advanced the thesis, probably valid at the time and in the manner in which he advanced it, that the Oglala were WARRIORS WITHOUT WEAPONS.

The chase was on.

From every library stack in the nation anthropologists converged on the innocent Oglala Sioux to test this new thesis before the ink dried on the scholarly journals. Outfitting the anthropological expeditions to Pine Ridge became the number-one industry of the small off-reservation Nebraska towns south of Pine Ridge. Surely supplying the Third Crusade to the Holy Land was a minor feat compared with the task of keeping the anthropologists at Pine Ridge.

Every conceivable difference between the Oglala Sioux and the folks at Hyannisport was attributed to the quaint warrior tradition of the Oglala Sioux. From lack of roads to unshined shoes Sioux problems were generated, so the anthros discovered, by the refusal of the white man to recognize the great desire of the Oglalas to go to war. Why expect an Oglala to become a small businessman when he was only waiting for that wagon train to come around the bend?

The very real and human problems of the reservation were considered to be merely by-products of the failure of a warrior people to become domesticated. The fairly respectable thesis of past exploits in war, perhaps romanticized for morale purposes, became a demonic spiritual force all its own. Some Indians, in a tongue-in-cheek manner for which Indians are justly famous, suggested that a subsidized wagon train be run through the reservation each morning at 9 A.M. and the reservation people paid a minimum wage for attacking it.

By outlining this problem I am not deriding the Sioux. I lived eighteen years on that reservation and know many of the problems it suffers. How, I ask, can the Oglala Sioux make any headway in education when their lack of education is ascribed to a desire to go to war? Would not perhaps an incredibly low per capita income, virtually non-existent housing, extremely inadequate roads, and domination by white farmers and ranchers make some difference? If the little Sioux boy or girl had no breakfast, had to walk miles to a small school, and had no decent clothes and place to study in a one-room log cabin, should the level of education be comparable to New Trier High School?

What use would roads, houses, schools, businesses, income, be to a people that everyone expected would soon depart on the hunt or warpath? I would submit that a great deal of the lack of progress at Pine Ridge is occasioned by people who believe they are helping the Oglalas when they insist on seeing, in the life of the people of that reservation, only those things which they want to see. Real problems and real people become invisible before the great romantic notion that the Sioux yearn for the days of Crazy Horse and Red Cloud and will do nothing until those days return.

The logical conclusion of this rampage of "warriorism" was the creation of a type of education which claimed to make "modern Indians" out of these warriors. I will not argue right or wrong about the process, since too few Indian people on the Sioux reservations have become acquainted with it, and many of those who have, accept it as the latest revelation from on high.

The question of the Oglala Sioux is a question that plagues every Indian tribe in the nation, if it will closely examine itself. Tribes have been defined as one thing, the definition has been completely explored, test scores have been advanced promoting and deriding the thesis, and finally the conclusion has been reached—Indians must be redefined in terms that white men will accept, even if that means re-Indianizing them according to a white man's idea of what they were like in the past and should logically become in the future.

What, I ask, would a school board in Moline, Illinois, or Skokie, even, do if the scholarly community tried to reorient their educational system to conform with outmoded ideas of Sweden in the glory days of Gustavus Adolphus? Would they be expected to sing *"Ein Feste Burg"* and charge out of the mists at the Roman Catholics to save the Reformation every morning as school began?

Or the Irish? Would they submit to a group of Indians coming to Boston and telling them what a modern Irishman was like? Expecting them to dress in green and hunt leprechauns so as to live on the leprechaun's hidden gold would hardly provide a meaningful path for the future.

Again let us consider the implications of theories put forward to solve the problems of poverty among the blacks. Several years ago the word went forth across the land that black poverty was due to the disintegration of the black family, that the black father no longer had a prominent place in the home.

How incredibly short-sighted that thesis was. How typically Anglo-Saxon! How in the world could there have been a black family if people were sold like cattle for two hundred years, if there were large plantations that served merely as farms to breed more slaves, if white owners systematically ravaged black women? When did the black family unit ever become integrated? During the years of the grandfather clause, when post-Civil War Negroes were denied the vote because their grandfathers hadn't been eligible to vote? Thanks to the programs of the Ku Klux Klan?

Academia, and its by-products, continues to become more irrelevant to the needs of people. The rest of America had better beware of having little quaint mores that will attract anthropologists or it will soon become victim of the conceptual prison into which Indians have been thrown.

What difference does it make?

Several years ago an anthropologist stated that over a period of some twenty years he had spent, from all sources, close to ten million dollars studying a tribe of less than a thousand people! Imagine what that amount of money would have meant to that group of people had it been invested in buildings and businesses. There would have been no problems to study!

Therein lies the trap into which American society has fallen and into which we all unknowingly fall. There is an undefined expectation in American society that once a problem is defined, no matter how, and understood by a significant number of people who have some relation to the problem, there is no problem any more.

Poverty programs are the best contemporary example of this thesis. The poor, according to Harrington, are characterized by their invisibility. Once that thesis was accepted, discussions of poverty made the poor so visible that eventually solutions to poverty replaced the visible poor and the poor faded once again into obscurity. And everyone was outraged to discover that three years of discussion and underfunded programs had not solved the problem of poverty.

In defense of the anthropologist it must be recognized that those who do not publish, perish. That those who do not bring in a substantial sum of research money soon slide down the scale of university approval. What university is not equally balanced between the actual education of its students and a multitude of small bureaus, projects, institutes, and programs which are designed to harvest grants for the university?

The implications of the anthropologist, if not for all America, should be clear for the Indian. Compilation of useless knowledge "for knowledge's sake" should be utterly rejected by the Indian people. We should not be objects of observation for those who do nothing to help us. During the crucial days of 1954, when the Senate was pushing for termination of all Indian rights, not one single scholar, anthropologist, sociologist, historian, or economist came forward to support the tribes against the detrimental policy.

How much had scholars learned about Indians from 1492 to 1954 that would have placed termination in a more rational light? Why didn't the academic community march to the side of the tribes? Certainly the past few years have shown how much influence academia can exert when it feels impelled to enlist in a cause? Is Vietnam any more crucial to the moral stance of America than the great debt owed to the Indian tribes?

Perhaps we should suspect the real motives of the academic community. They have the Indian field well defined and under control. Their concern is not the ultimate policy that will affect the Indian people, but merely the creation of new slogans and doctrines by which they can climb the university totem pole. Reduction of people to ciphers for purposes of observation appears to be inconsequential to the anthropologist when compared with immediate benefits he can derive, the production of further prestige, and the chance to appear as the high priest of American society, orienting and manipulating to his heart's desire.

A couple of years ago Roger Jourdain, chairman of the Red Lake Chippewa tribe of Minnesota, casually had the anthropologists escorted from his reservation. This was the tip of the iceberg breaking through into visibility. If only more Indians had the insight of Jourdain. Why should we continue to be the private zoos for anthropologists? Why should tribes have to compete with scholars for funds when the scholarly productions are so useless and irrelevant to real life?

I would advocate a policy to be adopted by Indian tribes which would soon clarify the respective roles of anthropologists and tribes. Each anthro desiring to study a tribe should be made to apply to the tribal council for permission to do his study. He would be given such permission only if he raised as a contribution to the tribal budget an amount of money equal to the amount he proposed to spend in his study. Anthropologists would thus become productive members of Indian society instead of ideological vultures.

This proposal was discussed at one time in Indian circles. It curled no small number of anthropological hairdos. Irrational shrieks of "academic freedom" rose like rockets from launching pads. The very idea of putting a tax on useless information was intolerable to the anthros we talked with.

But the question is very simple. Are the anthros concerned about "freedom" or "license"? Academic freedom certainly does not imply that one group of people have to become chessmen for another group of people. Why should Indian communities be subjected to prying non-Indians any more than other communities? Should any group have a franchise to stick its nose into someone else's business? No.

Realistically, Indian people will continue to allow their communities to be turned inside out until they come to realize the damage that is being done them. Then they will seal up the reservations until no further knowledge, useless or otherwise, is created. Thus the pendulum will swing radically from one extreme to another, whereas with understanding between the two groups it would not have to swing at all.

Recently, the world of the anthropologist has produced a book the influence of which will be very great. And very detrimental to Indian people. Perhaps when the implications of this book reach the tribes in the form of government programs, they will finally awaken and push the parasitic scholars off the reservations and set up realistic guidelines by which they can control what is written and said about them.

The book is called *Man's Rise to Civilization as Shown by the Indians of North America from Primeval Times to the Coming of the Industrial State*. It exemplifies all the sacred innuendos by which Indians have been hidden from view over the years. The unexamined premises under which the book was written are many and the book will merely serve to reinforce existing stereotypes concerning Indians which have been so detrimental for years.

The explanation of the book, as found on the jacket, indicates sufficiently the assumptions under which the book was written. In the foreword, by Elman R. Service, Professor of Anthropology at Michigan, it is noted that "beginning with the most pitiful and primitive Indians found by explorers, the Digger Indians of Nevada and Utah, Mr. Farb shows that even they are much above the highest non-human primate." Thank you, Mr. Farb, we were pretty worried about that.

The back of the jacket describes Mr. Farb as having been acclaimed by Stewart Udall, former Secretary of the Interior, as "one of the finest conservation spokesmen of our period." This statement will raise the question in Indians' minds of who *read* the book to Stewart Udall.

Being acclaimed as a conservationist by Udall is not exactly gathering laurels either. Udall has allowed Pyramid Lake in Nevada to languish some eight years with a mere pittance of water although it is the finest natural water resource in the state. And although he has repeatedly promised the Pyramid Lake Paiute tribe water for the lake. In many people's minds the best way to eradicate a species is to authorize Udall to conserve it. In his own inimitable style he will accomplish the task posthaste.

Farb's basic assumption is that somehow Indians have risen to civilized heights by being the victims of four centuries of systematic genocide. Under these assumptions the European Jews should be the most civilized people on earth from their graduate course in gas ovens given by Eichmann.

The implications of Farb's book are even more frightening. Indians, people will feel, weren't really as good as we thought, *therefore* we must hurry them on their way to civilization. Indians weren't really conservationists, therefore all this business about them having an attachment to their lands is bunk. Why not, therefore, go ahead with the plan for wholesale mortgage of Indian lands, they aren't using them anyway.

One has only to read Stewart Udall's review of Farb's book to understand the implication of it for future Indian policy. It is a justification for all the irrational policy decisions which Udall had wished he had been able to make but which Indian people brought to a halt. Many Indians still remember Udall's frantic ramblings at Santa Fe in 1966 when he questioned and answered himself on why Indians had not made progress like his friends in Arizona. His answer: because they didn't have the management tools that IBM, General Motors, and Bell Telephone had.

The eventual solution, as proposed by the Department of the Interior, was the creation of a bill under which land could be mortgaged for development, with bureaucrats "giving" technical advice and sharing none of the responsibility for failure, should it occur. The Udall Omnibus Bill was basically to continue "man's rise to civilization" by systematic confiscation of existing capital owned by those-to-be-civilized, through the device of ill-advised mortgages.

Farb continues to use phrases such as "test tubes" and "living laboratories" in describing the development, or rather unfolding, of Indian cultural change. In essence, then, Indian communities exist primarily for people to experiment with. Bureaucratically this means "pilot projects." Anthropologically, as we have seen, it means the continued treatment of Indian people as objects for observation.

One classic statement—"Modern American society has little place for institutionalized rites of rebellion, because it is a democratic society; it is characteristic of a democratic society always to question and challenge, never to be certain of itself"—blithely dismisses social reality.

American society has, in fact, institutionalized rebellion by making it popular. Once popularized, rebellions become fads and are so universalized that *not* to be rebellious is to be square, out of it, irrelevant. Television ads make a big noise about the great rebellions going on in the auto industry. Deodorants and soaps are always new, a radical departure from the old. Cigarette smokers are cautioned to break away from the crowd. Unless a man is rebelling, he is not really a man. And to achieve relevance in American society a person must always be the pioneer, the innovator, against the establishment.

The import of institutionalizing rebellion is that when real rebellion occurs society climbs the walls in its fright. I keenly remember our confrontation with Department of the Interior officials at Santa Fe, when several advised us to go home or we would be "terminated." A democratic society is always up tight about real rebellions because its very operating premise is that rebellions are nice. When rebellions turn out to be not so nice, panic prevails.

Democratic society is always absolutely sure of itself. It could not be otherwise, for to be unsure would call into question the very basis of the political institutions which gave it existence. Even more horrifying would be an examination of the economic realities underlying the society.

With institutionalized rebellion a way of life, one of the major differences between white and Indians emerges—ingratitude. Whites always expect Indians to be grateful according to the whites' ideas of gratitude. Or else they expect ingratitude to be expressed in institutionalized behavior, as other members of society have been taught to do. When Indians do not respond in accustomed ways, because the way is irrelevant to Indian modes of expression, Indian response is attributed to the innate savagery of the Indian.

Sometimes Farb's anthropological references to the Plains Indians are irrelevant and ridden with historical mythologies in several respects. The Mandans, for example, are found to be extinct—which they will be happy to know about. Plains Indians in general are declared to be as make-believe as a movie set—which will make them welcome Farb warmly when he next appears in the plains.

Most unforgivable is the statement that Sitting Bull was accidentally killed. For if Sitting Bull was accidentally killed, then President Kennedy's death was merely the result of Oswald carelessly cleaning his rifle. The two deaths had the same motivation—political assassination.

Man's Rise to Civilization may have redeeming anthropological features; it certainly has sufficient footnotes to make it PURE rather than APPLIED research. The question for Indian people, and the ultimate question for Americans, is: What effect will it have over the lives of people?

There should be little doubt that this book tends to reinforce the anti-Indian school of thought and to sidestep the entire issue of Indian society, culture, or what have you. Unless there is a frank understanding between the two people, red and white, so that the relationship between them is honest, sincere, and equal, talk about culture will not really matter. The white man will continue to take Indian land because he will feel that he is HELPING to bring civilization to the poor savages.

Thus has it ever been with anthropologists. In believing they could find the key to man's behavior, they have, like the churches, become forerunners of destruction. Like the missionaries, anthropologists have become intolerably certain that they represent ultimate truth.

The rest of America had better wake up before their entire lives are secretly manipulated by the musings of this breed. For the time is coming when middle class America will become credit-card-carrying, turnpike-commuting, condominium-dwelling, fraternity-joining, churchgoing, sports-watching, time-purchase-buying, television-watching, magazine-subscribing, politically inert transmigrated urbanites who, through the phenomenon of the second car and the shopping center have become golf-playing, wife-swapping, etc., etc., etc., suburbanites. Or has that day dawned? If so, you will understand what has been happening to Indian communities for a long, long time.

I would expect an instantaneous rebuttal by the "knowledgeable" anthros that these sentiments do not "represent" all the Indians. They don't TODAY. They will TOMOR-

ROW. In the meantime it would be wise for anthropologists to get down from their thrones of authority and PURE research and begin helping Indian tribes instead of preying on them. For the wheel of Karma grinds slowly but it does grind finely. And it makes a complete circle.

5 ✦ MISSIONARIES

AND THE

RELIGIOUS VACUUM

ONE OF THE major problems of the Indian people is the missionary. It has been said of missionaries that when they arrived they had only the Book and we had the land; now we have the Book and they have the land. An old Indian once told me that when the missionaries arrived they fell on their knees and prayed. Then they got up, fell on the Indians, and preyed.

Columbus managed to combine religion and real estate in his proclamation of discovery, claiming the new world for Catholicism and Spain. Missionaries have been unable to distinguish between their religious mission and their hunger for land since that time.

The first concern of mission work was land on which to build churches, homes, storehouses, and other necessary religious monuments. Like the men from New England in *Hawaii* by Michener, missionaries on the North American continent came to preach and stayed to rule. Or at least prepared the way for others to conquer and exploit.

Sacrifices often matched mistakes. Missionaries did more to open up the West than any other group, but in doing so they increased the possibility of exploitation of the people they purported to save. Land acquisition and missionary work always went hand in hand in American history.

While the thrust of Christian missions was to save the individual Indian, its result was to shatter Indian societies and destroy the cohesiveness of the Indian communities. Tribes that resisted the overtures of the missionaries seemed to survive. Tribes that converted were never heard of again. Where Christianity failed, and insofar as it failed, Indians were able to withstand the cultural deluge that threatened to engulf them.

The conflict between the Indian and white religions was classic. Each religion expressed the outlook and understanding of its respective group. Religious ideas of the two groups never confronted each other directly. The conflict was one of rites and techniques. Christianity destroyed many Indian religious practices by offering a much easier and more practical religion. It was something one could immediately understand, not a paving of the way for what ultimately confronted one.

The credal rhetoric of Christianity filled the vacuum it had created by its redefinition of religion as a commodity to be controlled. Although prohibited for several generations, Indian beliefs have always retained the capacity to return from their exile because they have always related to the Indian's deepest concern.

Indian religion required a personal commitment to act. Holy men relied upon revelations experienced during fasting, sacrifices, and visions. Social in impact, most Indian religious experience was individualistic in origin. Visions defined vocations in this world rather than providing information concerning salvation in the other world.

Formulas of faith were anathema to Indian societies. Debate over implications of the existence of God and creation of subtleties related to deity were unknown. The substantial doctrines developed by Christian theologians to explain, define, and control deity were never contemplated in Indian religious life. Religion was an undefined sphere of influence in tribal society.

Tribes shared with the Hebrews of the Old Testament the concept of the covenant of the People with God. The majority of tribal names, when translated into English, mean the People, First Men, or Original People. From the belief that the tribe is the People of God to the exclusion of other peoples, it usually follows that tribal customs and religious ordinances are synonymous.

Laws as such did not exist within tribal societies. Law was rejected as being force imposed from without, whereas peoplehood required fulfillment from within the individual. Insofar as there were external controls, Indians accepted only the traditions and customs which were rooted in the tribe's distant past. Time itself became irrelevant because custom prevailed long enough to outlive any knowledge of its origin. Mystery and reverence gradually surrounded rites and ceremonies, giving them the necessary *mysterium tremendum* by which they were able to influence social behavior.

Most mysterious was the Indian reverence for land. When told to settle down and become farmers, most Indians rebelled. For centuries they had lived off the land as hunters, taking and giving in their dances and ceremonies. Earth, they believed, was mother of all. Most important was the land which their particular tribe dwelt on. The Crow are a good example of the Indian religious love for land. The Crow have a long prayer which thanks the Great Spirit for giving them their land. It is not too hot, they say, and not too cold. It is not too high and snowy and not too low and dusty. Animals enjoy the land of the Crow, men enjoy it also. The prayer ends by declaring that of all the possible lands in which happiness can be found, only in the land of the Crow is true happiness found.

Even today I have watched Indian people look sadly over the miles of plowed ground of South Dakota, wishing that the land were returned to its primitive beauty, undefiled and giving to man and animal alike the life only land can give. Instead of beauty one sees a dust storm in the distance, ribbons of dirty highway going west, and the earth cut into a giant perverted checkerboard with no beauty and hardly even any symmetry.

Contrast this living, undefined religion, where man is a comfortable part of his world, with the message brought by the Christian missionary. The Reformation had divided the world into two arenas: church and state. Morality of one was not necessarily related to morality in the other. Often acts of the state, immoral by any standard, were endorsed by the church in an effort to gain political power and influence. Other times the church, in striving to protect its economic base, would encourage the state to undertake projects it dared not conceive of in its own moral terms.

There is, of course, an analogy in the contemporary role of the late Cardinal Spellman in supporting the United States in the Vietnam situation and the original encouragement by the churches of possession of lands the different European nations had *discovered*.

At one time or another slavery, poverty, and treachery were all justified by Christianity as politically moral institutions of the state. Economic Darwinism, the survival of the fittest businessman, was seen as a process approved by God and the means by which He determined His Chosen for salvation.

Exploitation of one's fellows by any means became a religious exercise. Law became a trap for the unwary and a dangerous weapon in the hands of those who understood how to use it. Public disclosure of wrongdoing was the only punishment society acknowledged either side of the grave, although religious sentimentalists talked vaguely about playing harps for an infinite number of years in some undisclosed heaven. Few mastered the harp before departing for that better life, however.

When the two religious movements came into conflict, the Christian religion was able to overcome tribal beliefs because of its ability to differentiate life into segments which were unrelated. When a world view is broken into its compoment disciplines, these disciplines become things unto themselves and life turns into an unrelated group of categories each with its own morality and ethics.

Missionaries approached the Indian tribes in an effort to bring them into western European religious life. Their primary message sought to invalidate the totality of Indian life and replace it with Christian values. Because Christian reality had been broken into credal definitions, all the missionaries could present to the Indians were words and phrases that had a magical connotation.

Missionaries looked at the feats of the medicine men and proclaimed them to be works of the devil. They overlooked the fact that the medicine men were able to do marvelous things. Above all, they overlooked the fact that what the Indian medicine men did *worked*.

Most activity centered on teaching and preaching. The thrust was to get the Indians to memorize the Large Catechism, the Small Catechism, the Apostles Creed, the Nicene Creed, the Ten Commandments, and other magic rites and formulas dear to Christianity. Salvation became a matter of regurgitation of creeds. In a very real sense, then, Christianity replaced living religions with magic.

And the white man had much magic. Blessed with the gun, the printing press, the iron kettle, and whiskey, it was obvious to many Indians that the white man's god took pretty good care of his people. Since there were no distinctions made between religion and life's other activities by the Indian people, the natural tendency was to adopt the white religion of recitation and forego the rigors of fasting, sacrifice, and prayer.

Missionary activity became an earthly parallel of what Christians thought was happening in heaven. Like the rich burghers of Europe, whom God bribed with earthly treasures, missionaries bribed their way into Indian societies. Once established, they began the laborious task of imprinting two thousand years of sterile dogmas on the unstructured Indian psyche.

Warfare between white and red solidified Indian religion in the persons of a few great leaders such as Sitting Bull, the Prophet (who was the brother of Tecumseh), Handsome Lake, and Wovoka, creator of the Ghost Dance. When these great leaders died, Indian religion went underground and became, like its white competitor, unrelated to the social and political life of the tribe.

By the middle of the last century few tribes were untouched by Christianity. When a tribe had been thoroughly subjugated, Army, trappers, and missionaries moved on and permanent personnel moved in to take control of Indian communities.

From 1860 to 1880, tribes were confined to reservations, as the West was in its death throes. Churches began lobbying early in the 1860's at the Indian Bureau in Washington for franchises over the respective reservations. Thus one reservation would be assigned to the Roman Catholics, one to the Lutherans, one to the Methodists, and one to the Episcopalians. Other churches were prohibited from entry on a reservation once it had been assigned to a particular church and could enter only with permission from the other church. It always bothered me that these churches who would not share pulpits and regarded each other as children of the devil, should have so cold-bloodedly divided up the tribes as if they were choosing sides for touch football.

Many times rations due Indians were mysteriously late in arriving, until the tribes responded to the pleadings of the missionaries. Other times outrageous programs designed to farm desert land were equated with Christian missions. A crop failure was sometimes seen as comparable to a decline in converts because the two harvests were inseparable in the minds of the missionaries.

Indian religious life was forbidden. The Ghost Dance movement, a last attempt to bring back the old hunting days, was enough to convince the Indian Bureau and the Army that the sooner the Indian was Christianized the safer the old frontier would be. Soon the only social activity permitted on reservations was the church service. Signs of any other activity would call for a cavalry troop storming in to rescue civilization from some non-existent threat.

It always amuses me to hear some white missionary glamorize the reception of Christianity by the Plains tribes. He will tell how "two or three were gathered together and gladly heard the word of God preached." The simple fact is that had the two or three not been talking about the white god they probably would have been shot down for fomenting an uprising.

It was no feat, therefore, to convert Indians to a new religion. No missionary ever realized that it was less the reality of his religion and more the threat of extinction that brought converts to him. Or if he did realize it, he never acknowledged it.

Some churches patterned their work after existing social traits within the tribal culture. They were able to translate older Indian ceremonies and rites into Christian celebrations. Like the Gothic arches which took the place of the oak groves under which the European tribes had worshiped, the traditional gatherings of the tribes were made into annual meetings of the mission fields.

Particularly among the Sioux in the Dakotas, the Sun Dance was reinterpreted as the annual convocation of the missions on each reservation. And this type of accommodation to Indian life gave churches that used it built-in advantages over their competitors. But Christianity was presented in such a dogmatic form to the Sioux that it became frozen into a rigid structure. The religion, as it was presented in the 1870's, remains the religion of the Sioux today. This fact was brought home to me quite vividly in 1964.

That was the year that many church people became convinced that the Civil Rights movement was the only real Christian mission. Most of us secretly suspected that the opportunity for national publicity had more to do with this feeling than did God. But we accepted this message of the churches as valid.

Church officials from the East came out to the reservations to bring the new message and to get Indians involved in the struggle. A New Yorker attended a Sioux religious meeting in South Dakota and was treated to an evening of hymns and prayers sung in the Dakota language. And he was horrified.

Nowhere, he later stated, did he find the social concern for integration and equality which made up the bulk of the Christian message. God's number-one priority, he felt, was Civil Rights and here he had been overwhelmed with missionary hymns that had no relevance to the great struggle.

When this message was later related to the Sioux they were more outraged than was our friend from New York. They insisted that the missionaries had come out to them in the 1870's and taught them to sing "From Greenland's Icy Mountains" and had told them that this was God's word, and that, by God, they were going to keep on singing "From Greenland's Icy Mountains" regardless of what the rest of the world was doing.

Where, therefore, Christianity was accepted, it became so ingrained in the social life of the people that it often became impossible to change. And the tribes generally accepted what they felt was important and disregarded the rest.

Today it is fairly easy to tell which churches had which

reservations by the predominance of members of a certain church among the older Indians. Nowhere was the validity of one denomination over another demonstrated. It always causes me to wonder why the various church bodies fight over doctrines today when a century ago they were willing to commit the souls of their red brothers to pernicious doctrines on one reservation in return for the exclusive preaching franchise on another.

Various Lutheran bodies do not share communions or pulpits today. The Roman Catholics and Episcopalians are always engaged in a brawl over the Apostolic pedigree of their ministry. Methodists, Presbyterians, and Baptists continually struggle over concepts of congregational sovereignty. Yet one hundred years ago these churches deliberately ceded various tribes to doctrines they considered heretical in order to gain a captive audience from the federal government.

What each denomination did share, however, was the Anglo-Saxon social forms. These modes of behavior were what they really taught and preached about on the various reservations. Churches struggled to make the Indians cut their hair because they felt that wearing one's hair short was the civilized Christian thing to do. After the tribal elders had been fully sheared, they were ushered into church meeting, given pictures of Jesus and the Disciples, and told to follow these Holy Men. Looking down at the pictures, the ex-warriors were stunned to discover the Holy Dozen in shoulder-length hair!

Often rows of sullen former warriors filled rickety wooden chapels to hear sermons on the ways of peace. They were told that the life of war was the path of destruction. Eternal hell, they were assured, awaited the man of war. Then the service would be closed with the old favorite hymn, "Onward, Christian Soldiers, Marching as to War."

An objective consideration of missionary efforts would indicate that the major emphasis was not religious conversion but experimentation with a captive culture. Western religion had failed to influence the society within which it was created. It had become a commodity for export long before Columbus discovered America. It had no choice but to attempt to gain a stranglehold on other cultures to reinstate itself. But its influence on Indian culture was comparable to that of other trade goods. Where it was useful, it was used.

Indian people obediently followed the way of the white man because it was the path of least resistance. The Great Spirit was exchanged for Santa Claus with some misgivings. Substituting toys for spiritual powers created a vacuum, however, and the tribes secretly preferred their old religion over the religion of the Easter Bunny.

The years from 1870 to 1930 were prosperous times, producing record harvests of red souls. Indian congregations were established in nearly every reservation west of the Mississippi. Many became self-supporting in a short time. By 1930 the majority of the Indian people had a tradition of three generations of church life behind them. Religious controversy centered on doctrinal differences unsolved by the denominations during Reformation days. Missionary work concentrated on such glamorous exploits as stealing sheep from another missionary's fold rather than the de-paganization which had characterized the early mission work.

The flower of tribal leadership served in the reservation chapels as laymen and helpers to the white missionaries. Many people hoped and expected that the mission status of Indian churches would soon be ended and they would receive full parish and congregational equality. Little did they realize that the Indian mission field had become a hobby in and of itself.

Church piety required that the "finest young men" take up the White Man's Burden and go abroad to save the heathen from their great darkness. Indian missions provided the only opportunity whereby young white clergymen could serve God after the mandate of Kipling and still enjoy the comforts of home. To release the Indian congregations to their own devices would have meant closing the only field in which traditional heroics could be achieved. A state of inertia set in.

The white missionaries of the Depression years and later frantically tried to duplicate the exploits of Whipple, Whitman, Father DeSmet, and Charles Cook. There was still glory to be gained by being identified as *the* missionary to a certain tribe. This struggle meant an absolute rejection of Indian people as candidates for the ministry. Recognition of an Indian as an equal or possibly a superior in the missionary venture would have acknowledged that the Indian people had already accepted Christianity. Paganism, per se, would have ceased to exist and there would have been no need for white missionaries.

The Depression missionaries were succeeded by a generation in which the mission field had been the glory spot of Christian work. Many arrived out West with the idea of finally completing the task started by the heroes of the faith two centuries ago. The new breed contemptuously announced that nothing had really been done by their predecessors. There were still Indians around and Indians meant pagans.

The new breed was something to behold. Almost universally they expected the Indian people to come to them for spiritual advice. The older missionaries had made the rounds of their chapels faithfully. After a time, most of the old timers were converted to the Indian way of life and spent their declining years ministering in an Indian way to the people.

But the new breed felt that the Indians were damn lucky they had come. Universally they downgraded Indian laymen. Often they changed patterns of worship and services that had been established for nearly a century. Quite a few had "days off," when they refused to do anything, and most spent a great deal of their time either on vacations or at conferences learning about the relevant new movements of the modern world.

The situation has not changed greatly over the past few years. Several years ago at a conference of missionary workers, a female missionary (somehow missionaries are able to achieve an asexual status) asked my advice on a problem she was having. It seemed that no matter how hard she tried, she couldn't get her little Choctaw pupils in Sunday School to understand the "technical side of being saved."

In her church, it turned out, there were seven steps to salvation. When one understood the seven steps to salvation and was able to recite the sequence correctly, he was saved. Then his task was to teach others the seven steps until Jesus came. Apparently the Lord would ask all people to recite the seven steps on Judgment Day.

Unfortunately I was not able to give her any insight into the task of getting six-year-old Choctaws to walk the seven steps to salvation, let alone memorize them. I asked her why, if it was so difficult to get them to understand, didn't she move to a field which the Lord had spent more time preparing. She replied that the Baptists had had the children for some time and had left them terribly confused. Her first task had been to correct all the heretical theology the Baptists had taught them. She said that she wouldn't dream of leaving and letting some other church come in after her and again confuse the children. On such incisive insights is Christian mission to the Indians founded.

The determination of white churches to keep Indian congregations in a mission status is their greatest sin. But it is more a sin against themselves than it is against Indian people. For the national churches do not realize how obsolete their conceptions have become and they continue to tread the same path they walked centuries ago.

The epitome of this blithe ignorance is the work of the Presbyterian Church among the Shinnecocks on Long Island. At a missionary conference two years ago, a Presbyterian minister, in charge of the Indian work for his denomination, described his church's work among this tribe. Then he asked for questions.

I asked him how long the Presbyterians intended to conduct mission activities among a tribe that had lived as Christians for over three hundred and fifty years. His answer to my question was representative of Christian attitudes toward Indian people today: "Until the job is done."

Christianity, which had laid the ancient world prostrate in less than three hundred years and conquered the mighty Roman Empire, has not been able in the same time period to subdue one hundred Indians huddled on Long Island. Needless to say, my faith was shaken to the core by this statement.

The impotence and irrelevancy of the Christian message has meant a return to traditional religion by Indian people. Tribal religions are making a strong comeback on most reservations. Only in the past few years have the Oglala Sioux and Rosebud Sioux revived their ancient Sioux Sun Dance. And this revival is not simply a re-enactment for tourists. The dance is done in the most reverent manner and with the old custom of piercing the dancers' breasts.

Pathetically, the response of the white missionaries has been to set up tipis and attempt to compete with the Indian religion by holding Masses and communions during the celebration. Nervously they try to convince the Indians that the Sun Dance and the Holy Communion are really the same thing and that Christianity is therefore "relevant" to the Indian people.

In the Great Lakes area the old Medicine Lodge religion has been making inroads with the Chippewas and Winnebagos. Two years ago at an annual conference of the Wisconsin tribes, a panel of Indians discussed native religions. Eagerly the younger conference participants listened to the old men talk. They left that conference with the conviction that Indian religion was for Indian people and Christian religion was for whites.

The Native American Church, famed for its use of the peyote button in its sacramental worship life, has doubled its membership in the last few years. It appears to be the religion of the future among the Indian people. At first a southwestern-based religion, it has spread since the last world war into a great number of northern tribes. Eventually it will replace Christianity among the Indian people.

When I was growing up on the Pine Ridge reservation before and during World War II, the Native American Church was something far away and officially "bad." Few adherents to this faith could be found among the two large Sioux reservations in southern South Dakota. Today a reasonable estimate would be that some 40 percent of the people are members of the Native American Church there.

Indian people have always been confused at the public stance of the Christian churches. The churches preached peace for years yet have always endorsed the wars in which the nation has been engaged. While the missionaries have never spoken about this obvious inconsistency, Indian people have been curious about it for some time. So the element of Indian people who believe deeply in pacifism have looked to other places for a religion of peace.

From the Hopi reservation has come a prophet of peace named Thomas Banyaca. He stands within the old Hopi religion and preaches to all Indians of their need to return to a life of peace and purity before the world ends. In 1967 Banyaca and some members of the Iroquois tribes traveled throughout the nation visiting the different reservations, bringing a message based on the prophecies of the Hopi and Iroquois. In June of 1968 Banyaca, "Mad Bear" Anderson, a Tuscarora prophet, and many of the traditional leaders of different tribes had two National Aborigine conventions in Oklahoma and New York to discuss prophecies of their religion.

Banyaca's message, and its ultimate influence, appears to me to be the most significant movement in religion in Indian Affairs today. Banyaca is very spiritual and highly traditional. He stands solidly within Hopi legend which looks at world history as a catastrophic series of events all of which the Hopi have been saved from. In the late fifties a Hopi delegation went to the United Nations to deliver a message of peace, as Hopi prophecies had required them to do. Legends said that should the Hopi delegation be refused entrance—as they were—the series of events foretelling the end of the world would begin. Banyaca's message to other Indian people is to orient them as to the number of prophecies now fulfilled.

The best statement of Hopi prophecy is contained in Frank Waters' *Book of the Hopi* in which the end of the world as we know it is foretold. There is great similarity between Hopi prophecy and Iroquois prophecy regarding the end of the white man and the restoration of the red man to dominance on this continent. Many people, especially whites, laugh when they hear the Hopi prophecy, feeling that they are so powerful that nothing can overcome them. They forget that Indian gods still roam these lands and do not realize that the Hopi have incredible gifts from their gods which cannot be duplicated by any Christian missionaries; not even, people tell me, by the Pope.

Even in the Northwest, Indian religions are on the move. The Northwest was supposedly converted by Marcus Whitman, early missionary to Oregon Territory. But those tribes, by and large, did not succumb to the word as easily as did tribes in other regions. People from Shoshone country tell me that the medicine men are more powerful there today than they were a century ago. Among the Yakimas the old religion still holds an honored place among the people. If and when native religion combines with political activism among the small tribes in western Washington, they are going to become extremely active in the coming Indian religious revival that many tribes expect in the next decade.

Perhaps only in eastern Oklahoma has Christianity been able to hold its ground. Among the Five Civilized Tribes, Cherokee, Choctaw, Creek, Seminole, and Chickasaw— called civilized because they were most like white men a century ago and have surpassed them in whiteness today —the Baptist denomination exerts great influence. This strength is due primarily to the large number of native clergy among the tribes. The Creeks particularly seem to have taken the Christian doctrines and made them their own. Native preachers exert tremendous influence among the Creeks and Cherokees. If Christianity is to have an Indian base of survival, it will be among the Creeks.

The dilemma of Christian missions today is great. National churches have committed two great mistakes, the solution of which depends upon their foresight and ability to reconcile themselves to what they have been preaching to Indian people for years.

The different denominations have, over the years, invested an enormous amount of money in mission buildings and property. In the closing years of the last century, churches could receive a piece of tribal land simply by promising to conduct certain operations such as a school, hospital, or mission station. Consequently many of them applied for and received a great deal of tribal land.

Now they are caught with property which is suitable only for religious use and with a declining religious following. What use has a church building other than as a church? National churches have continued to pour thousands of dollars annually into their mission programs simply to keep up the value of their investments. They must soon be prepared either to take a devastating paper loss as their congregations vanish or give the properties to the Indian people for their own use. Either solution is distasteful to the materialistic instincts of the churches.

Added to the question of property is the obvious racial discrimination of the denominations against the Indian people, which is becoming apparent to the reservation people. Try as they might, the churches cannot admit that an Indian minister speaking in his native tongue to his own people is more efficient and more effective than a highly trained white missionary talking nonsense.

The major denominations are adamant in their determination to exclude Indian people from the ministry. A number of devices, which skirt "official" pronouncements of concern for an indigenous ministry, are used to bar Indian candidates.

One church refuses to admit Indians to the ministry because it is afraid that someday an Indian priest or clergyman may want to serve in a white parish. Indian ministers would not, by definition, be able to serve in a white parish. Therefore, the reasoning goes, they are not suitable for work among Indian congregations either. While they are welcome, I have been told, they don't seem to be able to qualify.

Other churches are frightened that when the sacred doctrines are translated into the native tongue, the subtle nuances created by theologians of the Reformation will lose some of their distinctions. A perfect example of this attitude happened at an orientation session for new missionaries which I attended in 1963.

A Navajo interpreter was asked to demonstrate how the missionary's sermon was translated into Navajo. So the white missionary gave a few homilies and the interpreter spoke a few words of Navajo. The trainees cooed with satisfaction that meaning could actually be transferred into a barbaric tongue like Navajo.

One missionary was skeptical, however, and asked if there were specific words in Navajo that were comparable to English words. He was afraid, he said, that the wrong messages might be transmitted. So he asked what the Navajo word for "faith" was. Quickly the Navajo replied with the desired word.

"Yes," the missionary commented, "that's all very nice. Now what does that word mean?"

"Faith," said the Navajo smiling.

Nevertheless, many denominations are skeptical about letting Indians enter the ministry because of the possibility that doctrine may become impure. So they continue to send white missionaries for posts in Indian country to insure that the proper theological distinctions be drawn.

With the necessity of keeping large missions open and by refusing to bring Indian people into the ministry, churches have had great difficulty in filling their mission posts. The glory of intrepid pioneering is now gone, and the glory seekers as well as the devoted have long since written off Indian country as the place for service and advancement. Staff positions go unfilled for months and often the first white who comes wandering in across the desert is hired to operate the mission stations.

Some churches have an incredible turnover each spring and try all summer to fill their posts. Eventually they find some white who is a former basketball coach, a retired editor, an interested layman, or an ex-schoolteacher and promptly hand over the mission lock, stock, and barrel without further inquiry. The fact that the new appointee is white is sufficient to cover any theological or professional shortcomings.

Thus the quality of mission workers is at an all-time low. Most are not interested in their work and regard it as a job rather than a calling. Generally they have great contempt for the Indian people they are supposed to be helping.

But probably worse, much mission work is done by white clergymen who are not capable enough to run white parishes. In most cases, the Indian field is their last stop before leaving the ministry altogether. They are hauled from pillar to post by frantic church officials desperately trying to shore up the sagging fortunes of their mission fields. A great deal of money is spent covering up disasters created by these white misfits. When they cause too much controversy in one place they are transferred to another and turned loose again. More money is spent on them than on recruitment and training of Indian people for church work.

Pay is not high in mission work for either white or Indian workers. But it is universally higher for whites than it is for Indians. In the past there was some justification for a pay difference. Many Indian workers were only part-time workers and had another source of income. Gradually, however, Indian clergymen were assigned to remote areas and received less compensation.

Often the pay scale is based primarily upon whether a man is white or Indian. Indians receive less pay, even with seminary training. And Indians are still assigned to the remote areas with the poorest housing and least facilities. Go out to any mission field today and examine the placement of church workers and clergymen. You will discover that white workers have the best assignments, the best houses, the best fringe benefits, and receive the most consideration for advancement from their superiors.

No other field of endeavor in America today has as much blatant racial discrimination as does the field of Christian missions to the American Indian people. It is a marvel that so many Indian people still want to do work for the churches.

Documentation of discrimination and favoritism would be fairly easy were it not for the fantastic ability of the churches to cover their tracks. Instead of forcing resignations from the ministry, church officials transfer incompetents from station to station in order to protect the good name of the church. Thus some tribes are visited with a problem missionary who should have been sent on his way years ago but who has managed to hang on to his ministerial status by periodic transfer and the lack of moral courage by church officials to take action.

The Indian people have come a long way in the last generation. For a long time they accepted the missionary because he seemed to want to do the right thing. But there has always been a desire for the Indian people to take over their own churches. Now they no longer have the expectation that there will be native clergy in their churches. More and more they are returning to Indian dances and celebrations for their religious expressions. They now wait only for a religious leader to rise from among the people and lead them to total religious independence. Thomas

Banyaca or Frank Takes Gun, leader of the Native American Church, or someone yet unknown may suddenly find a way to integrate religion with tribalism as it exists today and become that leader.

Indian religion appears to many of us as the only ultimate salvation for the Indian people. Religion formerly held an important place in Indian tribal life. It integrated the functions of tribal society so that life was experienced as a unity. Christianity has proved to be a disintegrating force by confining its influence to the field of formula recitation and allowing the important movements of living go their separate ways until life has become separated into a number of unrelated categories.

Religion today, or at least Christianity, does not provide the understanding with which society makes sense. Nor does it provide any means by which the life of the individual has value. Christianity fights unreal crises which it creates by its fascination with its own abstractions.

I remember going to an Indian home shortly after the death of a child. There was a Roman Catholic priest admonishing the mother not to cry because the child was now with Jesus. Automatically, he insisted, because it had been baptized. Grief, he declared, was unnatural to man ever since Jesus had died on the cross. He went on to tell how God had decided on a great mission for the child and had called it home to Him and that the mother could see the hand of God in the child's death and needn't wonder about its cause.

In fact, the mother had not wondered about the reason for the child's death. Her child had fallen from a second-story window and suffered internal injuries. It had lingered several days with a number of ruptured organs and had eventually and mercifully died.

I could never believe that the priest was comforting the mother. It seemed rather that he was trying frantically to reinforce what had been taught to him in seminary, doctrines that now seemed shaken to their roots. The whole scene was frightening in its abstract cruelty. I felt sorrier for the priest than for the mother. His obvious disbelief in what he was telling her and his inability to face death in its bitterest moment made *him* the tragic figure.

That is why I believe that Indian religion will be the salvation of the Indian people. In Indian religions, regardless of the tribe, death is a natural occurrence and not a special punishment from an arbitrary God. Indian people do not try to reason themselves out of their grief. Nor do they try to make a natural but sad event an occasion for probing the rationale of whatever reality exists beyond ourselves.

Indians know that people die. They accept death as a fact of life. Rather than build a series of logical syllogisms that reason away grief, Indian people have a ceremony of mourning by which grief can properly be expressed. Depending on the tribal traditions, grief is usually accompanied by specific acts of mourning, which is then ended by giving a feast for the community. After the feast, there is no more official mourning. When expression of grief is channeled into behavioral patterns—as it is, also, in the Jewish religion—it can be adequately understood and felt. When it is suppressed—as it is in the Christian religion—death becomes an entity in itself and is something to be feared. But death also becomes unreal and the act of an arbitrary God.

When death is unreal, violence also becomes unreal, and human life has no value in and of itself. Consider the last talk you had with an insurance salesman. Remember how he told you that you would be covered "if" you died. An Indian salesman would have said "when," but then an Indian would have known how to die and both "if" and "when" would have held no terror for him.

Many tribes have kept their puberty ceremonies, and these ceremonies are very much alive today in the Southwest. Childhood and adolescence are marked off by these ceremonies so that the natural growth processes are recognized and young people growing up will be sure of their place in society.

Contrast the value of these ceremonies with the confusion of suburban America where children are pushed into imitations of adults in their younger years and then later denied the privileges of adults. Certainly the pressures on boys in the Little League are comparable in intensity and form with those professional ballplayers face. But after ten years of being treated like adults, young people begin to demand adult status and they are clubbed into submission by police at Columbia University and in Chicago.

The largest difference I can see between Indian religion and Christian religions is in inter-personal relationships. Indian society had a religion that taught respect for all members of the society. Remember, Indians had a religion that produced a society in which there were no locks on doors, no orphanages, no need for oaths, and no hungry people. Indian religion taught that sharing one's goods with another human being was the highest form of behavior. The Indian people have tenaciously held to this tradition of sharing their goods with other people in spite of all attempts by churches, government agencies, and schools to break them of the custom.

Christianity came along and tried to substitute "giving" for sharing. There was only one catch: giving meant giving to the church, not to other people. Giving, in the modern Christian sense, is simply a method of shearing the sheep, not of tending them.

Several years ago a Roman Catholic priest on the Wind River reservation complained bitterly about the Indian custom of sharing as being "un-Christian" because it distributed the wealth so well no middle class could be established. Hence "bad" Indians dragged the "good" ones down to a lower economic level and the reservation remained economically static.

The initial object of the Roman Catholic priest's outburst was an Indian woman who had a telephone and let all her neighbors use it. The bill ran as high as one hundred dollars some months. Often the woman was behind on her bill. But she didn't mind letting her neighbors use the phone when they wanted to.

The priest was furious when he reminded himself that of a Sunday the collection plate was not filled by the Indians. He felt that was intolerable and he wanted to teach the Indians "stewardship." Stewardship meant saving money and giving a percentage of the savings in the plate.

There was no difference, for the missionary, between sharing one's goods with the community and squandering resources. He preferred that the people give their money to the church, which would, in turn, efficiently define who was in need of help. Indians looked at the missionary's form of sharing as a sophisticated attempt to bribe the Great Spirit.

The onus is not on the Roman Catholics alone. The Protestants have devised a scheme whereby sharing is reduced to a painless sixty minutes a year. It is called One Great Hour of Sharing. Once a year they remind themselves how lucky they are to be Protestants and call for an outpouring of money so that others might receive the same privilege. Tough social problems always go unsolved.

Sharing, the great Indian tradition, can be the basis of a new thrust in religious development. Religion is not synonymous with a large organizational structure in Indian eyes. Spontaneous communal activity is more important. Thus any religious movement of the future would be wise to model itself on existing Indian behavioral patterns. This would mean returning religion to the Indian people.

The best thing that the national denominations could do to ensure the revitalization of Christian missions among Indian people would be to assist in the creation of a national Indian Christian Church. Such a church would incorporate all existing missions and programs into one national church to be wholly in the hands of Indian people.

Such a church would include all ordained Indian clergymen now serving as church workers in the Indian field. The actual form of the ministry would not be determined by obsolete theological distinctions preserved from the middle ages, but would rather incorporate the most feasible role that religion can now play in the expanding reservation societies.

Each denomination that has been putting funds into Indian work would contribute toward the total budget of the new church. Existing buildings and church structures would be evaluated by the new Indian church and the tribal council of the reservation on which the property is located. Congregations of the various denominations would be consolidated and reservation-wide boards of laymen would direct activities on each reservation.

With the religious function integrated into the ongoing life of the tribe, the Indian church would be able to achieve self-support in a short time as the role of religion clarified itself to the reservation communities. Religious competition, which fractures present tribal life, would disappear and the movement toward ancient religions might not be so crucial.

Such a proposal is too comprehensive for most denominations to accept at the present time. The primary fear of turning over the sacred white religion to a group of pagans would probably outrage most denominations, too few of whom realize how ridiculous denominational competition really is.

The best example I can mention of denominational competition existed at Farmington, New Mexico, a couple of years ago. The situation has probably changed since 1965. But that year there were twenty-six different churches serving an estimated Navajo population of 250. That's less than ten Indians per denomination! Assuming each church had a choir of eight, the congregations must have totaled one or two people per Sunday. Which does not indicate a field ready for harvest.

I estimated that the total mission budget for the Farmington area that year was in excess of $250,000. Christianity, not tourism, was Farmington's most profitable industry in 1965.

Churches face literal dissolution on the reservations unless they radically change their method of operation. Younger Indians are finding in Indian nationalism and tribal religions sufficient meaning to continue their drift away from the established churches. Even though many churches had chaplaincies in the government boarding schools, the young are not accepting missionary overtures like their fathers and mothers did.

As Indian nationalism continues to rise, bumper stickers like "God is Red" will take on new meanings. Originally put out at the height of Altizer's "God is Dead" theological pronouncements, the slogan characterizes the trend in Indian religion today.

Many Indians believe that the Indian gods will return when the Indian people throw out the white man's religion and return to the ways of their fathers. Whether or not this thinking is realistic is not the question. Rather the question is one of response and responsibility of the missionaries today. Will they continue to be a burden or not?

Can the white man's religion make one final effort to be

real, or must it too vanish like its predecessors from the old world? I personally would like to see Indians return to their old religions wherever possible. For me at least, Christianity has been a sham to cover over the white man's shortcomings. Yet I spent four years in a seminary finding out for myself where Christianity had fallen short.

I believe that an Indian version of Christianity could do much for our society. But there is little chance for such a melding of cards. Everyone in the religious sphere wants his trump to play on the last trick. In the meantime, Banyaca, Mad Bear Anderson, and others are silently changing the game from pinochle to one where all fifty-two cards are wild. They may, if the breaks fall their way, introduce religion to this continent once again.

6 ✦ GOVERNMENT AGENCIES

PEOPLE HAVE FOUND it hard to think of Indians without conjuring up the picture of a massive bureaucracy oppressing a helpless people. Right-wing news commentators delight in picturing the Indian as a captive of the evil forces of socialism and leftist policy. Liberals view the bureaucracy as an evil denial of the inherent rights of a free man.

It would be fair to say that the Indian people are ambivalent about all this. They fully realize that with no funds for investment in social services they are dependent upon the federal government for services which the ordinary citizen provides for himself and which other poor do not receive except under demeaning circumstances. Yet they are also fully aware that the services they receive are not gratis services. Many services are set out in early treaties and statutes by which Indians bargained and received these rights to services in return for enormous land cessions.

Some Indian people want desperately to get rid of the Bureau of Indian Affairs. Others want increased bureau services to help solve problems of long standing. In order to understand this ambivalence it is necessary to understand the history and present organization of the government agencies that provide services for Indian people.

The bureau is a creature of history. It was originally an

128

agency of the War Department because the early relations between the tribes and the government were more those of war than peace. In 1819 Congress authorized the President to begin to provide services for the Indian people "to prevent their extinction" and from this statute the basic programs which are now found in the Bureau of Indian Affairs began.

When the Department of the Interior was organized in 1849, the bureau was transferred to that agency. Fortunately Interior was able to take better care of the Indian than it subsequently did the buffalo and passenger pigeon, although some Indians would tell you that the policies which led to the demise of the other two species still reign supreme in Interior.

For nearly a century the bureau struggled along, subject to the whims of Congress, churches, and pressure groups. It gradually developed programs which covered all the possible needs of the Indian people. During the 1950's, in the midst of the drive for termination, the Health Service was transferred to the Department of Health, Education and Welfare. More recently proposals have been made to transfer the remainder of the BIA to HEW but these ideas have generally been rejected by both Indians and Congress, though for differing reasons.

At present the Bureau of Indian Affairs is divided into ten area offices which are scattered throughout the country. Each area office provides supervision for a number of tribes in the different states. One day an Interior Department official told me that the area offices were scattered "strategically" to serve the tribes. If that is strategy, we should all be thankful these people are in Interior instead of the State Department.

The area office in Minneapolis serves tribes in Minnesota, Wisconsin, Iowa, and Michigan. In fact, that area office ignores the Michigan Indians, persecutes the little Indian settlement at Tama, Iowa, and muddles around in Wisconsin and Minnesota. The last Interior official to visit Michigan came in a covered wagon shortly before Custer organized his famous Michigan regiment. It is unfortunate for the Michigan tribes that he was too late to join the outfit.

In 1968, after two years of loudly proclaiming that the

bureau would have thorough consultations with tribes before changing any services, it abruptly closed the grade school at Tama, Iowa, without even mentioning it to the tribe. The tribe fought back and, at this writing, was beginning to get promises from the bureau that it could have its school again.

The area office in Aberdeen, South Dakota, serves the tribes of the Dakotas and Nebraska. It is notorious for its inability to provide services to the tribes for land consolidation purposes. The reservations are all divided into small allotments and the people want to buy all of the land owned by individuals and put it into tribal ownership. During a hearing on the land problem in the 1950's it was revealed that when the Rosebud Sioux tribe had been fairly successful at land consolidation the bureau area office in Aberdeen suddenly discovered that the process they had been using to provide land consolidation was not legal.

The same hearing brought out that the same bureau office was advocating to the Oglala Sioux, the neighboring reservation to Rosebud, the same process of land purchase they had just denied use of to the Rosebud Sioux. Aberdeen is the most religious of the area offices. The right hand never knows what the left hand is doing.

Billings, Montana, area office serves the tribes of Wyoming and Montana. Although other area offices have been able to find means by which small groups of Indians could be organized under the provisions of the Indian Reorganization Act, Billings has been unable to do anything with the landless Indians of Montana, a remnant of Chief Little Shell's band of Chippewas who wandered into the state in the closing years of the last century. They have been lingering ever since.

The state of Oklahoma has two area offices, Muskogee for the "civilized" tribes in the east and Anadarko for the "wild" tribes of the west. Somewhere in the operations of the two offices the tribes of Kansas and the Choctaws of Mississippi are handled.

Albuquerque, New Mexico, provides services for the Apaches and Pueblos of New Mexico. They also used to provide services for the Tiguas of El Paso, Texas, in the early years of the present century but one day they decided the trip was too long for them to make. So they simply forgot about that tribe. It took half a century for the Tiguas to get their status as Indians back, and then they had to become a state-serviced tribe, not a federal tribe.

Phoenix, Arizona, is the area office which serves the tribes of Arizona (except the Navajo), Utah, and Nevada. The tribes of Utah and Nevada are some thousand miles from Phoenix, which makes it easy for them to run down to the area office to check on things. It was this arrangement that was described to me as "strategic."

Sacramento area office covers the state of California. For decades people have been trying to figure out if it has any relationship to Indians living in that state. Finally someone decided that it was placed there to hide information from Indians which they might otherwise ferret out from other agencies. In recent years this area office has begun to do something for Indians after a long siesta. Whether it will manage to get a program off the ground before California is dumped in the sea by an earthquake is a matter of serious speculation by Indians of that state.

The Pacific Northwest is serviced by the area office of Portland, Oregon. The tribes of Washington, Oregon, and Idaho receive services from Portland. Tribes have told me that tribal resolutions, leases, land sales, and programs disappear into the Portland area office never to be seen again. At one time a rumor spread that Judge Crater and Amelia Earhart were hidden somewhere in the Portland area office. And this rumor was never denied.

Alaska has its own area office in Juneau to take care of the natives of that state. Continental tribes have gotten the impression that the Juneau office is fairly responsive to tribal needs. It has probably the best reputation for service to native peoples of any of the area offices.

The Washington headquarters of the bureau serves the federal tribes that live east of the Mississippi, except the Choctaws of Mississippi. The tribes of New York, the Iroquois, were made the responsibility of the state in 1948, leaving only two tribes, the Eastern Band of Cherokees in North Carolina and the Seminole reservations in Florida, at the mercy of the bureau.

The function of the area office is to serve as an intermediary for the various agencies in the decision-making process. In some ways the area office fulfills its intended function. It can always decide *not to* do something, leaving the choice up to the tribe to go to Washington and fight out the decision where decisions are made. Perhaps the best service provided by the area offices is keeping records. The area office has copies of all the records kept by the local agency and the Washington headquarters.

When a decision has to be made, it must go from the agency to the area office, lie in state there for a decent period of time, then be stamped "disapproved" and sent on to Washington. In Washington the tribe and the Commissioner get together and try to solve the problem.

Once a decision is reached, the tribe goes back to its reservation, the Commissioner goes to lunch while the decision is mimeographed and sent down to the area office for distribution to the agencies. The agency personnel then interpret the decision according to their local policies, which usually makes the tribe mad enough to go back to see the Commissioner.

The process described above is the area office at its worst. In fact, most area offices operate quite smoothly and are in touch with tribes continuously. But one unpleasant incident can ruin the reputation of an area office quicker than one would imagine.

One of the biggest stumbling blocks facing the area office is the lack of funds to carry out their assigned tasks. In the Minneapolis area, for example, there are no funds to begin a comprehensive program for the Michigan tribes. The tribes of that state do not demand programs from their Senators and Congressmen and so do not receive consideration. In those areas where tribes are fairly sophisticated about using their Senators and Congressmen to pressure for programs, the area office can generally offer a great many more programs to the tribes because funds are made available to it.

Many area offices do not use tribes in a partnership to secure programs. They often lose sight of the reservations' needs and plan programs according to the funds they have available. If area offices would work more closely with people to support tribal programs, they would soon find the tribes out seeking more funds for programs.

Within each area are a number of agencies. Larger

tribes have agencies of their own and a number of smaller tribes may be gathered together under a general agency. An example of the general agency serving many tribes is Everett, Washington, which is designed to handle the small tribes of the Puget Sound area. The agency provides all of the basic services except health. Thus the agency may be large or small depending upon the size of the tribe to be serviced.

On the whole, the organizational structure of the Bureau of Indian Affairs provides one important feature which makes it capable of handling matters in a manner beneficial to the Indian people. That feature is that tribes are recognized as legal entities of equivalent rank by the office regardless of what level the office is on. Thus a tribe is able to exercise its fundamental sovereignty at all levels of government.

This feature contrasts sharply with agencies serving other American citizens. Social service agencies may be influential on the county level, but when people get to the state and regional levels they become merely another applicant, till at the national level they may be virtual nonentities. Tribes, however, never lose their basic legal rights as governing bodies.

Thus tribes have become eligible for a great variety of programs by qualifying as local sponsoring bodies and then using their federal status in Washington, D.C., as a competitive edge over other applicants for funding. Under the old Area Redevelopment Administration and its successor, the Economic Development Administration, tribes have been able to enjoy a great variety of projects. It would be fair to say that of any agency in the government in the last few years EDA has been the most responsive to tribal programs.

Wherein, you may ask, does all of the controversy—particularly the charge of paternalism—originate, if everything is operating so smoothly in the bureau?

The answer lies, I believe, in understanding the nature of the Bureau of Indian Affairs in the political sense. Unless one understands the outside pressures that operate on the bureau, one does not understand the flaws in the system which give rise to the various charges that are leveled against it.

To begin with, the bureau should not be characterized as paternalistic. It should be characterized as "fear-ridden," for the circle of fear that operates within it is much more detrimental to its efficiency than is its desire to paternalize.

America has been brainwashed to define government programs as paternalistic per se. Part of this tendency originates from the natural reluctance to pay higher taxes. People grumbling against taxes generally find some irrelevant thing their government is doing and place on it the entire blame. It becomes a paternalistic program simply because it is unpopular. Often an agency, bureau, or program is defined as paternalistic whether it accomplishes anything or not.

Over the years the average citizen has come to accept the Federal Deposit Insurance Corporation, the Federal Housing Authority, the Social Security system, the Federal Reserve, and other programs as essential services of government. Few would want to eliminate these programs because they serve general needs.

With the Bureau of Indian Affairs only Indians receive services, not citizens in general. The BIA is therefore tagged as paternalistic because people feel that its services are holding Indians back. Few have ever defined "back" for me. I would define it, as did Congress in 1819, back from extinction.

The Bureau of Indian Affairs is one of twenty-six odd bureaus within the Department of the Interior. Its top job, the Commissionership, is a job filled by appointment, a survivor of the political spoils system of the last century. The Commissioner has one basic task—to keep the members of the Interior and Insular Affairs committees of the House and Senate happy—not to serve Indians or even to run his own bureau.

Members serving on the Interior and Insular Affairs committees have little time to worry about Indians. Indian legislation is a chore that distracts the Congressmen and Senators from other legislation which is much more important to their careers. Most members of the two committees are from the West, where few electoral votes are available to the national parties. Their only chance for national political advancement is, therefore, as Vice-Presidential candidate or cabinet officer. Consequently they spend as little time on Indians as possible and concentrate on areas like Foreign Relations, Armed Services, and Commerce.

When tribes are unhappy, they traditionally contact their representatives for redress. When people become concerned about how Indians are being treated, they write their representatives in Congress demanding an answer. All of these pressures fall upon the few members of the two Interior committees.

Imagine, therefore, a Senator from the West, busy with Foreign Relations Committee work, being interrupted by newspaper reports that Indians are starving in West Elbow, Utah, or Baby Bear Butte, Nevada. He has to put away work he enjoys to answer questions on the starving Indians. Chances are that the newspaper reports are highly exaggerated but the Senator has to handle all accusations about how the federal government is not treating Indians right.

The next time an Indian bill is heard before the Interior Committee the Senator makes sure that the Commissioner hears about the starving Indians. In turn, when the Commissioner gets back to his office, field personnel find out rather quickly about the treatment of the Commissioner before the committee.

Thus fear in massive quantities is injected into the field operations of the bureau. Subsequent dealings with tribes begin to reveal a real lack of enthusiasm for taking chances. The possibility of backfire is a real consideration. Decisions are made according to the book in case any fracas results.

The tribe eventually gets furious at the attitude of the bureau and comes into Washington to complain to their Senator and the cycle begins once again. When one considers that this type of movement has been pounded into an organization for over a century then one can understand why things move at a snail's pace within the Bureau of Indian Affairs.

In my experience there are several incidents that stick out vividly as examples of bureaucratic fear. One day I got a call from a tribe that was trying to find out if its attorney contract had been approved. The Secretary of the Interior, or his delegate, has to approve all attorney contracts and tribes. I called the Phoenix area office for information and was told to check with Washington because the area office had sent the contract to the Bureau of Indian Affairs there to be approved. At the bureau in Washington I was told that all attorney contracts were approved out in the area office and none were sent east. I called Phoenix again and was again told that the area office had sent the contract to D.C. So I went in to see the Commissioner and asked his help in finding the contract. Nearly two weeks later the tribe informed me it had finally gotten the contract approved. The contract was, of course, in Phoenix all the time. But there was a duplicate copy in Washington also. In both places the bureau had failed to notify anyone that the contract had been approved. So rather than admit they were behind on their correspondence, both offices pushed the problem to and fro in an effort to absolve themselves from the blame, if any.

When I was working with the United Scholarship service my job was to find capable Indian high school students for our secondary school placement program. I visited several schools and looked at achievement tests and grades. At one bureau school I found several students of above-average ability who could easily qualify for our program. I asked for assistance from the bureau teachers in getting these students to apply for the program, but they refused to do anything to help. Their big argument was that they had to produce certain marks and standards or their school would fall below that of other bureau schools. To let these better students go on to schools in the East would have meant fewer students capable of doing college work in their school.

So a number of Indian students were denied an opportunity to get a better education because local bureau employees wanted to make a respectable record for themselves. The teachers were actually afraid to tell any of the students about our program because they were afraid the students might decide to enter it. That would have meant fewer capable students enrolled in the bureau high school and the subsequent questioning by higher bureau officials of the school's program.

Another time while I was working for the United Scholarship Service, Tillie Walker, the director of the program, and myself stopped in an area office to check on scholarship money that might be available that fall for Indian students. We were dumbfounded to learn that the bureau had seventeen thousand dollars on hand, expected another seventeen thousand dollars before the end of the year, and didn't expect to give any of it out.

We asked the man in charge of scholarships why the bureau, which had nearly one million dollars in scholarship money, couldn't use its funds to pick up eligible Indian students and let the USS with its meager resources provide funds for ineligible Indian students, those living off the reservation.

His explanation was a classic statement of the fear that pervades the bureau. He stated that he had worked in that job for some ten years, through both Democratic and Republican administrations. The Republicans, he said, frowned on expenditures, the Democrats encouraged them. And although it was a Democratic administration at present, someday, he said, the Republicans would be in office. They might, he told us, examine the books of that area office and discover that he had spent to the limit every year he had the money. He was laying the groundwork for his defense years before it would be necessary!

Bureau officials are very reluctant to defend tribal rights. Time and again tribes have come more than part way in pushing for a vital issue only to have the bureau fall back in fear at the last moment. Classic in this field has been the failure of the bureau to defend the fishing rights of the Northwest tribes. Although it is federal law that the bureau is responsible for defending Indian treaty rights as trustee, the bureau dodged the fishing rights issue for years. Finally, when Robert Bennett became Commissioner he took the bull by the horns and got the bureau to intervene. But the attitude of local bureau personnel, western Washington people told me, was to compromise Indian rights as much as possible.

Since the days of termination in the 1950's the situation in Indian Affairs has bordered on the irrational. There have been few changes on the Congressional committees, the bureau has changed little, tribes and the general public have been more vocal about their problems. Fear has increased proportionately.

One of the favorite games of the Congressional committees has been to threaten termination every time the bureau requests anything. I say games because it has been well known in Congress that, since 1960, tribes have petitioned for removal of the area offices and a concentration of personnel and decision-making authority at the local level. If Congress were serious about termination it would help the tribes to dismantle the bureau office by office, function by function.

Threats of termination have been disastrous from the Indian point of view. Tribes rarely know where they are in terms of national policy. They seldom know which tribe is programmed for new roads, new schools, new hospitals. No one knows until the dirt is turned. So tribes have come to take the word of bureau people as to their place in the overall program for development.

When it is known nationally that Congress is considering termination once again, bureau employees use this threat to keep tribes in line. Whenever a tribe begins to show a bit of independence, a BIA official will throw broad "hints" that the tribe had better forget it or be recommended for termination.

Recommendation for termination is no idle threat. As we have seen, in the 1950's the bureau offered every possible excuse for terminating tribes. No Indian is so foolish as to believe that it can't happen again. So the tribe generally gives in and follows the bureau line. The risk of total destruction of the Indian community is too great to treat lightly.

When I was Director of the National Congress of American Indians, the bureaucrats would tell me that the NCAI was advocating termination by following a course opposite to the BIA. Fortunately we always had an active tribal membership that thrived on combat and never took the threats seriously. But had I been leading a small tribe in western Washington, Wisconsin, or Nevada, the threat would have been enough to stop me cold.

One of the main problems of the bureau operations in the field has been the lack of Congressional policy directives. Tribes are obviously incapable of doing without federal services at present. Yet with proper training and development of community facilities many tribes could become self-sufficient and federal services and supervision would become nominal.

As long as the bureau is expected to prepare the tribes for termination it will fail in its programs. Many tribes have said that there is no incentive in building up their reservations if there is a chance they will be sold out unexpectedly in the near future. If there was a change in Congressional policy to promote the development of human and natural resources on the reservations, programs would be philosophically oriented to total development. There would be a means by which development could be evaluated—that of self-sufficiency. Motivation would change from fear to enthusiasm as programs became oriented to realistic goals based upon the expectation that the Indian people were building for the future instead of playing for time.

The annual process of budgeting also provides a great stumbling block for the bureau in its attempts to provide services to Indian people. Budgets too often reflect ongoing administrative overhead rather than funds which can be used to do a specific job. Thus an area office may have a surplus in education funds and a deficit in funds for roads or law and order. Funds must be spent for the purpose for which they are appropriated. So it may take a number of years to work an item up to the point where there is sufficient money available to do a job.

During 1968 Senator Clinton Anderson announced that the federal government was spending nearly a half billion dollars a year on Indian people and therefore he didn't think they were so neglected. The general public probably heard the figure and wondered what was happening in the bureau with all those funds.

In reality the funds were probably so earmarked that it was impossible for the bureau to do much with the money to overcome existing problems. Most area offices probably broke about even last year without being able to start new projects.

One glaring example of allocated funds being a detriment to Indian people is the school construction fund which is used to build new schools on the reservations. For years the bureau knew that the Navajo population was exploding and that classroom space would soon be at a premium. Yet nothing was done to reallocate funds for school construction on the Navajo reservations until Philleo Nash became Commissioner and by then it was too late.

For the past several years Navajos have been shipped all over the country in an effort to get the Navajo children in school. This policy resulted in the widespread displacement of children from other Indian tribes in schools near them. Thus northwestern tribes were denied entrance to the school in Chemawa, Oregon, and Nevada Indians were denied school space at Stewart, Nevada, a school they had used for decades.

The Navajo situation has begun to ease now, but the dropout rate of the other tribes who had to send their children to public and parochial schools increased during that period so that nationally the Indian education picture is about the same as it was years ago. The same story exists with regard to roads on several reservations.

In 1966 Commissioner Bennett was sent around Indian country to determine the needs of the tribes in order to plan Udall's great legislative masterpiece. In Minneapolis, Minnesota, site of the first of the regional meetings, several tribes presented their ideas on welfare. They complained that handouts undermined the educational programs they were conducting to encourage people to work. They asked that all welfare be turned into a work program so that people would not be idle all day long and then spend their welfare and unemployment checks carelessly.

Unfortunately this idea was never adopted. It couldn't be adopted under the present laws. And when the idea was subsequently discussed, various "liberal"-minded people said that it would be demeaning for people to have to work for welfare. So all possible avenues for development of this idea were blocked from the very beginning. It should be no wonder that the bureau has a hard time getting things done.

The other agencies working with Indian people—the Public Health Service, the Office of Economic Opportunity, the Labor Department, the Federal Housing Authority, and the Economic Development Administration—have a great deal more flexibility than does the bureau. They operate primarily on the grant basis. Funds are allocated by tribe according to projects. Primary responsibility for programming is on the tribe, and tribes who do not project a well-reasoned feasible plan for development do not get funds.

These agencies have had great success in assisting Indian tribes with their programs. One can hardly visit a reservation today without finding some new project under way. Many people arriving on a reservation for the first time bemoan the apparent lack of progress being made by the Indians. They are horrified by the poverty and living conditions. Automatically people seem to agree that the bureau had been incredibly derelict in its duty. Oh, if they had only seen these same reservations twenty years ago, they would have known what poverty was.

Consider for a moment, when did the reservations ever have the benefit of a program of major investment? Tribes went on the reservations in the late 1870's. For the most part the people lived in log cabins and tents. Indian Affairs was regarded as merely a matter of administration and record-keeping until the Meriam Report in 1928. Under the Indian Reorganization Act during the 1930's tribes were finally beginning to move, but World War II stopped all progress and funds were very scarce during those years.

In the 1950's and early 1960's tribes had to spend all of their time defending their lands and treaty rights from the whims of the terminationists. Little was done to develop the reservations because all energies went into saving them from obliteration. Finally in the 1960's, after nearly a century of neglect, funds began to become available for capital improvements such as tribal buildings, community halls, roads, and housing. The past few years have been the first time there has been money available for development of the reservations.

Deploring the lack of modern conveniences on the reservations is like beating your old horse for not being able to fly. If the tribes or the bureau could have developed the reservations any sooner, they would have done so.

In 1966, when the tribes met at Santa Fe, New Mexico,

to pressure the bureau for changes, they had a specific idea in mind. The programs of the OEO had taken hold on the reservations and the idea of granting funds directly to the tribes for specific programs was very popular.

At the meeting, Udall wandered around holding a paper written by a superintendent from Arizona who advocated a strict contract method of providing services comparable to the OEO programs. It was a radical departure from traditional policies and no one was sure that it could be sold to higher ups in the administration or Congress but the tribes all felt that it was the wave of the future.

Finally in 1968 the bureau set up a contracting project at the Salt River reservation in Arizona. After some two years in discussion it appeared that the way originally advocated by the tribes at Santa Fe would be tested on one reservation. To date the Salt River project has proved successful and plans are being made to expand the idea to other tribes.

Tribes today have a good grasp on the future. If they can work out the basic programs for contracting, they may be able to push on into new areas which have been unserviced or only partially serviced in the past. A lot depends upon the reactions within the bureaucracy and Congress as to whether or not the program will be continued.

The role of the Bureau of Indian Affairs must change radically if Indians are to make the progress necessary to keep them abreast of developments in the rest of society. It would be foolish to outline the basic problems of the bureau without offering alternative ideas by which it could be made more responsive.

There are a number of things the bureau could do immediately to completely change the rate and manner of progress of the Indian people. Here are some of them:

1. Programming by Size of Tribe

Too often tribes are simply lumped together as if they had identical profiles and it were merely a matter of tribal response to bureau programs which differentiated the tribes.

In fact there are about thirty-five tribes with sufficient population, land, and resources to make large programs feasible. These tribes average some two thousand people, generally have in excess of 100,000 acres of land, and have a large enough tribal income to provide a basic working budget for development.

These tribes should be given special consideration for funding from the major granting agencies within the federal government. Wherever possible they should be given responsibility for minor services which the bureau now provides. This could be done on a contract basis annually with a declining federal share as tribal income rises.

The rest of the two hundred odd tribes fall below one thousand people, have little natural resources, and have a small land base. As their tribal income ranges from zero to very little, certainly none would have sufficient income for programming.

These tribes should submit projects directly to the Bureau of Indian Affairs. The projects would include all areas now served by bureau programs and would be set up on a cost plus fixed-fee basis so that the tribe could conduct its own programs and have a little income for the tribe as well.

Special loan-grant funds would be made available to the tribes for land consolidation programs. In many cases federal lands, of submarginal or public domain character, would be added to tribal holdings to provide a decent land base for development.

These tribes would be encouraged to develop basic community strength and tribal income necessary for ongoing overhead expenses. They would receive declining grants according to projects completed until the basic community development plan had been realized. After that they would become eligible for grants in the same manner as the other larger tribes.

2. Discretionary Funds

Area offices and agencies should be given the bulk of their annual budgets in undesignated funds for total reservation development so that as tribes began to assume responsibilities they could set up immediate contracting arrangements. In addition the tribe and the bureau would set the priorities for expenditures each year instead of having the priorities set in Washington. In that way maximum flexibility in meeting local needs would be possible. Supplemental appropriations, now common to cover emergency situations, would become a thing of the past.

3. Tribal Employment Would Be Civil Service

As the tribes began to take over the programs on their reservations, need of top personnel would become critical as it is now with the various poverty programs on the reservations. Employment within the Bureau of Indian Affairs would be dropping as jobs were displaced through the contracting procedure. People leaving the bureau to seek employment with the tribes would be given Civil Service status. They would thus not lose their time in grade in federal service by leaving the bureau but would continue to work toward retirement while working for the tribe on a program contracted with a government agency.

Under this method of offering tribal employment to people in the bureau the most capable people would soon be hired for tribal programs. The remainder, obviously not in great demand by the Indian people, could be transferred to the Department of Agriculture where they could spend their remaining years in relative retirement.

4. Reorganization of the Bureau of Indian Affairs

As the programs of the tribes began to cut into the superstructure of the bureau the need for supervisory services would radically decrease. Thus there would be a great need for reorganization of the bureau to meet the changing situation.

At that time the bureau should be transferred, not to Health, Education and Welfare, but to Commerce. Since the bureau would be primarily a granting and technical assistance agency, it would need to be in a department where economic development was the primary mission. It could then become merged with the Economic Development Administration in a special Indian section where it would act as a fact-finding agency matching tribal projects with available programs in government and opportunities available in the private business sector.

5. Disposition of Federal Responsibility to Indians

Indian tribes would continue to be eligible for grants

from all federal agencies as long as the tribe remained functional. In this way the United States would be meeting its basic responsibilities to assist the Indian people and it would also fulfill now unfulfilled treaty promises of "free and undisturbed use" of reservation areas.

Income from tribal lands and tribal lands themselves would continue to be tax exempt as long as the lands and the income derived from them were used to provide social and community services to reservation residents. When all services had been provided, income could be distributed to enrolled members of the tribe. But then the tribe would no longer have eligibility for grants from federal agencies.

It remains to be seen what will happen to the Bureau of Indian Affairs in the future. Movements to abolish it continually interrupt the basic service programs so that it is very difficult for continuity of program to be achieved. Few people consider what would happen to the Indian people if the bureau were suddenly removed. Indians would be cast adrift in society at the mercy of sharp operators. Eventually they would be dispersed into the cities, having been cheated out of their lands.

Cities would all have ghettos of Indians on welfare. Conditions would rapidly deteriorate in the urban ghettos and eventually the issue would be joined with urban racial problems.

In recent years discussion has been going on in Indian Affairs advocating giving the Indians "more responsibility." This is useless talk. Designed to cover up a multitude of sins, particularly does it cover up the basic responsibility of the federal government toward the Indian people.

More, less, or no responsibility is irrelevant to the problem. When we talk about responsibility in these terms we are talking about play acting. Responsibility can never be given unless it is welcomed and desired. I could no more give my children responsibility than I could give them the far side of the moon. They must have a real status and stake in the process or they will recognize my overtures as tricks.

That was the primary misunderstanding of the Interior thesis over the past several years. People continued to talk about giving the tribes more responsibility. But they could not define for themselves what that responsibility should be, where it should be exercised, and what limits would be placed on it.

If responsibility is irrelevant, sovereignty is not. States have sovereignty, counties have sovereignty, cities and towns have sovereignty, water districts have sovereignty, school boards have sovereignty. Why shouldn't tribes have total sovereignty? Originally they did. Treaties recognize this basic fact of legal existence. Tribes agreed to go to the reservations provided they could have their basic community rights and self-government.

As the system of providing services to the tribes grew up, ideas of the government and the tribes grew farther apart. Much of the problem was caused by the agitation of the churches for franchises to hunt souls on the reservations. This demand created the feeling that Indians were to be pawns in the great experiment of civilizing a savage people.

Over the years programs have been designed to accomplish secretly what cannot be accomplished openly, the de-Indianization of the Indian. In 1934, John Collier began to move the Bureau of Indian Affairs in a new direction. He figured that the movement to make white men out of Indians had not succeeded in four centuries and there was no reason to expect it to succeed in his lifetime.

But Collier also realized that Indians were already Indians. It was a simple matter, therefore, for Collier to advocate the creation of a legal status whereby tribes could become competitive in modern society and undertake development programs which would be a result of community desires. So the official tribal status of the Indian Reorganization Act was created and each tribe was given a right to have a constitution and charter under the law. It was then up to the tribe to plan its own development to fit its own needs.

Congressional policy should recognize the basic right to tribal sovereignty. Such sovereignty should include all promises contained in treaties and should recognize the eligibility of tribal governments for all federal programs which are opened to counties and cities. In this way the onus of having failed the Indian people would not be placed on Interior or Congress. Tribes would be free to develop or not, according to the desires of the people in the tribe.

The charge has frequently been leveled at the bureau that it has set up puppet governments on the reservations and somehow mysteriously governs all aspects of tribal life by remote control. As long as policies remain so nebulous with respect to the actual status of tribal governments this charge will continue to be made. Recognition of basic sovereignty would provide a solution for this problem. The integrity of the tribal entity would be guaranteed by Congressional fiat in much the same manner as Congress makes a certain type of soldier an officer and a gentleman by fiat.

Until a new ideological basis is placed under the federal-Indian relationship it seems certain that the bureau will struggle along on one cylinder, carrying the burdens of misinformation and acting as the scapegoat for the collective sins of both red and white. It is unfortunate that one agency has to be designated as the target for the frustrations of people who have not recognized their confusion between culture and technique. Perhaps the future will be brighter.

7 ❖ INDIAN HUMOR

ONE OF THE best ways to understand a people is to know what makes them laugh. Laughter encompasses the limits of the soul. In humor life is redefined and accepted. Irony and satire provide much keener insights into a group's collective psyche and values than do years of research.

It has always been a great disappointment to Indian people that the humorous side of Indian life has not been mentioned by professed experts on Indian Affairs. Rather the image of the granite-faced grunting redskin has been perpetuated by American mythology.

People have little sympathy with stolid groups. Dick Gregory did much more than is believed when he introduced humor into the Civil Rights struggle. He enabled non-blacks to enter into the thought world of the black community and experience the hurt it suffered. When all people shared the humorous but ironic situation of the black, the urgency and morality of Civil Rights was communicated.

The Indian people are exactly opposite of the popular stereotype. I sometimes wonder how anything is accomplished by Indians because of the apparent overemphasis on humor within the Indian world. Indians have found a humorous side of nearly every problem and the experiences of life have generally been so well defined through jokes and stories that they have become a thing in themselves.

For centuries before the white invasion, teasing was a method of control of social situations by Indian people. Rather than embarrass members of the tribe publicly, people used to tease individuals they considered out of step with the consensus of tribal opinion. In this way egos were preserved and disputes within the tribe of a personal nature were held to a minimum.

Gradually people learned to anticipate teasing and began to tease themselves as a means of showing humility and at the same time advocating a course of action they deeply believed in. Men would depreciate their feats to show they were not trying to run roughshod over tribal desires. This method of behavior served to highlight their true virtues and gain them a place of influence in tribal policy-making circles.

Humor has come to occupy such a prominent place in national Indian affairs that any kind of movement is impossible without it. Tribes are being brought together by sharing humor of the past. Columbus jokes gain great sympathy among all tribes, yet there are no tribes extant who had anything to do with Columbus. But the fact of white invasion from which all tribes have suffered has created a common bond in relation to Columbus jokes that gives a solid feeling of unity and purpose to the tribes.

The more desperate the problem, the more humor is directed to describe it. Satirical remarks often circumscribe problems so that possible solutions are drawn from the circumstances that would not make sense if presented in other than a humorous form.

Often people are awakened and brought to a militant edge through funny remarks. I often counseled people to run for the Bureau of Indian Affairs in case of an earthquake because nothing could shake the BIA. And I would watch as younger Indians set their jaws, determined that they, if nobody else, would shake it. We also had a saying that in case of fire call the BIA and they would handle it because they put a wet blanket on everything. This also got a warm reception from people.

Columbus and Custer jokes are the best for penetration into the heart of the matter, however. Rumor has it that Columbus began his journey with four ships. But one went over the edge so he arrived in the new world with only three. Another version states that Columbus didn't know where he was going, didn't know where he had been, and did it all on someone else's money. And the white man has been following Columbus ever since.

It is said that when Columbus landed, one Indian turned to another and said, "Well, there goes the neighborhood." Another version has two Indians watching Columbus land and one saying to the other, "Maybe if we leave them alone they will go away." A favorite cartoon in Indian country a few years back showed a flying saucer landing while an Indian watched. The caption was "Oh, no, not again."

The most popular and enduring subject of Indian humor is, of course, General Custer. There are probably more jokes about Custer and the Indians than there were participants in the battle. All tribes, even those thousands of miles from Montana, feel a sense of accomplishment when thinking of Custer. Custer binds together implacable foes because he represented the Ugly American of the last century and he got what was coming to him.

Some years ago we put out a bumper sticker which read "Custer Died for Your Sins." It was originally meant as a dig at the National Council of Churches. But as it spread around the nation it took on additional meaning until everyone claimed to understand it and each interpretation was different.

Originally, the Custer bumper sticker referred to the Sioux Treaty of 1868 signed at Fort Laramie in which the United States pledged to give free and undisturbed use of the lands claimed by Red Cloud in return for peace. Under the covenants of the Old Testament, breaking a covenant called for a blood sacrifice for atonement. Custer was the blood sacrifice for the United States breaking the Sioux treaty. That, at least originally, was the meaning of the slogan.

Custer jokes, however, can barely be categorized, let alone sloganized. Indians say that Custer was well-dressed for the occasion. When the Sioux found his body after the battle, he had on an Arrow shirt.

Many stories are derived from the details of the battle itself. Custer is said to have boasted that he could ride through the entire Sioux nation with his Seventh Cavalry and he was half right. He got half-way through.

One story concerns the period immediately after Custer's contingent had been wiped out and the Sioux and Cheyennes were zeroing in on Major Reno and his troops several miles to the south of the Custer battlefield.

The Indians had Reno's troopers surrounded on a bluff. Water was scarce, ammunition was nearly exhausted, and it looked like the next attack would mean certain extinction.

One of the white soldiers quickly analyzed the situation and shed his clothes. He covered himself with mud, painted his face like an Indian, and began to creep toward the Indian lines.

A Cheyenne heard some rustling in the grass and was just about to shoot.

"Hey, chief," the soldier whispered, "don't shoot, I'm coming over to join you. I'm going to be on your side."

The warrior looked puzzled and asked the soldier why he wanted to change sides.

"Well," he replied, "better red than dead."

Custer's Last Words occupy a revered place in Indian humor. One source states that as he was falling mortally wounded he cried, "Take no prisoners!" Other versions, most of them off color, concentrate on where those **** Indians are coming from. My favorite last saying pictures Custer on top of the hill looking at a multitude of warriors charging up the slope at him. He turns resignedly to his aide and says, "Well, it's better than going back to North Dakota."

Since the battle it has been a favorite technique to boost the numbers on the Indian side and reduce the numbers on the white side so that Custer stands out as a man fighting against insurmountable odds. One question no pseudo-historian has attempted to answer, when changing the odds to make the little boy in blue more heroic, is how what they say were twenty thousand Indians could be fed when gathered into one camp. What a tremendous pony herd must have been gathered there, what a fantastic herd of buffalo must have been nearby to feed that amount of Indians, what an incredible source of drinking water must have been available for fifty thousand animals and some twenty thousand Indians!

Just figuring water-needs to keep that many people and animals alive for a number of days must have been incredible. If you have estimated correctly, you will see that the Little Big Horn was the last great *naval* engagement of the Indian wars.

The Sioux tease other tribes a great deal for not having been at the Little Big Horn. The Crows, traditional enemies of the Sioux, explain their role as Custer's scouts as one of bringing Custer where the Sioux could get at him! Arapahos and Cheyennes, allies of the Sioux in that battle, refer to the time they "bailed the Sioux out" when they got in trouble with the cavalry.

Even today variations of the Custer legend are bywords in Indian country. When an Indian gets too old and becomes inactive, people say he is "too old to muss the Custer anymore."

The early reservation days were times when humorous incidents abounded as Indians tried to adapt to the strange new white ways and occasionally found themselves in great dilemmas.

At Fort Sisseton, in Dakota territory, Indians were encouraged to enlist as scouts for the Army after the Minnesota Wars. Among the requirements for enlistment were a working knowledge of English and having attained twenty-one years of age. But these requirements were rarely met. Scouts were scarce and the goal was to keep a company of scouts at full strength, not to follow regulations from Washington to the letter.

In a short time the Army had a company of scouts who were very efficient but didn't know enough English to understand a complete sentence. Washington, finding out about the situation, as bureaucracies occasionally do, sent an inspector to check on the situation. While he was en route, orders to disband the scouts arrived, and so his task became one of closing the unit and making the mustering-out payments.

The scouts had lined up outside the command officer's quarters and were interviewed one by one. They were given their choice of taking money, horses, or a combination of the two as their final severance pay from the

Army. Those who could not speak English were severely reprimanded and tended to get poorer horses in payment because of their obvious disregard of the regulations.

One young scout, who was obviously in violation of both requirements, was very worried about his interview. He quizzed the scouts who came from the room about the interview. To a man they repeated the same story: "You will be asked three questions, how old are you, how long have you been with the scouts, and whether you want money or horses for your mustering-out pay."

The young scout memorized the appropriate answers and prepared himself for his turn with the inspector. When his turn came he entered the room, scared to death but determined to do his best. He stood at attention before the man from Washington, eager to give his answers and get out of there.

The inspector, tired after a number of interviews, wearily looked up and inquired:

"How long have you been in the scouts?"

"Twenty years," the Indian replied with a grin.

The inspector stopped short and looked at the young man. Here was a man who looked only eighteen or twenty, yet he had served some twenty years in the scouts. He must have been one of the earliest recruits. It just didn't seem possible. Yet, the inspector thought, you can't tell an Indian's age from the way he looks, they sure can fool you sometimes. Or was he losing his mind after interviewing so many people in so short a time? Perhaps it was the Dakota heat. At any rate, he continued the interview.

"How old are you?" he continued.

"Three years."

A look of shock rippled across the inspector's face. Could this be some mysterious Indian way of keeping time? Or was he now delirious?

"Am I crazy or are you?" he angrily asked the scout.

"Both" was the reply and the scout relaxed, smiled, and leaned over the desk, reaching out to receive his money.

The horrified inspector cleared the window in one leap. He was seen in Washington, D.C., the following morning, having run full speed during the night. It was the last time Indian scouts were required to know English and applications for interpreter were being taken the following morning.

The problems of the missionaries in the early days provided stories which have become classics in Indian country. They are retold over and over again wherever Indians gather.

One story concerns a very obnoxious missionary who delighted in scaring the people with tales of hell, eternal fires, and everlasting damnation. This man was very unpopular and people went out of their way to avoid him. But he persisted to contrast heaven and hell as a carrot-and-stick technique of conversion.

One Sunday after a particularly fearful description of hell he asked an old chief, the main holdout of the tribe against Christianity, where he wanted to go. The old chief asked the missionary where *he* was going. And the missionary replied that, of course, he as a missionary of the gospel was going to heaven.

"Then I'll go to hell," the old chief said, intent on having peace in the world to come if not in this world.

On the Standing Rock reservation in South Dakota my grandfather served as the Episcopal missionary for years after his conversion to Christianity. He spent a great deal of his time trying to convert old Chief Gall, one of the strategists of Custer's demise, and a very famous and influential member of the tribe.

My grandfather gave Gall every argument in the book and some outside the book but the old man was adamant in keeping his old Indian ways. Neither the joys of heaven nor the perils of hell would sway the old man. But finally, because he was fond of my grandfather, he decided to become an Episcopalian.

He was baptized and by Christmas of that year was ready to take his first communion. He fasted all day and attended the Christmas Eve services that evening.

The weather was bitterly cold and the little church was heated by an old wood stove placed in the center of the church. Gall, as the most respected member of the community, was given the seat of honor next to the stove where he could keep warm.

In deference to the old man, my grandfather offered him communion first. Gall took the chalice and drained the entire supply of wine before returning to his seat. The wine had been intended for the entire congregation and so the old man had a substantial amount of spiritual refreshment.

Upon returning to his warm seat by the stove, it was not long before the wine took its toll on the old man who by now had had nothing to eat for nearly a day.

"Grandson," he called to my grandfather, "now I see why you wanted me to become a Christian. I feel fine, so nice and warm and happy. Why didn't you tell me that Christians did this every Sunday. If you had told me about this, I would have joined your church years ago."

Needless to say, the service was concluded as rapidly as possible and attendance skyrocketed the following Sunday.

Another missionary was traveling from Gallup to Albuquerque in the early days. Along the way he offered a ride to an Indian who was walking to town. Feeling he had a captive audience, he began cautiously to promote his message, using a soft-sell approach.

"Do you realize," he said, "that you are going to a place where sinners abound?"

The Indian nodded his head in assent.

"And the wicked dwell in the depths of their iniquities?"

Again a nod.

"And sinful women who have lived a bad life go?"

A smile and then another nod.

"And no one who lives a good life goes there?"

A possible conversion, thought the missionary, and so he pulled out his punch line: "And do you know what we call that place?"

The Indian turned, looked the missionary in the eye, and said, "Albuquerque."

Times may have changed but difficulties in communications seem to remain the same. At Santee, Nebraska, the people tell of a full blood who had a great deal of trouble understanding English. He used the foreign tongue as little as possible and managed to get along. But he knew only phrases of broken English, which he used when bargaining for his necessities of life.

One day he approached a white farmer and began bargaining for a fine rooster that the farmer owned. The old timer had brought two large bags filled with new potatoes and he motioned to the farmer that he wanted to trade them for the rooster.

Pointing from one to the other, he anxiously inquired, "potato rooster, potato rooster?" Soon the white farmer got the message and decided that it would be a good trade.

"Sure, chief," he replied, "I'll trade you."

So the Indian picked up the rooster, looked at it with satisfaction, tucked the rooster under his arm, and started to walk away.

As he was leaving, the white farmer began to think about the exchange. Obviously the rooster would be of little value without some hens for it. The potatoes were more than adequate to pay for a number of chickens, so he called after the Indian:

"Chief, do you want a pullet?"

The Indian turned around, tucked the rooster tighter under his arm, and said, "No, I can carry it."

In the Southwest, Indians like to talk about a similar play on words. One favorite story concerns a time when the Apaches and the settlers were fighting it out for control of Arizona territory. The chief of one Apache band was the last one needed to sign the peace treaty. Scout after scout had urged him to sign so the territory could have peace. But to no avail.

One day the chief took sick and, because he realized his days were numbered, he called his three sons together and made them pledge not to make peace unless all three signed the treaty. Soon after that the old man died and his three sons, Deerfoot, Running Bear, and Falling Rocks, all left to seek their fortunes with portions of the original band.

Scouts quickly found Deerfoot and Running Bear and convinced them they should sign the treaty. But they were unable to find Falling Rocks. Years went by and everyone in the territory sought the missing band so the treaty could be concluded. Falling Rocks was not to be found.

Eventually everyone gave up except the state highway department. They continued looking for him. And that is why today as you drive through the mountain passes in Arizona you will see large signs that read, "Look out for Falling Rocks."

The years have not changed the basic conviction of the Indian people that they are still dealing with the United States as equals. At a hearing on Civil Rights in South Dakota a few years ago a white man asked a Sioux if they still considered themselves an independent nation. "Oh, yes," was the reply, "we could still declare war on you. We might lose but you'd know you'd been in a terrible fight. Remember the last time in Montana?"

During the 1964 elections Indians were talking in Arizona about the relative positions of the two candidates, Johnson and Goldwater. A white man told them to forget about domestic policies and concentrate on the foreign policies of the two men. One Indian looked at him coldly and said that from the Indian point of view it was all foreign policy.

The year 1964 also saw the emergence of the Indian vote on a national scale. Rumors reached us that on the Navajo reservation there was more enthusiasm than understanding of the political processes. Large signs announced, "All the Way with LJB."

The current joke is that a survey was taken and only 15 percent of the Indians thought that the United States should get out of Vietnam. Eighty-five percent thought they should get out of America!

One of the most popular topics of Indian humor is the Bureau of Indian Affairs. When asked what was the biggest joke in Indian country, a man once said, "The BIA." During the years of termination, no matter how many tribes were being terminated the BIA kept adding employees. Since the thrust of termination was to cut government expenditures, the continual hiring of additional people led Indians to believe that such was not the real purpose. The rumor began that the BIA was phasing out Indians and would henceforth provide services only for its own employees.

A favorite story about the BIA concerns the time when Interior tried to merge the Standing Rock and Cheyenne River Sioux agencies in an economy move. A Sioux from Cheyenne River told an investigating committee the following story.

One day an Indian went to the Public Health Service because he had a bad headache. The PHS doctor decided to operate on him and he cut the Indian's head open and took out the brain to examine it.

Just then a man came in the door and shouted, "Joe, your house in on fire."

Joe, lying on the operating table, urged the doctor to sew up his head so that he could go and fight the fire. The doctor did as requested and Joe headed for the door.

"Wait, Joe," the doctor yelled, "you forgot your brain."

"I don't need any brain," Joe answered as he went out the door. "After I get the fire put out, I'm going to work for the BIA."

An additional story about the BIA concerns the Indian who wanted a new brain. He walked into the PHS clinic and asked for an operation whereby he could exchange his brain for a better one.

The doctor took him into a room that contained many shelves upon which were rows of jars containing brains. Each jar had a price tag on it. A doctor's brain sold for ten dollars an ounce, a professor's brain sold for fifteen dollars an ounce. Similar brains from professional people ranged higher and higher until, at the very end of the back row of jars, there was a jar marked one thousand dollars an ounce.

The Indian asked why that type of brain was so expensive and wanted to know what kind of brain it was. The doctor said that the jar contained brains of the BIA, and added, "You know, it takes so many of them to make an ounce."

In 1967 we had a conference on manpower at Kansas City. One panel on employment had a well-known BIA representative moderating it. He made an excellent presentation and then asked for questions. For a long time the assembled delegates just sat and looked at him. So again he asked for questions, mentioned a few things he thought were important, and waited for response from the audience. Nothing.

Finally he said, "I really didn't want any discussion. I just wanted to show that the BIA can come to a conference and stand here without saying anything."

"You proved that during your speech," one of the Indians retorted.

Perhaps the most disastrous policy, outside of termination, ever undertaken by the Bureau of Indian Affairs was a program called Relocation. It began as a policy of the Eisenhower administration as a means of getting Indians off the reservation and into the city slums where they could fade away.

Considerable pressure was put on reservation Indians to move into the cities. Reservation people were continually harassed by bureau officials until they agreed to enter the program. Sometimes the BIA relocation officer was so eager to get the Indians moved off the reservation that he would take the entire family into the city himself.

But the Indians came back to the reservation as soon as they learned what the city had to offer. Many is the story by BIA people of how Indians got back to the reservations before the BIA officials who had taken them to the city returned.

When the space program began, there was a great deal of talk about sending men to the moon. Discussion often centered about the difficulty of returning the men from the moon to earth, as re-entry procedures were considered to be very tricky. One Indian suggested that they send an Indian to the moon on relocation. "He'll figure out some way to get back."

Chippewas always tease the Sioux about the old days when they ran the Sioux out of Minnesota. It was, they claim, the first successful relocation program. In turn, the tribes that were pushed aside by the Sioux when they invaded the plains are ribbed about the relocation program which the Sioux conducted.

One solution to the "Indian problem" advocated in the Eisenhower years was closing the rolls of Indians eligible to receive federal services. Instead of federal services, each Indian would receive a set per capita share of the total budget. As each Indian died off, the total budget would be reduced. When all of the eligible Indians died off, that would be the end of federal-Indian relationships.

This plan was the favorite solution of Commissioner Glenn Emmons, who was heading the bureau at that time. But try as he might, he couldn't sell the program to anyone.

An agency superintendent from the Rosebud Sioux reservation in South Dakota had to go to Washington on business and so he decided to drive. As long as he was going he decided to take an old full blood with him to let the old man see the nation's capital.

The old man was very excited to be going to Washington and he made up his mind to see the Commissioner when he arrived there. So the superintendent began to suggest that the old man might have some solution to the Indian problem that he could share with the Commissioner. The old Indian discussed several ideas but admitted that they would probably be rejected.

Finally the superintendent outlined Emmon's plan to distribute the federal budget being spent on Indians among those then eligible for services. The old man pondered the idea for some time. Then he said, "That's the craziest idea I ever heard of. If I said something like that to the Commissioner, he would have me thrown out of his office."

Later the superintendent said he had always wished that the old man had suggested the plan to Emmons. "I always wanted," he told me, "to see the look on Emmon's face when an uneducated full blood suggested his own plan to him. I'd bet my last dollar that things would have changed at the BIA."

Frequently, without intending any humor, Indians can create a situation that is so funny that it is nearly impossible to believe. At the Manpower Conference in Kansas City in 1967 a series of events set up a hilarious incident. At least, looking back at it, Indians still chuckle over the results of the conference.

In 1966, after Philleo Nash had been Commissioner and had been fired for protecting the tribes, Udall gathered all of his top people and began to plan for a massive new program for "his" Indians. The administration also planned a comprehensive survey of Indian problems, perhaps realizing that Interior would once again draw a blank.

All of 1966 a secret Presidential Task Force surveyed Indian Affairs. By late December of that year they had compiled their report which, among other things, advocated a transfer of the Bureau of Indian Affairs from Interior to Health, Education and Welfare. Rumors began to fly in Indian country about the impending transfer and so the administration sent John Gardner, then Secretary of

HEW, to Kansas City to present the idea to the assembled tribes.

In spite of all we could do to get HEW to advance the idea to a series of small conferences made up of influential tribal leaders, HEW insisted on presenting the idea to the entire group of assembled tribes—cold. So Gardner embarked for Kansas City with the usual entourage of high officialdom to present the message.

The tribal chairmen were greatly concerned about the possible loss of treaty rights which might occur during the transfer. When Gardner finished his presentation he opened the floor for questions, and the concerned chairmen began.

The first man wanted to know if all treaty rights would be protected. The Secretary of HEW assured him that treaty rights would be protected by law. The second man said that he had had such assurances before and now he wanted Gardner to give him his personal assurance so he could go back and talk with his people. Gardner gave him the personal assurances he wanted.

The next chairman wanted Gardner's assurance that nothing would be changed in the method of operations. The third wanted Gardner's assurance that no part of the existing structure would be changed, but that only the name plates would be different. The man following again wanted assurance that nothing would be changed, absolutely nothing. Wearily Gardner explained that *nothing* would be changed, everything would remain the same, all personnel would remain the same.

Eight straight chairmen questioned Gardner, asking for assurances that the basic structure would remain absolutely as it had been under Interior. Not a jot or tittle, according to Gardner, would be changed at all. There was no possible way that anything could be changed. Everything was to remain just as it was.

The ninth questioner brought down the house. "Why," he inquired, "if there are to be no changes at all, do you want to transfer the bureau to HEW? It would be the same as it is now," he concluded.

It suddenly occurred to everyone that the chairman had successfully trapped Gardner in a neat box from which there was no escape. Suffice it to say, there was no transfer.

Not only the bureau, but other agencies, became the subject of Indian humor. When the War on Poverty was announced, Indians were justly skeptical about the extravagant promises of the bureaucrats. The private organizations in the Indian field, organized as the Council on Indian Affairs, sponsored a Capital Conference on Poverty in Washington in May of 1966 to ensure that Indian poverty would be highlighted just prior to the passage of the poverty program in Congress.

Tribes from all over the nation attended the conference to present papers on the poverty existing on their reservations. Two Indians from the plains area were asked about their feelings on the proposed program.

"Well," one said, "if they bring that War on Poverty to our reservation, they'll know they've been in a fight."

At the same conference, Alex Chasing Hawk, a nationally famous Indian leader from Cheyenne River and a classic storyteller, related the following tale about poverty.

It seemed that a white man was introduced to an old chief in New York City. Taking a liking to the old man, the white man invited him to dinner. The old chief hadn't eaten a good steak in a long time and eagerly accepted. He finished one steak in no time and still looked hungry. So the white man offered to buy him another steak.

As they were waiting for the steak, the white man said, "Chief, I sure wish I had your appetite."

"I don't doubt it, white man," the chief said. "You took my land, you took my mountains and streams, you took my salmon and my buffalo. You took everything I had except my appetite and now you want that. Aren't you ever going to be satisfied?"

At one conference on urban renewal, an Indian startled the audience when he endorsed the program. All day he had advocated using the poverty program to solve Indian problems on the reservation. Then, when the discussion got around to urban renewal, he abruptly supported the program.

He was asked why he wanted the program. It was, he was assured, perfectly natural for black and Mexican people to support urban renewal because so many of their people lived in the cities. But it didn't make sense to the conference participants what good an urban program would do for reservation Indians.

"I know," the Indian replied, "that a great many blacks and Mexicans want the program because so many of their people live in the cities and these cities must be rebuilt to give them a better life. But the program would also mean a better life for my people. You see, after the cities are rebuilt and everyone is settled there, we are going to fence them off and run our buffalo all over the country again."

People are always puzzled when they learn that Indians are not involved in the Civil Rights struggle. Many expect Indians to be marching up and down like other people, feeling that all problems of poor groups are basically the same.

But Indian people, having treaty rights of long standing, rightly feel that protection of existing rights is much more important to them. Yet intra-group jokes have been increasing since the beginning of the Civil Rights movement and few Indians do not wryly comment on movements among the other groups.

An Indian and a black man were in a bar one day talking about the problems of their respective groups. The black man reviewed all of the progress his people had made over the past decade and tried to get the Indian inspired to start a similar movement of activism among the tribes.

Finally the black man concluded, "Well, I guess you can't do much, there are so few of you."

"Yes," said the Indian, "and there won't be very many of you if they decide to play cowboys and blacks."

Another time, an Indian and a black man were talking about the respective races and how they had been treated by the white man. Each was trying to console the other about the problem and each felt the other group had been treated worse.

The Indian reminded the black man how his people had been slaves, how they had not had a chance to have a good family life, and how they were so persecuted in the South.

The black man admitted all of the sufferings of his people, but he was far more eloquent in reciting the wrongs against the Indians. He reviewed the broken treaties, the great land thefts, the smallpox infected blankets given to the tribes by the English, and the current movement to relocate all the Indians in the cities, far from their homelands.

Listening to the vivid description, the Indian got completely carried away in remorse. As each wrong was recited he nodded sorrowfully and was soon convinced that there was practically no hope at all for his people. Finally he could stand no more.

"And do you know," he told the black man, "there was a time in the history of this country when they used to shoot us *just to get the feathers!*"

During the riots, an Indian and a black man were talking about the terrible things going on. The black man said that the Indians could have prevented all of this grief if they had only stopped the white men at the Allegheny Mountains in the early days. Then there would have been no expansion of white influence and perhaps even slavery would not have been started. Why, the black man wanted to know, hadn't the Indians stopped the white man when it was possible for them to do so.

"I know, I know," the Indian answered, "but every time we tried to attack their forts, they had 'Soul Brother' painted on them, and so we never got the job done."

Because there is so little communication between minority communities, inter-group jokes always have the great danger of being misunderstood. In 1966, beside the Custer cards, we put out a card which read "We Shall Overrun," which, at least to us, harked to the scenes in Western movies where a small group of Indians mysteriously grows as it is outlined along the rim of a canyon until it appears as if several thousand warriors have sprung from the initial group of a dozen.

When we showed the card to various blacks in the Civil Rights movement, they didn't know how to take it and several times there was a tense situation until the card was explained.

Such is not the case when tribes tease each other. Then everything is up for grabs. Sioux announce that safe-conduct passes are available to Chippewas at the registration desk. Chippewas retort that if the Sioux don't behave they will relocate them again. Southwestern tribes innocently proclaim that their chili is very mild when in reality they are using asbestos pottery to serve it in. And the northern tribes seem always to take large helpings, which they somehow manage to get down amid tears and burnt mouths.

In the old days, after the buffalo were gone, the Sioux were reduced to eating dogs to keep alive. They had no meat of any kind and rabbits on the reservation were rare. Other tribes keep up the ribbing by announcing that the chef has prepared a special treat for the Sioux present at the annual banquet through the special cooperation of the local dog pound.

In 1964, Billy Mills, a Sioux from Pine Ridge, South Dakota, won the ten thousand meter run at the Olympics in Tokyo. Justly proud of Billy, the Sioux went all out to inform other tribes of his achievement. One day we were bragging about Billy's feat to the Coeur d'Alenes of Idaho, who politely nodded their heads in agreement.

Finally the wife of the chairman, Leona Garry, announced that Mills' running ability did not really surprise the Coeur d'Alenes. "After all," she said, "up here in Idaho, Sioux have to run far, fast, and often if they mean to stay alive." That ended the discussion of Sioux athletic ability for the evening.

Clyde Warrior, during his time, was perhaps the single greatest wit in Indian country. One day he announced that the bureau was preparing a special training program for the other tribes. When quizzed about how it differed from other programs in existence, he noted that it had a restriction of only a half-hour lunch period. "Otherwise," Clyde said, "they would have to be retrained after lunch."

Providing information to inquisitive whites has also proved humorous on occasion. At a night club in Washington, D.C., a group of Indians from North Dakota were gathered, taking the edge off their trip before returning home. One man, a very shy and handsome Chippewa, caught the eye of one of the entertainers. She began to talk with him about Indian life.

Did Indians still live in tents, she inquired. He admitted shyly that he sometimes lived in a tent in the summer time because it was cooler than a house. Question after question came and was answered by the same polite responses. The girl took quite a fancy to the Chippewa and he got more and more embarrassed at the attention.

Finally she wanted to know if Indians still raided wagon trains. He said no, they had stopped doing that a long time ago. She was heartbroken at hearing the news. "I sure would like to be raided by you," she said, and brought down the house.

Louie Sitting Crow, an old timer from Crow Creek, South Dakota, used to go into town and watch the tourists who traveled along Highway 16 in South Dakota to get to the Black Hills. One day at a filling station a car from New York pulled up and began filling its tank for the long drive.

A girl came over to talk with Louie. She asked him a great many questions about the Sioux and Louie answered as best he could. Yes, the Sioux were fierce warriors. Yes, the Sioux had once owned all of the state. Yes, they still wished for the old days.

Finally the girl asked if the Indians still scalped people. Louie, weary of the questions, replied, "Lady, remember, when you cross that river and head west, you will be in the land of the fiercest Indians on earth and you will be very lucky to get to the Black Hills alive. And you ask me if they still scalp. Let me tell you, it's worse than that. Now they take the whole head."

As Louie recalled, the car turned around and headed east after the tank was full of gas.

Southwestern Indians can get off a good one when they are inspired. A couple of years ago I was riding a bus from Santa Fe to Albuquerque late at night. The bus was late in leaving Santa Fe and seemed like it was taking forever to get on its way.

Two old men from one of the pueblos between the two cities were aboard and were obviously feeling contented after their night in town. They filled the time we were waiting for the bus to depart telling stories and as the bus got under way they began to make comments on its snail's pace.

The bus driver was in no humor to withstand a running commentary on the speed of the bus that night and so he turned around and said, "If you don't like the speed we're making, why don't you get out and walk?"

"Oh, we couldn't do that," one of the men said. "They don't expect us home until the bus gets in."

An Indian in Montana was arrested for driving while intoxicated and he was thrown in jail for the night. The following morning he was hauled before the judge for his hearing. Not knowing English very well, the Indian worried about the hearing, but he was determined to do the best he could.

The judge, accustomed to articulate, English-speaking people appearing before him, waited for the man to make his plea. The Indian stood silently waiting for the judge to say something. As the two looked at each other the silence began to become unbearable and the judge completely forgot what the man was being tried for.

Finally he said, "Well, speak up, Indian, why are you here?"

The Indian, who had been planning to plead not guilty, was also completely off balance. He gulped, looked at the judge, and said, "Your honor, I was arrested for driving a drunken car."

One-line retorts are common in Indian country. Popovi Da, the great Pueblo artist, was quizzed one day on why the Indians were the first ones on this continent. "We had reservations," was his reply. Another time, when questioned by an anthropologist on what the Indians called America before the white man came, an Indian said simply, *"Ours."* A young Indian was asked one day at a conference what a peace treaty was. He replied, "That's when the white man wants a piece of your land."

The best example of Indian humor and militancy I have ever heard was given by Clyde Warrior one day. He was talking with a group of people about the National Indian Youth Council, of which he was then president, and its program for a revitalization of Indian life. Several in the crowd were skeptical about the idea of rebuilding Indian communities along traditional Indian lines.

"Do you realize," he said, "that when the United States was founded, it was only 5 percent urban and 95 percent rural and now it is 70 percent urban and 30 percent rural?"

His listeners nodded solemnly but didn't seem to understand what he was driving at.

"Don't you realize what this means?" he rapidly continued. "It means we are pushing them into the cities. Soon we will have the country back again."

Whether Indian jokes will eventually come to have more significance than that, I cannot speculate. Humor, all Indians will agree, is the cement by which the coming Indian movement is held together. When a people can laugh at themselves and laugh at others and hold all aspects of life together without letting anybody drive them to extremes, then it seems to me that that people can survive.

8 ❖ THE RED

AND THE BLACK

CIVIL RIGHTS HAS been the most important and least understood movement of our generation. To some it has seemed to be a simple matter of fulfilling rights outlined by the Constitutional amendments after the Civil War. To others, particularly church people, Civil Rights has appeared to be a fulfillment of the brotherhood of man and the determination of humanity's relationship to God. To those opposing the movement, Civil Rights has been a foreign conspiracy which has threatened the fabric of our society.

For many years the movement to give the black people rights equal to those of their white neighbors was called Race Relations. The preoccupation with race obscured the real issues that were developing and meant that programs devised to explore the area of race always had a black orientation.

To the Indian people it has seemed quite unfair that churches and government agencies concentrated their efforts primarily on the blacks. By defining the problem as one of race and making race refer solely to black, Indians were systematically excluded from consideration. National church groups have particularly used race as a means of exploring minority-group relations. Whatever programs or policies outlined from national churches to their affiliates and parishes were generally black-oriented programs which had been adapted to include Indians.

There was probably a historical basis for this type of thinking. In many states in the last century, Indians were classified as white by laws passed to exclude blacks. So there was a connotation that Indians might in some way be like whites. But in other areas, particularly marriage laws, Indians were classified as blacks and this connotation really determined the role into which the white man forced the red man. Consequently, as far as most Race Relations were concerned, Indians were classified as non-whites.

There has been no way to positively determine in which category Indians belong when it comes to federal agencies. The Bureau of Indian Affairs consistently defined Indians as good guys who have too much dignity to demonstrate, hoping to keep the Indian people separate from the ongoing Civil Rights movement. Other agencies generally adopted a semi-black orientation. Sometimes Indians were treated as if they were blacks and other times not.

The Civil Rights Commission and the Community Relations Service always gave only lip service to Indians until it was necessary for them to write an annual report. At that time they always sought out some means of including Indians as a group with which they had worked the previous fiscal year. That was the extent of Indian relationship with the agency: a paragraph in the annual report and a promise to do something next year.

Older Indians, as a rule, have been content to play the passive role outlined for them by the bureau. They have wanted to avoid the rejection and bad publicity given activists.

The Indian people have generally avoided confrontations between the different minority groups and confrontations with the American public at large. They have felt that any publicity would inevitably have bad results and since the press seemed dedicated to the perpetuation of sensationalism rather than straight reporting of the facts, great care has been taken to avoid the spotlight. Because of this attitude, Indian people have not become well known in the field of inter-group and race relations. Consequently they have suffered from the attitudes of people who have only a superficial knowledge of minority groups and have attached a certain stigma to them.

The most common attitude Indians have faced has been the unthoughtful Johnny-come-lately liberal who equates certain goals with a dark skin. This type of individual generally defines the goals of all groups by the way he understands what he wants for the blacks. Foremost in this category have been younger social workers and clergymen entering the field directly out of college or seminary. For the most part they have been book-fed and lack experience in life. They depend primarily upon labels and categories of academic import rather than on any direct experience. Too often they have achieved positions of prominence as programs have been expanded to meet needs of people. In exercising their discretionary powers administratively, they have run roughshod over Indian people. They have not wanted to show their ignorance about Indians. Instead, they prefer to place all people with darker skin in the same category of basic goals, then develop their programs to fit these preconceived ideas.

Since the most numerous group has been the blacks, programs designed for blacks were thought adequate for all needs of all groups. When one asks a liberal about minority groups, he unconsciously seems to categorize them all together for purposes of problem solving. Hence, dark-skinned and minority group as categorical concepts have brought about the same basic results—the Indian is defined as a subcategory of the black.

Cultural differences have only seemed to emphasize the white liberal's point of view in lumping the different communities together. When Indians have pointed out real differences that do exist, liberals have tended to dismiss the differences as only minor aberrations which distinguish different racial groups.

At one conference on education of minority groups, I once mentioned the existence of some three hundred Indian languages which made bicultural and bilingual education a necessity. I was immediately challenged by several white educators who attempted to prove that blacks also have a language problem. I was never able to make the difference real to them. For the conference people the point had again been established that minority groups all had the same basic problems.

Recently, blacks and some Indians have defined racial problems as having one focal point—the White Man. This concept is a vast oversimplification of the real problem, as it centers on a racial theme rather than on specific facts. And it is simply the reversal of the old prejudicial attitude of the white who continues to define minority groups as problems of his—that is, Indian problem, Negro problem, and so on.

Rather than race or minority grouping, non-whites have often been defined according to their function within the American society. Negroes, as we have said, were considered draft animals, Indians wild animals. So too, Orientals were considered domestic animals and Mexicans humorous lazy animals. The white world has responded to the non-white groups in a number of ways, but primarily according to the manner in which it believed the non-whites could be rescued from their situation.

Thus Orientals were left alone once whites were convinced that they preferred to remain together and presented no basic threat to white social mores. Mexicans were similarly discarded and neglected when whites felt that they preferred to remain by themselves. In both cases there was no direct confrontation between whites and the two groups because there was no way that a significant number of them could be exploited. They owned little; they provided little which the white world coveted.

With the black and the Indian, however, tensions increased over the years. Both groups had been defined as animals with which the white had to have some relation and around whom some attitude must be formed. Blacks were ex-draft animals who somehow were required to become non-black. Indeed, respectability was possible for a black only by emphasizing characteristics and features that were non-black. Indians were the ex-wild animals who had provided the constant danger for the civilizing tendencies of the invading white. They always presented a foreign aspect to whites unfamiliar with the western hemisphere.

The white man adopted two basic approaches in handling blacks and Indians. He systematically excluded blacks from all programs, policies, social events, and economic schemes. He could not allow blacks to rise from their position because it would mean that the evolutionary scheme had superseded the Christian scheme and that man had perhaps truly descended from the ape.

With the Indian the process was simply reversed. The white man had been forced to deal with the Indian in treaties and agreements. It was difficult, therefore, to completely overlook the historical antecedents such as Thanksgiving, the plight of the early Pilgrims, and the desperate straits from which various Indian tribes had often rescued the whites. Indians were therefore subjected to the most intense pressure to become white. Laws passed by Congress had but one goal—the Anglo-Saxonization of the Indian. The antelope had to become a white man.

Between these two basic attitudes, the apelike draft animal and the wild free-running antelope, the white man was impaled on the horns of a dilemma he had created within himself.

It is well to keep these distinctions clearly in mind when talking about Indians and blacks. When the liberals equate the two they are overlooking obvious historical facts. Never did the white man systematically exclude Indians from his schools and meeting places. Nor did the white man ever kidnap black children from their homes and take them off to a government boarding school to be educated as whites. The white man signed no treaties with the black. Nor did he pass any amendments to the Constitution to guarantee the treaties of the Indian.

The basic problem which has existed between the various racial groups has not been one of race but of culture and legal status. The white man systematically destroyed Indian culture where it existed, but separated blacks from his midst so that they were forced to attempt the creation of their own culture.

The white man forbade the black to enter his own social and economic system and at the same time force-fed the Indian what he was denying the black. Yet the white man demanded that the black conform to white standards and insisted that the Indian don feathers and beads periodically to perform for him.

The white man presented the *problem* of each group in

contradictory ways so that neither black nor Indian could understand exactly where the problem existed or how to solve it. The Indian was always told that his problem was one of conflicting cultures. Yet, when solutions were offered by the white man, they turned out to be a reordering of the legal relationship between red and white. There was never a time when the white man said he was trying to help the Indian get into the mainstream of American life that he did not also demand that the Indian give up land, water, minerals, timber, and other resources which would enrich the white men.

The black also suffered from the same basic lie. Time after time legislation was introduced which purported to give the black equal rights with the white but which ultimately restricted his life and opportunities, even his acceptance by white people. The initial Civil Rights Act following the thirteenth, fourteenth, and fifteenth amendments was assumed to give the blacks equal rights with "white citizens." In fact, it was so twisted that it took nearly a century to bring about additional legislation to confirm black rights.

In June of 1968 the Supreme Court finally interpreted an ancient statute in favor of blacks in the matter of purchasing a house. Had the right existed for nearly a century without anyone knowing it? Of course not, the white had simply been unwilling to give in to the black. Can one blame the black athletes at the recent Olympic Games for their rebellion against the role cast for them by white society? Should they be considered as specially trained athletic animals suitable only for hauling away tons of gold medals for the United States every four years while equality remains as distant as it ever was?

It is time for both black and red to understand the ways of the white man. The white is after Indian lands and resources. He always has been and always will be. For Indians to continue to think of their basic conflict with the white man as cultural is the height of folly. The problem is and always has been the adjustment of the legal relationship between the Indian tribes and the federal government, between the true owners of the land and the usurpers.

The black must understand that whites are determined

to keep him out of their society. No matter how many Civil Rights laws are passed or how many are on the drawing board, the basic thrust is to keep the black out of society and harmless. The problem, therefore, is not one of legal status, it is one of culture and social and economic mobility. It is foolish for a black to depend upon a law to make acceptance of him by the white possible. Nor should he react to the rejection. His problem is social, and economic, and cultural, not one of adjusting the legal relationship between the two groups.

When the black seeks to change his role by adjusting the laws of the nation, he merely raises the hope that progress is being made. But for the majority of blacks progress is not being made. Simply because a middle-class black can eat at the Holiday Inn is not a gain. People who can afford the best generally get it. A socio-economic, rather than legal adjustment must consequently be the goal.

But the understanding of the racial question does not ultimately involve understanding by either blacks or Indians. It involves the white man himself. He must examine his past. He must face the problems he has created within himself and within others. The white man must no longer project his fears and insecurities onto other groups, races, and countries. Before the white man can relate to others he must forego the pleasure of defining them. The white man must learn to stop viewing history as a plot against himself.

It was more than religious intolerance that drove the early colonists across the ocean. More than a thousand years before Columbus, the barbaric tribes destroyed the Roman Empire. With utter lack of grace, they ignorantly obliterated classical civilization. Christianity swept across the conquerors like the white man later swept across North America, destroying native religions and leaving paralyzed groups of disoriented individuals in its wake. Then the combination of Christian theology, superstition, and forms of the old Roman civil government began to control the tamed barbaric tribes. Gone were the religious rites of the white tribesmen. Only the Gothic arches in the great cathedrals, symbolizing the oaks under which their ancestors worshiped, remained to remind them of the glories that had been.

Not only did the European tribes lose their religion, they were subjected to a new form of economics which totally destroyed them: feudalism. The freedom that had formerly been theirs became only the freedom to toil on the massive estates. Even their efforts to maintain their ancient ways fell to the requirements of the feudal state as power centered in a few royal houses.

Feudalism saw man as a function of land and not as something in himself. The European tribes, unable to withstand the chaos of medieval social and political forces, were eliminated as power consolidated in a few hands. Far easier than the Indian tribes of this continent, the Europeans gave up the ghost and accepted their fate without questioning it. And they remained in subjection for nearly a millenium.

The religious monolith which Christianity had deviously constructed over the Indo-European peasants eventually showed cracks in its foundations. The revolution in religious thought triggered by Martin Luther's challenge to Papal authority was merely an afterthought. It did no more than acknowledge that the gates had been opened a long time and that it was perfectly natural to walk through them into the new era.

In the sixteenth century Europe opened up the can of worms which had been carefully laid to rest a millenium earlier. The Reformation again brought up the question of the place of Western man in God's scheme of events. Because there was no way the individual could relate to the past, he was told to relate to the other world, leaving this world free for nationalistic exploitation—the real forger of identity.

Because tribes and groups had been unable to survive, the common denominator, the individual, became the focal point of the revolt. Instead of socially oriented individuals, the Reformation produced self-centered individuals. Social and economic Darwinism, the survival of the fittest at any cost, replaced the insipid brotherhood of Christianity not because Christianity's basic thrust was invalid, but because it had been corrupted for so long that it was no longer recognizable.

The centuries following the Reformation were marked with incredible turmoil. But the turmoil was not so much over religious issues as it was over interpretation of religious doctrines. Correctness of belief was preferred over truth itself. Man charged back into the historical mists to devise systems of thought which would connect him with the greats of the past. Fear of the unfamiliar became standard operating procedure.

Today Europe is still feeling the effects of the submersion of its original tribes following the demise of the Roman Empire. Western man smashes that which he does not understand because he never had the opportunity to evolve his own culture. Instead ancient cultures were thrust upon him while he was yet unprepared for them.

There lingers still the unsolved question of the primacy of the Roman Empire as contrasted with the simpler more relaxed life of the Goths, Celts, Franks, and Vikings.

Where feudalism conceived man as a function of land, the early colonists reversed the situation in their efforts to create "new" versions of their motherlands. Early settlers made land a function of man, and with a plentitude of land, democracy appeared to be the inevitable desire of God. It was relatively simple, once they had made this juxtaposition, to define Indians, blacks, and other groups in relation to land.

The first organizing efforts of the new immigrants were directed toward the process of transplanting European social and political systems in the new areas they settled. Thus New England, New France, New Spain, New Sweden, New Haven, New London, New York, New Jersey, Troy, Ithaca, and other names expressed their desire to relive the life they had known on the other side of the Atlantic—but to relive it on their own terms. No one seriously wanted to return to the status of peasant, but people certainly entertained the idea of indigenous royalty. If your ancestor got off the boat, you were one step up the ladder of respectability. Many Indians, of course, believe it would have been better if Plymouth Rock had landed on the Pilgrims than the Pilgrims on Plymouth Rock.

The early colonists did not flee religious persecution so much as they wished to perpetuate religious persecution under circumstances more favorable to them. They wanted to be the persecutors. The rigorous theocracies which quickly originated in New England certainly belie the myth that the first settlers wanted only religious freedom. Nothing was more destructive of man than the early settlements on this continent.

It would have been far better for the development of this continent had the first settlers had no illusions as to their motives. We have seen nearly five centuries of white settlement on this continent, yet the problems brought over from Europe remain unsolved and grow in basic intensity daily. And violence as an answer to the problem of identity has only covered discussion of the problem.

In transplanting Europe to these peaceful shores, the colonists violated the most basic principle of man's history: certain lands are given to certain peoples. It is these peoples only who can flourish, thrive, and survive on the land. Intruders may hold sway for centuries but they will eventually be pushed from the land or the land itself will destroy them. The Holy Land, having been periodically conquered and beaten into submission by a multitude of invaders, today remains the land which God gave to Abraham and his descendants. So will America return to the red man.

The message of the Old Testament, the Hebrew-Jewish conception of the Homeland, has been completely overlooked. Culture, if any exists, is a function of the homeland, not a function of the economic system that appears to hold temporary sway over a region.

Thus the fundamental error of believing a transplant possible practically canceled any chances for significant evolution of a homogeneous people. Even more so, it canceled the potentiality of making the new settlements the land of the free and the home of the brave—not when it was already the home of the Indian brave.

There never really was a transplant. There was only a three-hundred-year orgy of exploitation. The most feverish activity in America has been land speculation. Nearly all transactions between Indian and white have been land transactions. With Emancipation, the first program offered the black was one hundred dollars, forty acres, and a mule! But when it appeared the black might be able to create something on the land, that was immediately taken away from him.

Land has been the basis on which racial relations have been defined ever since the first settlers got off the boat. Minority groups, denominated as such, have always been victims of economic forces rather than beneficiaries of the lofty ideals proclaimed in the Constitution and elsewhere. One hundred years of persecution after Emancipation, the Civil Rights laws of the 1950's and 1960's were all passed by use of the Interstate Commerce Clause of the Constitution. Humanity, at least on this continent, has been subject to the whims of the marketplace.

When we begin to talk of Civil Rights, therefore, it greatly confuses the issue and lessens our chances of understanding the forces involved in the rights of human beings. Rather, we should begin talking about actual economic problems; and in realistic terms we are talking about land.

No movement can sustain itself, no people can continue, no government can function, and no religion can become a reality except it be bound to a land area of its own. The Jews have managed to sustain themselves in the Diaspora for over two thousand years, but in the expectation of their homeland's restoration. So-called *power* movements are primarily the urge of peoples to find their homeland and to channel their psychic energies through their land into social and economic reality. Without land and a homeland no movement can survive. And any movement attempting to build without clarifying its goals usually ends in violence, the energy from which could have been channeled toward sinking the necessary roots for the movement's existence.

Civil Rights is a function of man's desire for self-respect, not of his desire for equality. The dilemma is not one of tolerance or intolerance but one of respect or contempt. The tragedy of the early days of the Civil Rights movement is that many people, black, white, red, and yellow, were sold a bill of goods which said that *equality* was the eventual goal of the movement. But no one had considered the implications of so simple a slogan. Equality became sameness. Nobody noticed it, but everyone was trained to expect it. When equality did not come, black power did come and everybody began to climb the walls in despair.

In 1963, when the Civil Rights drive was at its peak, many of us who occupied positions of influence in Indian Affairs were severely chastised by the more militant churchmen for not having participated in the March on Washington. One churchman told me rather harshly that unless Indians *got with it* there would be no place for us in America's future. Equality, he assured me, was going to be given to us whether we want it or not.

We knew, of course, that he had equality confused with sameness, but there was no way to make him understand. In the minds of most people in 1963, legal equality and cultural conformity were identical.

We refused to participate in the Washington March. In out hearts and minds we could not believe that blacks wanted to be the same as whites. And we knew that even if they did want that, the whites would never allow it to happen. As far as we could determine, white culture, if it existed, depended primarily upon the exploitation of land, people, and life itself. It relied upon novelties and fads to provide an appearance of change but it was basically an economic Darwinism that destroyed rather than created.

It was therefore no surprise to us when Stokely Carmichael began his black power escapade. We only wondered why it had taken so long to articulate and why blacks had not been able to understand their situation better at the beginning.

A year earlier, during the Selma March, Abernathy introduced Martin Luther King with a stirring speech. He reminded his audience that "God never leaves His people without a leader." When we heard those words we knew where the Civil Rights movement was heading. It was then merely a question of waiting until the blacks began to explore *peoplehood*, toy with that idea for awhile, and then consider tribalism and nationalism.

Peoplehood is impossible without cultural independence, which in turn is impossible without a land base. Civil Rights as a movement for legal equality ended when the blacks dug beneath the equality fictions which white liberals had used to justify their great crusade. Black power, as a communications phenomenon, was a godsend to other groups. It clarified the intellectual concepts which had kept Indians and Mexicans confused and allowed the concept of self-determination suddenly to become valid.

In 1954, when the tribes were faced with the threat of termination as outlined in House Concurrent Resolution 108, the National Congress of American Indians had developed a Point Four Program aimed at creating self-determinative Indian communities. This program was ignored by Congress, bitterly opposed by the national church bodies and government agencies, undercut by white interest groups, and derided by the Uncle Tomahawks who had found security in being the household pets of the white establishment.

So, for many people, particularly those Indian people who had supported self-determination a decade earlier, Stokely Carmichael was the first black who said anything significant. Indian leadership quickly took the initiative, certain that with pressures developing from many points the goal of Indian development on the basis of tribal integrity could be realized. Using political leverage, the NCAI painstakingly began to apply itself to force change within the Bureau of Indian Affairs.

In April of 1966, following the forced resignation of Philleo Nash as Commissioner of Indian Affairs, Stewart Udall, Secretary of the Interior, held a conference to determine what "they" could do for "their" Indians. The tribe balked at the idea of bureaucrats planning the future of Indian people without so much as a polite bow in their direction. So sixty-two tribes arrived at Santa Fe for their own meeting and forced Interior to realize that the days of casually making Indian policy at two-day conferences was officially over. It took, unfortunately, another two years for Udall to get the message that the Indian people meant business.

All through 1966 and 1967 Interior tried one scheme after another in an effort to sell an incredibly bad piece of legislation, the Omnibus Bill, to the tribes. In May of 1966 an embryo bill was conceived within Interior, which purported to solve all existing Indian problems. September of that year saw the Commissioner of Indian Affairs embark on a tour of the West to gather tribal suggestions "in case the Interior Department wanted to suggest some legislation"—coincidentally the bill of May, 1966.

In July of 1966, however, the National Congress of American Indians obtained a copy of the Interior bill. By September all of the tribes had versions of the proposed legislation—the same legislation which Interior claimed couldn't even be on the drawing boards until after the regional meetings to gather tribal opinions on legislative needs.

Commissioner Bennett's task of presenting a façade of consultation while Udall rammed the bill down the Indians' throats later that year dissolved in smoke as irate tribal chairmen shot down the proposal before it left the launching pad.

As success followed success, Indians began to talk playfully of *red power* in terms similar to what SNCC was saying. The bureaucrats became confused as to which path the tribes would take next. After all, a two-year skirmish with the Secretary of the Interior and achievement of a standoff is enough to whet one's appetite for combat.

As 1968 opened, national Indian Affairs appeared to be heading faster and faster toward real involvement with other minority groups. In January, twenty-six urban centers met at Seattle, Washington, to begin to plan for participation of urban Indians in national Indian affairs. Seattle was the high point of the red power movement. But Indians quickly veered away from "power" as a movement. We knew we had a certain amount of power developing. There was no need to advocate it. The task was now to use it.

Too, black power, as many Indian people began to understand it, was not so much an affirmation of black people as it was an anti-white reaction. Blacks, many Indian people felt, had fallen into the legal-cultural trap. They obviously had power in many respects. In some instances, publicity for example, blacks had much more power than anyone dreamed possible. Indians began to question why blacks did not use their impetus in decisive ways within the current administration, which was then sympathetic to the different minority groups.

As spring came Martin Luther King had begun to organize the Poor People's Campaign. The thesis of the movement, as many of us understood it, was to be built around the existing poverty among the minority groups.

Indians had understood when Carmichael talked about racial and national integrity and the need for fine distinctions to be made between white and black. But when King began to indiscriminately lump together as one all minority communities on the basis of their economic status, Indians became extremely suspicious. The real issue for Indians—tribal existence within the homeland reservation—appeared to have been completely ignored. So where Indians could possibly have come into the continuing social movement of the 1960's, the Poor People's Campaign was too radical a departure from Indian thinking for the tribes to bridge.

Some Indians, under the name of Coalition of Indian Citizens, did attend the Washington encampment, but they remained by themselves, away from Resurrection City. By and large they did not have the support of the Indian community and were largely the creation of some national churches who wished to get Indians involved in the Poor People's Campaign. With church funding, these individuals wandered around Washington vainly trying to bring about a "confrontation" with Interior officials. They were sitting ducks for the pros of Interior, however, and the effects of their visits were negligible.

The remainder of 1968 was a traumatic experience for Indian tribes. Ideology shifted rapidly from topic to topic and dared not solidify itself in any one place for fear of rejection. National leaders trod softly when discussing issues. No one seemed to know which direction the country would take. Return to the old integration movement seemed out of the question. Continuing to push power movements against the whole of society seemed just as senseless.

Cautiously the subject of capital began to come into discussions. Too many Indian people realized the gulf that existed between the various groups in American society. A tremendous undefined need for consolidation, capitalization, and withdrawal took hold of Indian Affairs. Many tribal chairmen began to withdraw from conferences and others began to hedge their bets by remaining close to the reservation.

Tribal leaders became concerned about ongoing economic development which would be aimed at eventual economic independence for their tribes, rather than accepting every grant they could squeeze out of government agencies.

The National Congress of American Indians refused to join the Poor People's March because the goals were too generalized. Instead the NCAI began a systematic national program aimed at upgrading tribal financial independence.

In 1968 Indian leadership finally accepted the thesis that they would have to match dollar for dollar in income and program to fight the great clash between white and non-white that was coming in the months ahead. And Indian leaders began to realize that they had a fair chance of winning.

Many tribes began to shift their funds from the U.S. Treasury into the stock market. Mutual funds and stocks and bonds became the primary interest of the tribal councils. Those tribes with funds available put them into high-paying investment programs. Other tribes ordered a general cutback on overhead to give them additional funds for programming and investment.

In the move toward capitalization the tribes followed the basic ideas outlined years before by Clyde Warrior and others when the National Indian Youth Council first began to concentrate on building viable Indian communities. But it was too late for the National Indian Youth Council to take advantage of their success. Warrior died in July of 1968, some say of alcohol, most say of a broken heart.

Warrior had already been a rebel in 1964 when the majority of the tribes had lined up to support the Johnson-Humphrey ticket in the general election. Clyde supported Goldwater. His basic thesis in supporting Goldwater was that emotional reliance on a Civil Rights bill to solve the black's particular cultural question was the way to intergroup disaster. Warrior had been right.

What the different racial and minority groups had needed was not a new legal device for obliterating differences but mutual respect with economic and political independence. By not encouraging any change in the status quo, Goldwater had offered the chance for consolidation of gains at a time when the Indian people had great need to consolidate. Now consolidation was a move that may have started too late.

When a person understands the basic position developed by Warrior in 1964, one comes to realize the horror with which the Indian people contemplated their situation in 1968.

All the white man could offer, all that Johnson offered, was a minor adjustment in the massive legal machinery that had been created over a period of three hundred years. Rights of minority groups and reactions of the white majority depended solely on which parts of the machinery were being adjusted.

For many Indians the white had no culture other than one of continual exploitation. How then, they wondered, could an adjustment in methods of exploitation which had prevented formation of a culture solve their cultural problem? Thoughtful Indians, young and old, began to withdraw as they saw America building up toward a period of violent conflict. The basic problems which the colonists had brought over from Europe had not been solved and many felt there was a great danger that they would be solved violently in the future.

Culture, as Indian people understood it, was basically a life-style by which a people acted. It was self-expression but not a conscious self-expression. Rather, it was an expression of the essence of a people.

All the white man had succeeded in creating in his time on this continent had been a violent conglomerate of individuals, not a people. Being a people is more a state of mind than it is a definable quality. Indians had it and now they began to give much consideration to strengthening that state of mind before racial conflict engulfed them.

When one is an integral part of the Indian world view, his values are oriented according to the social values inherent in the culture itself. Social relations become not merely patterns of behavior but customs which dominate behavior so that the culture becomes self-perpetuating. Once the cultural values take hold, crises do not cause disorientation. Thus the Indian enters a state of mind and behavior in which many things of secondary concern to him would ordinarily cause a non-Indian great emotional turmoil. Once a person is a vital part of the Indian frame of mind, it is impossible to leave. Like an old cavalry or circus horse, the call to action invoked by some distant echo produces certain action which everyone accepts as Indian. Since definition, any definition, is canceled by experience, Indian people have tended to equate behavior patterns with culture. Racial conflicts have not tended to be as important as have actual events.

There is, therefore, basically no way in which the ideology of the Civil Rights movement could reach Indian communities in a communicative sense. Outside of black power nothing that the Civil Rights people could have said would have indicated their meaning or opened lines of interaction by which the Indian people would have understood what the movement was all about.

The sight of blacks carrying TV sets through riot-torn streets completely turned off those Indian people who were trying to understand Civil Rights. America, rioters seemed to be saying, is a color TV and this is what we want from her.

Where we were hopeful of eventual peace, friendship, and cooperation between the various groups, many of us felt betrayed and confused. For years we had fought the fight for cultural survival only to find the situation reversed on us when we thought we were beginning to understand it.

It was incomprehensible to us that a people would rebel against a system that they felt was irrelevant and unresponsive to their needs. Blacks seemed to be saying that white society was bad, but they wanted it anyway.

Consequently, when a number of young Indians joined the Poor People's Campaign, they seemed to be betraying the Indian fight for survival. Feelings ran extremely high during the Poor People's March, particularly when Indian people were shown on television conducting demonstrations for fishing rights and food. Too many Indian people confused the means used with the ends to be achieved. Ideologically, Indian participation in the Poor People's March seemed to be a surrender to white society because the basic thrust of the campaign was to endorse middle-class values through pointing out their absence in the life of the poor.

Resistance to Civil Rights ideas by tribal leaders has proved a catalyst to some Indian participants in the Poor People's Campaign. Discussions with some of these Indians have convinced tribal leaders that dangerous times lie ahead for reservation people. The new militants appear ready to destroy the legal status of the tribes in order to introduce change. This attitude frightens tribal councils immensely and their fright convinces the new militants that their way is right. There appears to be very little leeway for compromise between the two groups.

Frightened tribal councils are beginning to create an atmosphere within which issues can be brought forward for solution, however. One good tangible result of Indian participation in the Poor People's Campaign is that Indian people all over have begun to question the nature of their situation. They are asking what their specific rights and benefits are and what the Poor People's March could possibly do to improve their situation.

In the defensive gesture of counting their blessings to show that the new militants should not have participated in the campaign, Indians have spent much time suffering new insights and attempting to digest what they have learned.

To many young Indians it has come through quite clearly that the problem of the Indian people is legal and not cultural, although the problem between Indians and other groups insofar as they inter-relate is cultural. That is to say, the white always presents opportunities for cultural enrichment when he is trying to steal Indian land. When the white sincerely wants to develop capital resources of the Indian people he invariably strengthens Indian cultural traits.

One has only to hear speeches by leading Democratic Senators who want to *help Indians,* to realize that there is a quiet move against the Indian land base. On the other hand, when attempts are made to develop Indian resources these thoughts are interpreted by Indian people as an affirmation of their way of life.

When we talk about basic solutions to the problems of each group, we talk about a startling reversal of concepts.

Indian tribes need the basic gift of the white to the Negro —readjustment of tribal rights to protect person and property from exploitation by the federal government and private persons. Treaties need to be reaffirmed as the law of the land. Gurantees of free and undisturbed use of the reservation lands need to be enforced. Congressional pressure to destroy the Indian tribes and communities needs to be lifted.

On the other hand, the federal government needs to be the main supporter of the black quest for cultural development. The black does not need more legal rights so much as he needs the freedom to develop himself through experimentation. Prejudicial practices in law enforcement continually impinge upon the black communities, with cessions of police power and law to the local communities. During the riots after the assassination of Martin Luther King, those cities where militant black nationalists were strongest were the quietest because the young blacks kept order in spite of the white police.

White culture destroys other culture because of its abstractness. As a destroyer of culture it is not a culture but a cancer. In order to keep the country from complete divisiveness, separatism must be accepted as a means to achieve equality of personality both for groups and individuals. Separatism can be the means by which blacks gain time for reflection, meditation, and eventual understanding of themselves as a people.

The black needs time to develop his roots, to create his sacred places, to understand the mystery of himself and his history, to understand his own purpose. These things the Indian has and is able to maintain through his tribal life. The Indian now needs to create techniques to provide the economic strength needed to guarantee the survival of what he has.

In a real way, white culture, if there is such, is already doomed to its own destruction. Continual emphasis on racial rather than cultural problems will not only bring down white society but may also endanger ancient Indian society and newly emerging black and Mexican social movements.

The white man has the marvelous ability to conceptualize. He has also the marvelous inability to distinguish be-

tween sacred and profane. He therefore arbitrarily concep-
tualizes all things and understands none of them. His science creates gimmicks for his use. Little effort is made to
relate the gimmicks to the nature of life or to see them in
a historical context.

The white man is problem-solving. His conceptuali-
zations merge into science and then emerge in his social
life as problems, the solutions of which are the adjustments of his social machine. Slavery, prohibition, Civil
Rights, and social services are all important adjustments of
the white man's social machine. No solution he has
reached has proven adequate. Indeed, it has often proven
demonic.

White solutions fail because *white* itself is an abstraction of an attitude of mind, not a racial or group reality.
The white as we know him in America is an amalgam of
European immigrants, not a racial phenomenon. But the
temptation has always been present to define groups according to their most superficial aspect. Hence we have
white, black, red, and the Yellow Peril. And we are taught
to speak of the *Negro problem,* the *Indian problem,* and
so forth.

White has been abstracted into a magical nebulous mythology that dominates all inhabitants of our country in
their attitudes toward one another. We are, consequently,
all prisoners of that mythology so far as we rebel against
it. It is our misfortune that our economic system reflects
uncritical acceptance of the mythology and that economic
movements tend to reinforce the myth.

There is basically nothing real about our economic system. It is neither good nor bad, but neutral. Only when we
place connotations on it and use it to manipulate people
does it become a thing in itself.

Our welfare system demonstrates better than anything
else the means to which uncritical *white* economics can be
used. We have all types of welfare programs: old age, dis-
ability, aid to dependent children, orphanages, and unemployment. There is continual controversy in the halls of
Congress, state legislatures, and city halls over the welfare
programs.

Conservatives insist that those receiving welfare are lazy
and are getting a free ride at the expense of hard-working

citizens. Liberals insist that all citizens have a basic right to life and that it is the government's responsibility to provide for those unable to provide for themselves.

What are we really saying?

Welfare is based upon the norm set up by the Puritans long ago. A man is defined as a white, Anglo-Saxon Protestant, healthy, ambitious, earnest, and honest, a man whom the Lord smiles upon by increasing the fruits of his labor. Welfare is designed to compensate people insofar as they deviate from that norm. Insofar as a woman has an illegitimate child, she receives compensation. Insofar as a man is disabled, he receives compensation. Insofar as a person is too old to work, he receives compensation.

Welfare buys that portion of a person which does not match the stereotype of the real man. Welfare payments are never sufficient, never adequate. This is because each person bears some relation to the norm and in proportion to their resemblance, they receive less.

When this attitude is applied to groups, it is best seen in the political parties. The Republicans represent the best of the white economics. The Democrats represent all of the deviations.

The Republican Party has ostensibly stood for less government as a political philosophical position. But when you listen carefully to the Republicans you do not really hear less government, you hear a strange religion of early Puritan mythology. The Republican Party is in reality the truest expression of America's religion of progress and white respectability. It stands for the white superman who never existed. The peddler's grandson who conquered the unknown by inheriting a department store—such is the basic American religion unmasked. The measure of America's willingness to examine the basis of its existence is to be counted in the number of registered voters who claim to be Republicans.

The measure of truth in the above assertion is the Republican willingness to lose elections rather than depart from cherished doctrines and myths. Only a religion can attract and hold such loyalty.

The other party is something else. Popular conceptions gloss over reality and continue the Rooseveltian myth that the Democrats are the party of the people. The old Roosevelt coalition of labor, minority and ethnic groups, and farmers fails to acknowledge one unpublicized member—the special interests.

More than the Republicans, the Democrats are the party of the special interests. Who else defends the oil-depletion allowance more than the Democrats? Who else creates farm subsidies, tariffs, foreign aid, large development projects? Who else piles special programs on top of special programs? Could the Republicans create the poor as a class in themselves? For, the Republicans know no poor because it is not within their religious comprehension. Nixon's election was the last gasp of this quasi-religious nineteenth-century, Horatio Alger, WASP ethic.

Until 1968 the Democrats won election after election by gathering the rejected into an amalgam of special interests for the sole purpose of splitting the pie which they would then attempt to create. The pie never exists; it is continually being created by the adjustment of the governmental machinery to include additional special interests, while eligible parties participate in the American religion carefully being nurtured by the Republicans in their isolation.

Recent elections tend to show the reality of this analysis. Eisenhower proved that a President was not necessary for the true American religion to progress. Kennedy proved that if enough special interests are combined, even Americans will desert the long-term goals of progress for the immediacy of splitting the pie which was to be created. The New Frontier promised a new chance to be cut in on the action, a short cut into Republican heaven for those groups who had deviated from the norm either by birth, place of origin, or failure to deal themselves in at some previous point in history.

Johnson simply dealt more cards to more people than had ever been dealt before. And his opponent was out preaching salvation by works alone. No wonder there was a religious revolt! The election of 1964 was comparable to the Protestant Reformation, for never had the choices been so clear between faith and works.

Politically, most minority groups have shifted to the Democrats and remained loyal through thick and thin. Margins compiled by blacks, Indians, and Mexicans for

Democratic candidates have been incredible. In 1964 it took a strong Indian to support Goldwater in spite of his publicized heroic flights to the Navajo and his superb collection of Hopi Kachina dolls.

The Kennedys increased the normal margins which minority groups gave to the Democrats because of their apparent interest in minority groups. Few members of the Indian community realize or will admit how little the Kennedys really did for the Indians. Although the mythology of the Kennedys has made them appear as the only saviors of minority communities, the legislative record compiled by both Jack and Robert Kennedy shows another story.

Jack Kennedy broke the Pickering Treaty and had accomplished little besides the usual Interior Task Force study of Indians before his death. Robert Kennedy did little for Indians legislatively or administratively. He drew some fire and spotlighted some of the problems, but in doing so he practically pre-empted any chance of action because of his many political enemies and their outright rejection of causes he advocated.

Robert Kennedy did prove that race was not the real thing bothering this country and that the turmoil over Civil Rights was misunderstood. He presented himself as a person who could move from world to world and never be a stranger anywhere. His genius was that he personified the best traits of his Irish heritage and made an attempt to define *white* in a different way.

Other people were frightened at Kennedy's obvious attempt to re-create the days of the New Frontier. White mythology sees the kingship as demonic, as against the American religion of ostensible equality.

Indian people loved the idea of Robert Kennedy replacing Jack. For them it was an affirmation of the great war chief from the great family leading his people in his brother's place. Robert Kennedy became as great a hero as the most famous Indian war chiefs precisely because of his ruthlessness. Indians saw him as a warrior, the white Crazy Horse. He somehow validated obscure undefined feelings of Indian people which they had been unwilling to admit to themselves. Spiritually, he was an Indian!

Robert Kennedy's death has completely changed the na-

ture of the Civil Rights movement and has altered the outlook of the American Indian toward American society.

Winds of caution have set in and sails are being
trimmed. There appears to be no means by which the cultural crisis can be understood by those outside the group.
Indian people are becoming more and more reluctant to
consider alternatives. They are becoming distrustful of
people who talk equality because they do not see how
equality can be achieved without cultural separateness. To
the degree that other groups demand material ransoms for
peace and order, Indian people are fearful of the ultimate
goals of the different movements.

There is no basic antagonism between black and red, or
even between red and white. Conflicts are created when
Indians feel they are being defined out of existence by the
other groups. Historically, each group has its own road to
travel. All roads lead to personal and group affirmation.
But the obstacles faced by each group are different and
call for different solutions and techniques.

While it is wrong and harmful to define all dark-skinned
people by certain criteria, it is also wrong to pretend that
they have nothing in common. It is what Indians, blacks,
and Mexicans have in common and where their differences
lie which should be carefully studied.

Time and again blacks have told me how lucky they
were not to have been placed on reservations after the
Civil War. I don't think they were lucky at all. I think it
was absolute disaster that blacks were not given reservations.

Indian tribes have been able to deal directly with the
federal government because they had a recognized status
within the Constitutional scheme. Leadership falls into
legal patterns on each reservation through the elective process. A tribal chairman is recognized by federal agencies.
Congressional committees, and private agencies as the
representative of the group. Quarrels over programs, rivalry between leaders, defense of rights, and expressions
of the mood of the people are all channeled through the
official governing body. Indian people have the opportunity to deal officially with the rest of the world as a corporate body.

The blacks, on the other hand, are not defined with

their own community. Leadership too often depends upon newspaper coverage. Black communities do not receive the deference tribes receive, because they are agencies in the private arena and not quasi-governmental. Law and order is something imposed brutally from without, not a housekeeping function of the group.

Above all, Indian people have the possibility of total withdrawal from American society because of their special legal status. They can, when necessary, return to a recognized homeland where time is static and the world becomes a psychic unity again.

To survive, blacks must have a homeland where they can withdraw, drop the façade of integration, and be themselves. Whites are inevitably torn because they have no roots, they do not understand the past, and they have already mortgaged their future. Unless they can renew their psychic selves and achieve a sense of historical participation as a people they will be unable to survive.

Already the cracks are showing. The berserk sniper characterizes the dilemma of the white man. Government by selective assassination is already well established as the true elective process.

All groups must come to understand themselves as their situation defines them and not as other groups see them. By accepting ourselves and defining the values within which we can be most comfortable we can find peace. In essence, we must all create social isolates which have economic bases that support creative and innovative efforts to customize values we need.

Myths must be re-examined and clarified. Where they are detrimental, sharp and necessary distinctions must be made. The fear of the unknown must be eliminated. The white mythologizes the racial minorities because of his lack of knowledge of them. These myths then create barriers for communication between the various segments of society.

What the white cannot understand he destroys lest it prove harmful. What the Indian cannot understand he withdraws from. But the black tries everything and fears nothing. He is therefore at liberty to build or destroy both what he knows and what he does not know or understand.

The red and the black must not be fooled either by

themselves, by each other, or by the white man. The black has moved in a circle from *Plessy v. Ferguson,* where Separate but Equal was affirmed, to *Brown v. the Board of Education,* where it was denied by the Supreme Court, to Birmingham, Washington, Selma, and the tragedies of Memphis and Los Angeles. Now, Separate but Equal has become a battle cry of the black activists.

It makes a great deal of difference who carries this cry into battle. Is it the cry of a dying amalgam of European immigrants who are plagued by the European past? Or is it the lusty cry of a new culture impatient to be born?

The American Indian meditates on these things and waits for their solution. People fool themselves when they visualize a great coalition of the minority groups to pressure Congress for additional programs and rights. Indians will not work within an ideological basis which is foreign to them. Any cooperative movement must come to terms with tribalism in the Indian context before it will gain Indian support.

The future, therefore, as between the red, white, and black, will depend primarily upon whether white and black begin to understand Indian nationalism. Once having left the wild animal status, Indians will not revert to their old position on the totem pole. Hopefully black militancy will return to nationalistic philosophies which relate to the ongoing conception of the tribe as a nation extending in time and occupying space. If such is possible within the black community, it may be possible to bring the problems of minority groups into a more realistic focus and possible solution in the years ahead.

9 ❖ THE PROBLEM

OF INDIAN

LEADERSHIP

QUITE EARLY IN the Civil Rights struggle certain individuals emerged and were accepted as representative leaders of the Negro people. Martin Luther King, James Farmer, Bayard Rustin, Whitney Young, John Lewis, and others were able to attract the attention of the communications media. It was largely through identification with these, individuals that vast numbers of Americans began to be concerned about Civil Rights. By vicariously experiencing the exploits of King and others, people participated in the great marches and felt they had an important emotional investment in the outcome. For a time, at least, racial themes were submerged by the common appeal for simple justice.

When the Civil Rights goals became blurred and a multitude of leaders appeared to be saying contradictory things, public sympathy vanished as quickly as it had arisen. No longer could people identify with simply understood individuals who stood for simple goals.

Indians experienced an era similar to the Civil Rights movement in the closing years of the last century. Then Indian tribes and their great leaders dominated the news and attracted the attention of the public. The Indian struggle for freedom was symbolized by the great war chiefs

Crazy Horse, Sitting Bull, Chief Joseph, and Geronimo. They were better known than the important statesmen of those days. Public interest often reached a fever pitch and opinions were as evenly divided as to solutions to the Indian problem then as they are today about the Negro problem.

Public opinion was fickle. When Custer was wiped out the impulse was to exterminate the Sioux. Yet several years later Sitting Bull was so popular that he appeared in Wild West shows. Chief Joseph, the great Nez Perce chief, left his reservation in Oregon with his people and headed for the Canadian border. Whites were terrified at first. Later they cheered for the Nez Perces as they eluded troop after troop of cavalry. When they were finally caught twelve miles from the Canadian border nearly everyone in the nation was on their side. Even the opposing generals, who had the task of catching the tribe, were attracted by Joseph's obvious ability to command.

The Cheyennes were corraled on a dusty reservation in Oklahoma and longed for their homeland in Montana. Facing starvation on their desert lands in the South, the tribe broke for freedom. They managed to elude the major cavalry forces that were sent out to catch them and got through Kansas unnoticed. In Nebraska the troops finally caught up and killed most of them. A few kept going and reached Montana. Some hid with Red Cloud's Oglala Sioux at Pine Ridge, South Dakota, where they were given refuge. When the public realized the tragedy of Dull Knife and his starving band of homeward-fleeing Cheyennes, the tide turned in favor of the tribes. They were able to survive by submitting to confined reservations and the ration system, and were eventually freed from the fear of physical extermination.

For a time the government attempted to break the power of the great war chiefs and failing, adopted the tactic of exile and assassination to render the Indian people completely docile. Once they were restricted to the reservations the might of the government was applied to the Indians to destroy their political and social institutions. Missionaries and government agents worked to undermine the influence of the old people and the medicine men. Of all the great Indian leaders perhaps only Red Cloud of the

Oglala Sioux maintained his influence in his tribe until his death.

After the war chiefs had been killed or rendered harmless, Indians seemed to drift into a timeless mist. There appeared to be no leaders with which the general public could identify. The status of the Indian became a nebulous question which seemed familiar and important but for which there was apparently no answer.

Missionaries soon filled the vacuum through clever exploitation of natives who had turned Christian. There began in the East the great round of testimonial appearances of native clergymen who made speeches appealing for more missionary work among their tribes. Church congregations, indoctrinated with the message of the White Man's Burden, cooed with satisfaction to hear formerly fierce and feathered warriors relate how they had found the Lord and been brought out of their pagan darkness.

Poor things, so great had been the pressure on them to conform to the white man's way that they could do nothing else if they and their people were to survive. Only the fickle sentimentality of the churches often stood between them and the government policy of total dispersal or extinction of their people.

But the Christianized warrior role did not provide any significant means by which white people could identify with the real desires and needs of the Indian people. The post-pagans simply recited what they had been taught concerning their people's needs. Indian beliefs held most tenaciously were forbidden subjects and there was no way to attract the sympathy of the public to support ideas that were considered foreign.

After the turn of the century, Jim Thorpe almost overnight changed the image of the Indian in the mind of the public. Suddenly the Indian as the superathlete dominated the scene. This concept was soon replaced by the Indian as a show business personality with the rise to popularity of Will Rogers, the Cherokee humorist.

In large measure the Indian path to visibility has been paralleled by the Negro. A mythology created to explain Jim Thorpe and Will Rogers was later applied to Joe Louis and Dick Gregory in order to make Negroes comprehensible when they began to appear in American life. After the Indian had been accepted as a humorous, athletic, subspecies of white man, historians and popular writers revisited the past and carved out a role for the Indian that overlooked the centuries of bloodshed between white and red, effectively neutralizing historical betrayals of the Indian by the government.

The supreme archetype of the white Indian was born one day in the pulp magazines. This figure would not only dominate the pattern of what Indians had been and would be, but also actually block efforts to bring into focus the crises being suffered by Indian tribes.

It was Tonto—the friendly Indian Companion—who galloped onto the scene, pushing the historical and the contemporary Indians into obscurity.

Tonto was everything that the white man had always wanted the Indian to be. He was a little slower, a little dumber, had much less vocabulary, and rode a darker horse. Somehow Tonto was always *there*. Like the Negro butler and the Oriental gardener, Tonto represented a silent subservient subspecies of Anglo-Saxon whose duty was to do the bidding of the all-wise white hero.

The standard joke, developed as group consciousness arose, had the Lone Ranger and Tonto surrounded by a tribe of hostile Indians, with Tonto inquiring of the Lone Ranger, "Well, White Man?" The humor came from Tonto's complete departure from his stereotype. The real Tonto would have cut down his relatives with a Gatling gun rather than have a hair on said Ranger's head mussed.

But Tonto never rebelled, never questioned the Lone Ranger's judgment, never longed to go back to the tribe for the annual Sun Dance. Tonto was a cultureless Indian for Indians and an uncultured Indian for whites.

Tonto cemented in the minds of the America public the cherished falsehood that all Indians were basically the same—friendly and stupid. Indeed, the legend grew, not only were tribes the same, but all Indians could be brought to a state of grace—a reasonable facsimile of the white—by a little understanding.

But Tonto also had another quality about him. Although inarticulate to a fault, he occasionally called upon his primitive wisdom to get the Lone Ranger out of a tight spot. Tonto had some indefinable aboriginal knowledge that operated deus ex machina in certain situations. It was almost as if the Lone Ranger had some tragic flaw with respect to the mysterious in nature which Tonto could easily handle and understand.

In those crises where Tonto had to extricate the Lone Ranger by some impossibly Indian trick, a glimmer of hope was planted in the subconscious of the Indian that someday he would come into his own. Few whites realized what this was, or that it existed; but to Indians it was an affirmation of the old Indian way. In an undefined sense, Tonto was able to universalize Indianness for Indians and lay the groundwork for the eventual rejection of the white man and his strange ways.

And so when no one succeeded Thorpe and Rogers, Tonto cornered the market as the credible Indian personality. Turncoats of history who could be resurrected as examples of the "friendly Indian companion" were publicized in an attempt to elaborate on the Tonto image.

Squanto, who had welcomed the Pilgrims and helped them destroy the tribes in Connecticut and Long Island, was reworked as a "friendly" Indian as opposed to Massasoit, the father of King Philip the Wampanoag chief, who had suspicions about the Pilgrims from the very start.

Keokuk, the Sac and Fox subchief who had betrayed Black Hawk during the war which bears his name, was also brought back to life as a friendly companion. Washakie, the Shoshone chief who tattled on the other tribes every chance he got and finally received a nice reservation in Wyoming, was another early fink who was honored posthumously as a good guy.

Eastern society matrons somehow began to acquire blood from John Smith and Pocahontas. The real Indian leaders who had resisted the encroachments of the white man and died protecting their homes, became sullen renegades unworthy of note.

Both whites and Indians were buried under the weight of popular pseudo-history in which good guys dominated the scene and tribes were indiscriminately scattered throughout the West in an effort to liven up the story. Contemporary Indian leadership was suppressed by tales of the folk heroes of the past. Attempts to communicate contemporary problems were brushed aside in favor of the convenient and comfortable pigeonhole into which Indians had been placed. The Sioux warbonnet, pride of the Plains Indians, became the universal symbol of Indianism. Even tribes that had never seen an eagle were required to wear a warbonnet to prove their lineage as Indians.

It was probably only because Indians were conveniently forgotten that a movement for national unity of all three tribes became a possibility. So rigid was the stereotype of a friendly childlike Indian that all efforts by Indians to come together were passed off as the prattling of children who could not possibly do anything without instructions from their white friends.

Indian tribes were thus freed to experiment with the concept of inter-tribal unity because they were considered irrelevant. First on regional levels, occasionally with regional congresses, then finally on a national basis, tribes began to come together. They soon learned to use the prejudices of the friendly whites to their own advantage.

Reconstruction of past traitors as good Indians also brought with it remembrances of previous attempts to unify the tribes and repel the white invaders. Indian unity had been an old dream. Deganawidah had forged the great Iroquois confederacy out of a miscellaneous group of refugee tribes who had been driven out of the Missouri-Arkansas area in the fifteenth century by the stronger Osage and Quapaw tribes. Eventually this conglomeration dominated the northern portion of the United States completely. They were the balance of power in the colonial wars between England and France.

In the South the Creek confederacy had controlled a vast area in what is now Georgia, Mississippi, and Alabama with extensions of its power well into northern Florida. The Natchez confederacy ruled the Mississippi plains almost completely and extended its influence a considerable distance southwestward.

With the westward movement of whites, temporary alliances were formed for the purpose of protecting hunting grounds. Pontiac and later Tecumseh brought the tribes together for momentary successes against the whites. But always it was too late with too little. Nowhere was there enough time for effective groupings to be built which guaranteed more than sporadic success.

In the Great Plains, traditional hunting alliances did their best to prevent white encroachment on their hunting grounds, but they could not stem the tide. The Sioux, Cheyenne, and Arapaho united briefly to send Custer on his way. But shortly after the battle the tribes split into a number of small bands which were all rounded up and placed on reservations by the following winter.

In the southern plains the Kiowa and Comanche had occasional successes before being overcome and sent to their western Oklahoma reservation. The desert areas saw the Paiutes and Shoshones futilely oppose the white man but quickly give in. The Northwest had a brief Yakima war and an even briefer struggle by Chief Joseph and his Nez Perces.

By and large the hunting economy was so entrenched that the destruction of the buffalo eliminated the economic base by which tribal alliances were cemented. The tribes seemed doomed to follow the buffalo. No large number of people could be kept together because they could not be fed. Thus sustained warfare was impossible for the tribes while still a way of life for the white man. In separate groups the tribes were easily defeated and confined to reservations through a series of so-called peace treaties. In fact, treaties were ultimatums dictated by historical reality. While the tribes could have fought on, absolute extinction would have been their fate.

Because buffalo and other game were so essential to the tribes, hunting areas defined the manner in which tribes would fight and where. It was fairly easy to divide and conquer the various tribes by exploiting their rivalry over hunting grounds. This the white man did with deadly and consummate skill. Indian warfare was oriented toward protection of food supply and courageous exploits. Sustained warfare to protect or control territory which they could not settle was inconceivable to most of the tribes. Killing others simply to rid the land of them was even more unthinkable. Thus the white man's way of war was the deadly antithesis of the Indian's.

From Plymouth Rock to the lava beds of northern California, the white man divided and conquered as easily as if he were slicing bread. The technique was not used simply to keep different tribes from uniting, but also to keep factions of the same tribe quarreling so that when their time came they would be unable to defend themselves. And most important, the United States government used the treaty as an ultimate weapon to destroy the tribal political institutions by recognizing some men as chiefs and refusing to recognize others.

In treating for lands, rights of way, and minerals, commissioners negotiating for the government insisted on applying foreign political concepts to the tribes they were confronting. Used to dealing with kings, queens, and royalty, the early white men insisted on meeting the supreme political head of each tribe. When they found none, they created one and called the man they had chosen *the Chief*.

Finding a chief at treaty-signing time was no problem. The most pliable man who could be easily bribed was named chief and the treaty was signed. Land cessions were often made and a tribe found itself on the way to a treeless desert before it knew what had happened. Most of the Indian wars began because of this method of negotiation. The Indians were always at a loss to explain what had happened. They got mad when told to move off lands which they had never sold and so they fought. Thus were renegades created.

Most tribes had never defined power in authoritarian terms. A man consistently successful at war or hunting was likely to attract a following in direct proportion to his continuing successes. Eventually the men with the greatest followings composed an informal council which made important decisions for the group. Anyone was free to follow or not, depending upon his own best judgment. The people only followed a course of action if they were convinced it was best for them. This was as close as most tribes ever got to a formal government.

In an absolutely democratic social structure like the Indian tribe, formal legal negotiations and contractual arrangements were nearly out of the question. Once a man's word was given it bound him because of his integrity, not because of what he had written on a sheet of paper.

Men went to war because they had faith in a leader, not because they were drafted to do so or because they had signed a paper pledging themselves to be hired killers for a set period of time. Indians had little respect for white generals who did not lead their men into battle and contemptuously tagged the first white soldiers they saw as the "men who take orders from the chief who is afraid to fight."

The basic Indian political pattern has endured despite efforts by the federal government to change it. The people still follow a man simply because he produces. The only difference between two centuries ago and today is that now the Bureau of Indian Affairs defines certain ground rules by which leaders can be changed. These rules are called tribal elections. Otherwise, leadership patterns have not changed at all.

Today a man holds his chairmanship as long as he produces, or at least appears to produce, for his tribe. Without making substantial progress or having the ability to present a fighting image, a man's term in tribal office is short and severe. Demands are great. Some tribes have never had an incumbent re-elected because tribal goals far surpass any conceivable performance. A few tribes have had strong men dominate tribal affairs for long periods of time because of their tremendous following with the people.

Frank Ducheneaux of the Cheyenne River Sioux, Joe Garry, six-time President of the NCAI and long-time chairman of the Coeur d'Alenes of Idaho, Marvin Mull of the San Carlos Apaches, Roger Jourdain of the Red Lake Chippewas, and James Jackson of the Quinaults have all had many years as chairman of their respective tribes. Each man has been able to keep his chairmanship because of the progressive programs he has initiated, which have in turn created more respect and a greater following for him within the tribe. Success and respect go hand in hand in Indian affairs.

But other tribes throw out chairmen with such regularity it's almost an annual event, anticipated with pleasure by the reservation people. In those cases the tribe has no discernible goals except to throw the rascals out. The safest political position is always as member of the out group.

Unlike hunting days, production today depends upon

the ability to gain concessions from governmental agencies. Some tribes demand more from the bureau than others. Ability to produce the necessary demands in reasonable yet militant terms is sometimes enough to win and hold the chairmanship, even though the demands are not often met.

The more sophisticated the tribal demands, the better the chances a militant chairman has of remaining in office. The simpler the demands, the more criticism seems to be directed at the leader and the less his chances are for political survival.

This pattern of tribal behavior creates a basic insecurity which has a double edge when seen nationally in movements toward unification of the tribes. Some chairmen use state and national organizations as sounding boards for militant speeches that hopefully prove to reservation people they are not afraid to fight for Indian rights. Other chairmen withdraw from national and state inter-tribal organizations when they are elected to demonstrate that by their power alone the tribe is protected from its enemies.

Inter-tribal cooperation therefore has two aspects: one is to allow the chairman to fight paper tigers for the effect it will have on his critics; the other is for a chairman to advance his own plan for national unity which will give him such stature that his tribe will gain leverage in its dealings with private and governmental agencies.

It is on the national scene, however, that new and different forces, which alter the methods by which Indian leadership defines its goals, come into play.

Years ago churches, anthropologists, and bureaucrats all discovered that it was a good idea to have Indians attend a meeting on Indian problems. It looked better. But they certainly didn't have to invite the *wrong* kind of Indian. Like the treaty-makers of old, they could pick and choose who would represent the tribe and what philosophy he would support. Red leaders therefore had to adopt an official double-talk in order to bring reservation problems into the sphere of national communication.

For some time, conferences began to be set up, with white men outlining what would be accomplished and giving the background as to why their particular theory was best for Indians at that time. Some of these white men were so successful that they became the Great White Fathers who had almost total control of Indian policy. As for the Indians, while they were invited to the conferences, they were there only to agree with the proceedings or to enhance the white man's reputation as the *one* who knew what was best for the tribes.

Of all the white saviors, Oliver La Farge was perhaps the best known and most skillful manipulator of Indian people. La Farge dealt primarily with Uncle Tomahawks who would say anything to stay on the good side of him. Real Indian leadership was anathema to La Farge and the thought of a national union of the tribes was complete heresy in his eyes.

La Farge built his reputation through his novels. During the 1950's he was the white who always took it upon himself to come forward as the protector of Indian people in the press. But he also realized that he could not risk placing his organization in a position where its tax status might be questioned. So La Farge never made any appearances before Congressional committees during the termination period of legislation. Instead, the tribes had to bear the brunt of Congressional ire while La Farge reaped the benefits of national publicity as the defender of the lowly childlike Indian.

In 1954, when the NCAI met and began to plan its Point Four Development Program modeled after the experiment of Operation Bootstrap in Puerto Rico, La Farge hurriedly put together his own Point Four Program, which incorporated the basic points the tribes had been considering. He put forward his version after the tribes had fully discussed the proposal and before the Indians could publicize their efforts. Thus La Farge undercut Indian leadership in order to strengthen his own image as their savior.

Throughout his life La Farge looked contemptuously upon the Indian people as an inferior brand of human being who, if not properly controlled, would be certain to hurt himself. There was never any doubt in La Farge's mind that he knew best about Indians.

La Farge and his friends systematically undercut Indian leadership. National Indian leaders had to play ball or suffer the consequences. La Farge's successors, the Great

White Fathers of today, continually attempt to appear as people with some mysterious knowledge about Indians, derived either from their extensive travels or their research into "the Indian problem."

Indian people were kept in a stupor of self-acknowledged incompetency during La Farge's reign as Indian spokesman. Because of his prominence as a writer and his access to public relations media in the East, La Farge was able to effectively block efforts by the tribes to gain recognition as a people capable of self-determination. For all the eastern United States knew, Indians moved only because Oliver La Farge had shown them the way and there was, it appeared, no significant movement by Indians except that which he planned.

But gradually a more sophisticated type of white man came into Indian country. He actually wanted to solve some of the problems and was not awed by the status La Farge and others had achieved as protectors of the Indians.

This new trend meant that reservations were scoured for a successful Indian who could *motivate* others. The same game was played, but this time the values were derived from a liberal orientation rather than a conservative one. Many national Indian leaders of the last generation had made their reputations by demonstrating their ability to be non-Indian. They were comparable to the old timers who had toured the continent with Buffalo Bill and acted pseudo-warlike for Europeans rather than stay home as real warriors chased all day by the cavalry.

Many of today's leaders were attending high school and college during the heyday of liberal self-helpism. Many of us were dragged from conference to conference to hear nearly identical speeches by model Indians of the day. I call to mind bits and pieces of speeches I have heard and a composite speech runs as follows:

Well, I'm an INDIN, just like you. [Never INDIAN. They had to identify with us.] I was born in a one-room log cabin with a dirt floor [later a *rehab* shack], and I walked fifty miles a day to school, a little one-room [everything was one-room in those days] school where I got my education, and I went to a little one-room chapel where I met my Lord every Sunday and He replenished my soul. And then I went to college, and although I received scholarships from the government and my church, my parents still had to give me most of their money and I still had only one meal a day. But I persevered and graduated and then I got a job and started my climb upward and so after many years of hard work I am now a success. I am accepted by the best people and eat in the fanciest hotels. I believe all Indins could do the same if they would only apply themselves. I hope all of you young people are inspired by my success and that you will someday be as successful as I am.

And then we used to watch this INDIN meekly agree with the most outrageous and prepostrous schemes to solve "the Indian problem" and take his farewell.

With modest examples like that it is a shame that so many of us didn't make it. But we just didn't. Somehow we realized that the day of the successful individual was gone. Time had run out for the individualist and the days of the professional rebel had come into vogue.

The professional rebel was a younger person who was invited to conferences primarily to recite the wrongs of the white man, the real issue of the last century, never the current white man. The idea was that we could make the white feel guilty. When he felt guilty it would somehow make his efforts more real, and then he was happy again.

It would curl your hair to learn that the white man had perpetuated a colonial system, that he had done all sorts of irrational things to Indians; then made an about-face and tried to atone for the past, in order that his ancestors might sleep peacefully. Although this is what these conferences produced, we have yet to experience white atonement.

The funny thing about this era was that one subject was absolutely forbidden. And that was any attempt to compare the white man's treatment of Indians with that of other minority groups. That might have revealed a startling case against the whites' dealings with all dark-skinned peoples. Endless hours were spent to convince us that somehow, in a way neither we nor they understood, Indians were unique in relation to other minorities.

Little did we realize that the main tactic was to keep in our minds the fact that if we were separate, then only a certain group of whites could understand us, care for us, and work with us.

There was very little we could have done anyway. They controlled all the travel money, organized all the conferences, made all the chiefs. We had not yet learned how to bring Indian problems to the attention of the public, but we thought that there was some impelling reason why we should. In the meantime the white friend was busy with his own orgy of self-flagellation. Our role was to crystallize his guilt individually as if he alone had done all these things and to us personally.

After the conferences, missionaries, educators, and bureaucrats proceeded to do exactly as they had planned to do anyway. Some continued the very practices they had confessed were wrong, but with released vigor now that they had undergone a catharsis at the conference.

The guilt era ended when suddenly the skies opened and the money poured down. In 1964 there was talk about a great war that was to be waged. It was, we found out, a War on the Poor, officially designated as the War on Poverty.

The War on Poverty created a land office business (to use a painful phrase) in which everyone with a soft spot in his heart for the Indian, a desire for big money, and a plan to solve the *plight* of the reservations headed for the nearest tribe to offer his talents.

Universities that hadn't known that Indians existed outside of the textbooks charged into the forefront of social responsibility. Indian centers sprang up where no Indians had previously been allowed to loiter. Plans for massive archives, research, pilot projects, and developments mushroomed until we were convinced there would not be enough Indians to go around.

Washington was flooded with *grass roots* proposals to fight poverty on the different reservations. Looking out from a tribal office in the late afternoon, one could see a veritable wave of consultants treading their way to the motels. Evaluators greatly outnumbered workers. Feasibility replaced reality.

But plans were not automatically funded. Everyone was looking for *the* complete proposal that would solve every problem at once. Conferences dwelt on complete solutions. It sounded like the French Revolution, as proposal after proposal was presented to the assembled delegates only to be demolished by those experts on poverty.

It became popular to shoot down proposals with grass-roots sayings. The ultimate psych-out game of today's Indians was developed. Unity took a strange twist when proposals were gunned down because *all* tribes were not represented or because the tribes were so different that no one plan could serve them all.

Various tribal leaders would be asked to present their interpretation of tribal needs. After an Indian had finished speaking, educators, bureaucrats, sociologists, and anthropologists holding the opposing point of view would rise and, like a chorus in a Greek play, proclaim, "But he doesn't represent the *grass roots.*"

One educator constantly blasted me because NCAI didn't represent *all* the Indians. Then one day a fellow bureaucrat received a buffeting by urban Negroes and this same educator asked me to send a telegram of support because NCAI "represented all the Indian community." Such were the inconsistencies around which the national unity of Indian tribes was being predicated.

Indians who had spent their lives in Wounded Knee, Red Shirt, Cherry Creek, and Black River Falls were suddenly *unrepresentative* of the *real* Indian people and unceremoniously drummed out of consideration by conferees. Even full bloods who two years before would not have been invited because they were *too* Indian were brushed aside because they were thought not to know the reservation problems.

One full-blood acquaintance of mine had spent some thirty years on his tribal council. He was dismissed because he was part of the establishment!

Indian unity and Indian problems became the subjects for intense manipulation behind the scenes, as professional Indian-lovers fought to keep some semblance of cooperation among the tribes while arrayed against it were the universities, educators, and old-line bureaucrats. One friend of mine, a sociologist, suggested that we Indians be heeded "so far, but only insofar, as they represent all the Indians." After that remark I was tempted to rise at the next conference and state that I represented 107 of 315 tribes, so I could be trusted 107/315 of the time. And that the building was on fire.

The ultimate insult came at a conference at which about thirty of the most knowledgable Indians in the country were present to discuss Indian education. They were airily dismissed by a white educator because the *real Indians* were the ones he worked with and, since none of *them* were in attendance, the white felt he ought to represent them because he alone knew what *they* wanted.

In the last several years the very concept of unity has been used against the tribes to prevent their cooperation on national programs. Knowing that tribes are in all stages of development, whites have insisted upon uniformity of goals and definitions before they will accept Indian ideas as real. Because there cannot be such a concensus, Indian unity has been made to appear impossible.

National conferences, even National Congress conventions, have been confused by the whites' demand for that single answer which can then be passed on to government, church, or private agencies for the solution of Indian problems.

With the broad spectrum of tribes and the different levels of sophistication, plus the background maneuvering of whites with a financial or emotional interest in the outcome, you can imagine the impossible discussions that characterize national Indian meetings.

The first Indian will announce that he lives in a one-room shack. He will be rebutted by an Indian educator who has lost his identity between two cultures. Another will agree about the two cultures and will immediately be refuted by an old timer fighting for his treaty rights who is simultaneously challenged because he doesn't speak for all the Indians.

A national Indian meeting thus bears more resemblance to the Tower of Babel Improvement Association than it does to a strategy planning session.

The major problem, therefore, in unifying the tribes and supporting constructive leadership is that everyone is subject to judgment according to the standards of two distinct points of view. The white society is not satisfied with anything less than the efficiency of an Irish political machine. The Indian society expects little articulation, but infallible and successful exploits. And there is no attempt by either white or Indian to distinguish between the two.

Indians have no concept of teamwork as it is known by white society. Assignment of personnel to component jobs within an action plan leaves Indians cold. Rather, they expect leaders to charge ahead and complete the task. If anyone wants to assist in the job, so much the better. But there is no sense of urgency or need for efficiency in anything that is undertaken.

With their social structure largely undefined and modern society changing to data processing, Indians appear quite primitive. Charts, graphs, and statistics are irrelevant to most tribes. Their concern is the reality of the goals, the eventual effect a program will have on the tribe. Techniques and means of operation are left largely for staff considerations.

Whites who attempt to help Indians are constantly frustrated by their tragic lack of understanding of Indian people. For Indians always know exactly what position they will take on major issues, how far they can push certain concepts, and when to delay so as to wear out their opponents and eventually get their way.

There is usually not the slightest difference in what the tribes want for the future, though any detectable difference is immediately grasped by whites and used to form a major breach with the hopes of preventing any conclusion being reached.

While this dissension is superficially disheartening, understandings are quite often worked out through a technique which resolves issues without bringing matters to the floor. But there is a difference between the manner in which Indians use dissension and the way that conferences are manipulated by white onlookers.

Whites generally have some tangible motive for stalling an Indian meeting. Generally it is benign and relates to what they honestly think is best for the tribes. Other times it is simply to keep the tribes apart so the whites can eventually get their own programs approved.

Indians use dissension and controversy to guide the

sense of the meeting and also to maintain prestige among each other. It is a thrill to watch the psychological games played by Indians at a meeting. The most common game is an appeal to unity.

One Indian will get up and make a suggestion. He will be followed by another, who will agree completely with him but will phrase the speech in such a way as to create the impression that his predecessor is somehow against tribal unity. The second speaker creates such a sentiment in this audience that man after man gets up and speaks eloquently for unity of all Indians. Unity speeches roll down like a waterfall. Never did the Democrats unify like the Indians. If northern liberal Democrats and southern racist Democrats are cozy, Indians are stifling in their unity.

It would be fair to say that the best way to get a heated argument going in an Indian meeting is to speak on the need for unity. But the concern for unity serves to postpone divisions on the real issues in which unity is vital. It is far better to fight over unity than over something crucial to tribal existence.

Controversy over efforts to unify is naturally supported by Indian cultural motifs. In the old times as we have seen, a man's position rested primarily upon his ability to attract followers. Indians have come to rely on a strong leader and this in turn has created the War Chief complex.

The War Chief during the days of glory provided success or failure for the tribe. Leadership often depended upon a quasi-religious vocation and men were intimately concerned with the religious as well as political meaning of their lives.

In the Ghost Dance days, messiahship came to dominate Indian thought patterns and all expectations were tinged with this other-worldly hope of salvation. Every Indian leader of today must face the question of whether or not he is a great figure of the past reincarnated to lead his people to victory, for legends die hard among our people.

One in a leadership role is therefore constantly bothered by undefined doubts as to his ultimate role in his people's historical journey. He is inevitably drawn to compare himself in a mystical sense with Crazy Horse, Joseph, Geronimo, and others.

Initial spectacular success creates speculation as to how a leader compares with well-known tribal heros. If a man compares favorably, more work is placed upon him because of his capability and the people, satisfied with his performance, depend on him more and more and do less for themselves.

At my first convention of the NCAI there was very little for me to do because I was so new that no one had any confidence in me. A couple of years later I was fairly run to death doing minor errands because people had come to depend on me for a great many things.

Because Indian people place absolute dependence on their leaders, they exhaust more leaders every year than any other minority group. The useful national life of an Indian leader today is about two and a half years. After that he is physically and emotionally spent. His ideas have been digested and the tribes are ready to move on.

Unity, because of the ancient leadership patterns and the constant personal involvement between rival chiefs, becomes a function of personalities rather than issues. Unity as a team of experts is absolutely hopeless. Dynasties are impossible to maintain nationally and even temporary alliances are often destroyed by loss of a single individual.

National unification forms around popular leaders. But these people are generally worked to death by the time a significant number of people are supporting their program or before a large number of tribes accept them. The last three Executive Directors of the National Congress of American Indians achieved the largest number of member tribes the last year they held office.

When national or regional unification is based upon the personality of the leader, insane jealousies develop which are fed by white elements hoping to weaken tribal alliances. But Indians themselves do more to permanently weaken efforts to develop effective working relationships between tribes because of the intense rivalry which they develop by regions, states, tribes, and programs.

National Congress conventions are often split according to regional lines and the idea of capturing the presidency for a certain area becomes all consuming, pushing aside obvious real problems that face all the tribes.

Let no one say that only the white man is cruel with his

periodic assassinations and grief orgies. Or that blacks and Spanish cannot achieve unity. The Indian is so much more exquisitely skilled at political warfare and makes it so much more a casual game.

Indians know the human mind intimately. They can dwell for hours on slight nuances that others would completely miss or feel unworthy of their attention. I would put up an Indian brain-washing team against the Chinese Communists any day of the week.

Indians know the Indian mind best of all. They savor innuendo and inference above all. Consequently Indian meetings always have that undercurrent of psych-out that is a veritable preamble to existence as an Indian and the very antithesis of unity as the white man knows it.

I discovered this aspect of Indian politics at my second convention as NCAI Director. We had put together a very effective team the previous year, working hard to develop the organization and increase its ability to bring the tribes together. I had assumed that we would all be elected again because of our success in reconstituting the organization. To my chagrin I discovered that the tribes were systematically dissolving and reforming our team simply because they wanted to have an exciting election and feared that we would be re-elected without any real fight. They wanted action.

There is no way, therefore, that a person involved in national Indian politics can be assured of his position no matter how good he is and what his record has been. Dissidents often take advantage of the War Chief complex and lead their opponents down the road of messiahship— only to later accuse them of thinking they are really the Indian messiah. Slight hints here and there are often the tip of the iceberg of jealousy or discontent.

I have watched devoted, exhausted men cry because their tribe had totally rejected them at the height of their successes without so much as a backward glance.

With leadership and unity so intensely personal, unless a man is extremely charismatic, incredibly lucky, and hides his true purposes from inquisitive whites, his chances for success nationally are nil. Above all he must accept the social and ceremonial aspect of Indian politics and work within that framework to bring issues into focus for his people.

Among those people occupying national leadership roles there is a common tacit understanding of their common plight. Unless there is an impelling reason to go against another leader, Indians will generally support each other against the common enemy—the out group.

Many people would rather see a meeting come to no conclusion than embarrass a good man in public if such embarrassment would give his enemies weapons to be used against him. Most people realize that part of the chairman's job is to make a good showing for the tribe wherever he goes. Prestige committee assignments are handed out like presents at Christmas in an effort to maintain working relationships between tribal groups.

Most meetings held by Indians come to no conclusions which could be understood as agreements to do certain things. But every person attending a high-level meeting of Indians knows exactly what courses of action will be supported by the majority of tribes and exactly how to interpret the actions of the meeting to his people. Rarely do minutes of national meetings even need to be kept because of the silent understandings reached there.

The result of national meetings, therefore, is that there is mutual support and strength in the general consensus of tribes, from which each tribe gains more leverage and room to maneuver against the outsiders. It would be highly unlikely that an Indian meeting would or could develop a Poor People's Campaign or a March on Washington. Direct action is extrinsic to general understanding and traditional methods of problem-solving. But the tribes are able to get more for their people because of the insistence on indirect action.

When the Poor People camped in Washington the leadership left no room for retreat, placing themselves in a position of little negotiability with respect to government agencies. Tribes rarely box themselves into a position such as that. Rather, they always have such flexibility that they can change positions overnight and appear to be entirely consistent. For example the Hualapai tribe reversed its stand completely on the Marble Canyon Dam, finally supporting it, and no one thought a thing about it. Abernathy would not have dared make such a turnabout after his campaign began in Washington; the Hualapai could have changed every year and pulled it off.

The struggle is not so much one of unification but of who will eventually call the shots in Indian Affairs. Competition is thus multi-leveled and inter-group as well as racial. National and state Indian organizations are constantly being undercut by white interest groups in an effort to control the vast sums spent in Indian Affairs every year. No one wants a cut of the action for personal monetary gain; prestige, power, and emotional involvement play a much more vital role. Ego moves Indian Affairs in both white and red spheres much more than the dollar does.

The largest and most consistent national movement toward unification is the National Congress of American Indians. The NCAI is a small united nations of tribes with a past checkered from battles on every level. Its existence is only grudgingly admitted by white interest organizations because of their very reasonable fear that if the public found out Indians were doing things for themselves the annual fund appeals would look ridiculous. For the most part these people masquerade as friends of the Indian, presenting a distorted picture of the unbelievable poverty which they alone are fighting and perpetuating the image of the inarticulate incompetent savage who would be utterly destroyed save for their work. But like the buffalo, their days have been numbered. Each time an Indian organization wins a victory they must inevitably claim it partially for themselves in order to prevent, or at least postpone, the day when their downfall is complete.

Meanwhile, the National Congress charges through Indian country with sporadic successes and failures. Tribal membership varies from thirty tribes to over one hundred according to the climate for temporary unification. When times are plush, as they have been in the 1960's, the number of tribes participating is fairly high. When hard times come, membership dwindles and each tribe embarks on its own course to best determine its relationships with a menacing Congress.

It is this phenomenon of tribal membership that holds the key to understanding Indian unity and its twin, Indian leadership. The tribes do not depend upon the national organization for assistance on the local level. Where the NAACP, CORE, SNCC, and other Civil Rights groups have made use of local situations to highlight problems and work for their solutions, tribes totally reject assistance from the NCAI on the local level. It is inconceivable to most tribes that a national organization would work in localities to assist them. Rather, they look at the NCAI strictly in terms of the national scene. Consequently, membership is an abstraction whose mere presence heightens the total mystery of things.

The political effect of this behavior is just the opposite of what the tribes expect. Local difficulties bog them down and prevent progress in many areas of concern. Precedents that affect tribal rights all across the country are set on the local scene. Most of the problems Indians encounter are local, yet they refuse to face them on a realistic basis.

In recent years the NCAI has been able to sit back and pick its national battles. It has had considerable success in some scraps. If anything, leaders at the national level have set their sights too low and could have accomplished more with no more effort.

But with emphasis on creating a position for negotiating inside the government establishment and rejecting action programs used by the blacks, Indians have doomed themselves to political obscurity and impotence. Where SCLC could create pressure for a number of major laws through marches, Indians wait to take advantage of the tide of social legislation and gain a few crumbs when the goods are divided.

Unless Indians can adapt their tactics to place more emphasis on exploiting the local situation they will remain an unknown factor in American life. Always, it seems, issues detach themselves from the local situation and nebulously float off into the paragraphs of the perennial Task Force reports done by Interior and related agencies every few years.

So Indians are placed in the most inconsistent position for determining their own policy. They can very quickly reach a concensus on their problems. They are fairly sophisticated and experienced in getting their way with government agencies. But when they attempt to articulate what they are doing so that the white society can understand them, unity dissolves into chaos and the movement, along with the ideas supporting it, collapses.

Indians simply cannot externalize themselves. Externalization implies a concern for the future. Indians welcome the future but don't worry about it. Traditionally the tribes had pretty much what they wanted. There was no reason to get up tight about wealth and its creation. The land had plenty for everyone. Piling up gigantic surpluses implied a mistrust of the Great Spirit and a futile desire to control the future.

In addition no tribes had complex writing as did the white society. Winter counts and stories memorized by the favorite storytellers served to perpetuate the great events in tribal history. Other than that, there was no concern for recording events. Life thus had a contemporaneous aspect which meant immediate experiences of life, not continual analysis and dissection.

Attempts to force the tribes to expound on great themes for dispersion to non-Indian parties results in sheer chaos and disaster. Why, the people feel, should we explain anything to someone else, it is enough that we understand it.

Inability to use the white man's objective criteria most seriously hampers Indian programs. Resolutions passed at national meetings appear to be like white man's policy statements, but are actually only a polite nod to his way of doing business. It is almost as if by passing a resolution the tribes had fulfilled all righteousness for the express satisfaction of the whites who might be watching.

This type of operation creates the most baffling misunderstandings between Indians and the non-Indians with whom they must work. Actions of a tribal or national organization, although clear on the surface, seldom mean what they appear to mean and often mean something entirely different. If one cannot read between the lines he is at a loss to explain the apparent inconsistency.

In early 1967 there was a big meeting in Washington, D.C., to consider Udall's Omnibus Bill. Though this was heralded as the greatest thing ever to come down the pike, tribes universally rejected it. Yet for five days in January the tribes argued all around the point and, rather than rejecting it outright, sent a letter to President Johnson asking for more time. Everyone knew that another century would not suffice to change the mind of one tribe.

Many of our white friends have been ecstatic at some of our speeches, resolutions, and policy statements in the NCAI. Later, however, they've been horrified to see us take absolutely opposite stands on an issue.

To understand Indians and their unique place among the minority groups, one must look at unity through Indian eyes. Unity is strictly a social function of the tribes. Indians prefer to meet and have a good time; conventions are when you have a chance to get together and renew old friendships and learn to trust one another.

The real impact of the NCAI is the personal trust developed between people which in turn affects how each tribe views the others. The convention is merely a façade to confuse any wandering white man who should be in the neighborhood. After several days together, tribal leaders instinctively know how much they can depend upon each other, what a certain tribe is experimenting upon, and what issues are vital to their tribes. Then they are ready to go home again.

Social unification can best be illustrated by observation of the many powwows and celebrations held around Indian country each year. At a certain point in the program the announcer will proudly state that "eighty-three tribes are represented at this great event." Beware.

What the man means is that people from eighty-three different tribal backgrounds happened to have been in the neighborhood and decided to attend the doings; not that eighty-three tribes sent delegations to the event.

At one celebration a group of us each took turns adding up tribes and padded the total to well over one hundred tribes by simply stating that we had seen certain people from certain tribes present, although in fact we hadn't. Our announcer friend glowed at the prospect of so many tribes at powwow.

It is important to understand that the more tribes claimed, the better the powwow. This was an Indian doing and the more Indians involved the better everyone felt. This was unity for all of us.

What, after all, is unity but the fellowship of people? Too often, unified efforts are created simply to take advantage of people as one special interest group battles another for concessions from the government. America is certainly not a democracy when it is controlled by pressure groups. Rather, it is a pressure cooker waiting to explode when the wrong ingredients come together. Recent events show this tendency all too well.

After the latest Kennedy assassination, Congressman after Congressman came on TV and admitted that a vast majority of the American people wanted stricter gun control laws. But each stated that he couldn't do anything about it because of the big bad NRA lobby. Anyone swallowing that type of statement deserves to live in the land of the sniper.

Indians have always rejected unity as a weapon, though a number of younger Indians want unity precisely for that reason. Most of the tribes want unity as a fellowship of equals where they can play their Indian games with a minimum outside interference. Indian unity is what the churches mean when they say brotherhood, but which they dare not practice. It is what the white man seeks in his fraternities and exclusive clubs.

Like he has done everything else, the white man has turned the idea completely inside out when he has put unity into action. He has defined the right to be oneself as the right of exclusive privacy, never realizing that to be alone is to be dead. He has tried to create one society and has done so by creating an incredible number of pressure groups which control his society.

As Indians we will never have the efficient organization that gains great concessions from society in the marketplace. We will never have a powerful lobby or be a smashing political force. But we will have the intangible unity which has carried us through four centuries of persecution and we will survive. We will survive because we are a people unified by our humanity; not a pressure group unified for conquest. And from our greater strength we shall wear down the white man and finally outlast him. But above all, and this our strongest affirmation, we SHALL ENDURE as a people.

10 ✦ INDIANS AND MODERN SOCIETY

ONE OF THE intriguing little puzzles which anthropologists, Congressmen, missionaries, educators, and others often pose for themselves is whether an Indian tribe can survive in a modern setting. For the most part the question is posed as if the Indians were just coming out of the woods with their flint-tipped arrows and were demonstrating an unusual amount of curiosity about the printing press, the choochoo train, the pop machine, and other marvels of civilized man.

Black militants overbearingly tell Indians to "revolt, confront, destroy," the "powerstructure" that oppresses them. Confusing notoriety with success, they equate confusion with progress, draw on their vast storehouse of knowledge of the modern world, and advise Indians to become militant.

Everywhere an Indian turns he is deluged with offers of assistance, with good, bad, and irrelevant advice, and with proposals designed to cure everything from poverty to dandruff. Rarely does anyone ask an Indian what he thinks about the modern world. So assured is modern man that he has absolute control of himself and his society that there is never any question but what Indians are moving, albeit slowly and inefficiently, toward that great and blessed land of suburban America, the mecca for all people.

When an Indian considers the modern world, however, he sees it being inevitably drawn into social structures in which tribalism appears to be the only valid form of supra-individual participation. The humor becomes apparent when the Indian realizes that if he simply steps to the sidelines and watches the rat race go past him, soon people will be coming to him to advise him to return to tribalism. It appears to many Indians that someday soon the modern world will be ready to understand itself and, perhaps, the Indian people.

In March of 1968 the Southern Christian Leadership Conference began plans to have a massive march on Washington. The march was to be comparable, SCLC hoped, to the great marches of the past which had been instrumental in producing Civil Rights legislation. The purpose of the Poor People's Campaign was to bring attention to the plight of the poor with the hopes that Congress, which was then considering a six-billion-dollar cut in social welfare programs, would respond with a gigantic outpouring of funds to eradicate poverty. As the Poor People's Campaign gained momentum the purpose narrowed to the proposition of guaranteed jobs or a guaranteed annual income.

Notably absent from the list of supporting organizations in the campaign was the Congress of Racial Equality. CORE had been a leader in the Civil Rights struggles of the past. It was headed by black nationalists who endorsed black power. It was regarded as one of the militant left-leaning organizations of blacks in the nation. But CORE refused to fall into line with the campaign because it was busy taking another approach to the problems of black poverty.

The CORE solution was unveiled in July of 1968 at a joint news conference which featured Roy Innis, Acting Director of CORE, and four Republican Congressmen, Charles Goodell of New York, Robert Taft, Jr., of Ohio, Thomas Curtis of Missouri, and William Widnall of New Jersey. CORE proposed the Community Self Determination Act, which was designed to promote black capitalism of which CORE and Richard Nixon had both cooed approvingly earlier in the year.

The basic thrust of the Community Self-Determination Act of 1969 (which was not passed in the Ninetieth Congress but which has now been introduced again) was the Community Development Corporation. The Community Development Corporation, called affectionately CDC in the news conference, was to operate in six categories of activity:

1. Provider of neighborhood services and community improvement: basic education, child welfare, day care, pre-school training, health, consumer education, home ownership counseling, college placement, job finding, recreation, legal aid, and other services now available from federal sources.
2. Owner of stock of business enterprises.
3. Sponsor, owner, or manager of housing in the community.
4. Planning agency for neighborhood renewal.
5. Representative of community interests in areas of public policy.
6. Encourager of outside financial sources to assist self-help efforts of the community.

In short, the CDC was to be the all-purpose corporation by which black poverty was to be eliminated from the black ghettos and self-determination given to ghetto areas. The CDC was hailed as an important new step in the development of black pride and initiative in the private area.

If the CDC was brand-new for blacks it had a mighty familiar ring to the Indian people. The tribal council, as set up under the Indian Reorganization Act, had precisely the same powers, functions, and intents. Indians have been using the tribal council as organized under IRA for nearly a generation. As Indians viewed the "new" CDC, the blacks were finally ready to tribalize. One young Indian waggishly suggested that if they made up enrollments they might call them blacklists.

In the corporate structure, formal and informal, Indian tribalism has its greatest parallels and it is through this means that Indians believe that modern society and Indian tribes will finally reach a cultural truce. The corporation forms the closest attempt of the white man to socialize his individualism and become a tribal man. And certainly when one thinks back to what has been written over the last decade about corporate existence, one can see the startling parallels.

The devastating books of Vance Packard and William H. White outlined in detail how the corporation impinges upon individual man in his private life and reorients him toward non-individual goals. In the 1950's no existence was hated by the undergraduate as much as that of the organization man. The early beatnik and his descendant, the hippie, both abhorred the organization man. Many a career was nipped in the bud rather than let it develop in the insidious ways of corporate existence.

But in the corporation, man was offered a tribal existence of security and ease. The corporation provided everything a man might need if he were to maintain an affluent life over and above that of non-corporate man and befitting a person of vast educational achievement. The higher the degree, the more privileges bestowed upon corporate man. With untold fringe benefits covering all conceivable circumstances which might arise, organization man dwelt in an economic tribe to which he needed only give his allegiance and daylight hours. In return he had social and economic security rarely equalled since the days of feudalism.

Post-war developments of the corporation created the phenomenon of the merger. As corporations were piled together to form conglomerates, it became possible for a man to work for a great many corporations which were enclosed within one monstrous holding corporation so diversified that it rarely knew how far its tenacles extended.

The corporation became comparable to the great Indian coalitions such as the Iroquois and the Creek confederacies which stretched for thousands of square miles and in which a member was entirely safe and at home. And like the Indian tribes, success was measured against those outside the corporations, by prestige and honors. Where eagle feathers measured an Indian's successes, thickness of carpets measured executive success. Where a war chief might be given his choice of the loot of a war, the annual bonus and stock option became a regular means of rewarding the successful executive, home fresh from the competitive wars.

In short, corporate life since the last world war has structured itself along the lines taken a couple of centuries earlier by Indian tribes as they developed their customs and traditions of social existence. Totems have been replaced by trade marks, powwows by conventions, and beads by gray flannels. War songs have been replaced by advertising slogans. As in the tribe, so in the corporation the "chief" reigns supreme.

The life of the rugged individualist, beloved hero of Republican hymns, has now disappeared. The little family grocery or drug store, such as spawned the two chief contestants of the 1968 Presidential campaign, has now become the outpost, the frontier settlement, of the corporate conglomerate giant. Small businesses have all but vanished over the past two decades as the "chain" has driven them out of existence. Opportunity now exists within the corporate giant as a member of the tribe. The individual seeks fame only in bringing home the honors for his company.

Classifying the corporation as the tribe takes a little reorientation for most Americans because they are so quick to judge by outward appearances. Rarely do they meditate on how something really operates. Instead they want to believe that because something is shiny and appears new, it is new.

But in understanding the corporation as a form of tribalism, a number of new paths of understanding are made possible. The life of organization man is not simply one of allegiance to a cold unfeeling machine. Rather it becomes a path by which he can fulfill himself within certain limits. But going outside of the limits is taboo. It negates the existence by which organization man has defined himself and allowed himself to be defined. Just as a Cherokee or Sioux would have never done anything to eliminate himself from the tribe and accepted the limits by which the tribe governed itself, so the organization man must remain within the limits of his corporate existence.

The primary purpose of the tribe, then and now, was to ensure as beneficial a life as possible for members of the tribe. The hunting grounds of the tribe had to be defended at all costs. Outside of that, individual freedom ran rampant. Certainly the CDC proposed by CORE, which will cover all aspects of social existence, purports to do the same.

It would appear then that we are witnessing the gradual tribalization of the white man as his economic tribes become more and more oriented toward social services for their members. What is now needed is the frank admittance by the white man that he is tribalizing and the acknowledgment that his tribalism will gradually replace government as we now know it, submerging the differentiated society into a number of related economic social units.

When executives can admit what they are doing, then it will be possible to form programs around those left out of corporate existence—the poor—and organize them as tribes also, completing the circuit from Pilgrimish individualism to corporate tribalism. Preliminary treaty-making —price fixing—has been declared wrong because it infringed upon non-corporate victims. The government decreed that until these victims became sufficiently strong to embark on corporate warfare, it would protect them. Government thus stands as arbitrator between corporate and non-corporate man, a role previously occupied by the Onondagas in the Iroquois League.

It is not only in economic terms that America is tribalizing. Scholars and students of the modern family bemoan the fact that the family unit is disappearing and members of the family now have their primary interests outside the home. The old picture of the clan gathered around the fireplace or trooping through the snow to grandmother's house is fast fading into the historical mists.

In place of the traditional family has come the activist family in which each member spends the majority of his time outside the home "participating." Clubs, committees, and leagues devour the time of the individual so that family activity is extremely limited. Competition among clubs is keenly predicated upon the proposition that each member should bring his family into its sphere. Thus Boy Scouts is made a family affair. PTA, the YMCA, the country club, every activity, competes for total family participation although it demands entry of only one member of the family.

Clubs as social tribes wage fantastic warfare for the loyalties of the individuals of a community. Their selling point is that only by participating in their activity can a family partake of the snowy trips to grandmother's house in modern terms. The numena of American mythology is plastered indiscriminately over activities in order to catch unsuspecting participants and offer a substitute existence.

The American family is thus split into a number of individuals each claiming his blood relationship as a commitment on other members of the same biological source to support his tribe as against theirs. At best it is a standoff, with each member giving half-hearted recognition of the multitude of tribes to which the family as a conglomerate belongs.

The best example in intellectual circles of a tribal phenomenon is the magazine. *Playboy* early capitalized on tribal existence, although exemplified in the hutch instead of the tipi, and turned a magazine into a way of life. If ever there was a tribal cult oozing with contemporary mythology and tribal rites it is the Playboy club. Identity is the last concern of the Playboy, yet it is what his tribe offers him—and with a key.

Perhaps the only segment of American society to face tribalism head on has been the long-haired hippie and his cousins, yippies, zippies, and others. In 1966 strange beings began to appear on Indian land, proclaiming their kinship with the redskins in no uncertain terms. Some Indians thought that the earlier VISTA program had spoiled things for the hippies by their inept performance on the reservations, but no one had seen anything until the summer of 1966.

I used to sit in my office and suddenly find it invaded by a number of strange beings in gaudy costumes who would inform me of their blood-intellectual relationship with Indians. When one is used to the strange smells of legislation written by the Interior Department and is suddenly confronted by an even more exotic perfume, it is unsettling indeed.

Yet many hippies whom I met had some basic humanistic beliefs not unlike those of Indian people. Concern for the person and abhorrence for confining rules, regulations, and traditions seemed to characterize the early hippie movement. When the hippies began to call for a gathering of the tribes, to create free stores, to share goods, and to gather all of the lost into communities, it appeared as if they were on the threshold of tribal existence.

I remember spending a whole afternoon talking with a number of hippies who had stopped in Denver on the way west. They were tribally oriented but refused to consider customs as anything more than regulations in disguise. Yet it was by rejecting customs that the hippies failed to tribalize and became comical shadows rather than modern incarnations of tribes.

Indian tribes have always had two basic internal strengths, which can also be seen in corporations: customs and clans. Tribes are not simply composed of Indians. They are highly organized as clans, within which variations of tribal traditions and customs govern. While the tribe makes decisions on general affairs, clans handle specific problems. Trivia is thus kept out of tribal affairs by referring it to clan solutions.

Customs rise as clans meet specific problems and solve them. They overflow from the clan into general tribal usage as their capability and validity are recognized. Thus a custom can spread from a minor clan to the tribe as a whole and prove to be a significant basis for tribal behavior. In the same manner, methods and techniques found useful in one phase of corporate existence can become standard operating procedure for an entire corporation.

Hippies, at least as I came to understand them, had few stable clan structures. They lived too much on the experiential plane and refused to acknowledge that there really was a world outside of their own experiences. Experience thus became the primary criteria by which the movement was understood. Social and economic stability were never allowed to take root.

It seemed ridiculous to Indian people that hippies would refuse to incorporate prestige and social status into their tribalizing attempts. Indian society is founded on status and social prestige. This largely reduces competition to inter-personal relationships instead of allowing it to run rampant in economic circles. Were competition to be confined to economic concerns, the white conception of a person as a part of the production machine would take hold, destroying the necessary value of man in his social sense.

With competition confined within social events, each man must be judged according to his real self, not according to his wealth or educational prowess. Hence a holder of great wealth is merely selfish unless he has other redeeming qualities besides his material goods. Having a number of degrees and an impressive educational background is prerequisite to prestige in the white world. It is detrimental in the Indian world unless the person has the necessary wisdom to say meaningful things also.

Hippies, at least initially, appeared to throw off the white man's prestige symbols while refusing to accept the Indian prestige symbols. Hence there was no way in which tribalism, in its most lasting form, could take root in the hippie movement. What prestige they had, came with publicity. Quickly the media turned them into a fad and the hippie with something to say became no more than Batman or the Hoola Hoop.

Additional to hippie failure to tribalize was their inability to recognize the existence of tribal capital, particularly land. Tribal existence has always been predicated upon a land base, a homeland, within which tribal existence could take place. The primary concern of Indian tribes has been the protection of the land to which they are related. Once landless, a people must fall back upon religion, social values, or political power. But with a land base, nationalism in a tribal setting is more possible.

Only a very few hippies made an effort to develop a land base. A few communes are beginning to spring up around the country. But most of the flowers, unfortunately, have yet to be planted.

Inter-corporate competition has revealed the necessity of banding together for political purposes to defend hunting grounds, be it oil import quotas, tariffs, or subsidies. In this respect white corporations are more aware of the inevitability of conflict than are Indian tribes. Whites know how to best use the corporate structure in an infinite variety of ways. And they know how to manipulate the governmental structure to obtain the goals of their corporations.

Some corporations, particularly social corporations such as those listed annually in the various United Fund appeals, have already mastered the technique of taxing the rest of society to support their ventures. They are thus one step beyond even the profit-making corporations which offer a substantial number of fringe benefits to their employees.

The United Fund agencies have achieved a status comparable to the Magi of yesteryear. The Magi, conquered by the Persians, promptly set themselves up as religious experts and soon exercised incredible control over Persian society. They burrowed right into the fabric of Persian life and dominated it. In the same way, United Fund agencies have captured the priesthood of social activity and now exact their pound of flesh as necessary organizations upon which the lifeblood of the community depends.

Examine, if you will, the agencies listed in the United Fund appeal the next time you are called upon to give. By and large they all do what everyone else is doing. Only, they appear to be doing it somehow differently. Had they been active in a meaningful programmatic manner, it would have been unnecessary for the government to conduct a War on Poverty. But should the government win its War on Poverty tomorrow, United Fund agencies would continue on their merry way.

What then is the genius of the United Fund agency? We called them above, the priesthood of our society and they *are* priests in the mediating sense. Where fraternities, sororities, and service clubs have the same basic clientele, United Fund agencies have developed a mediating role between diverse segments of society. They collect from one set of clientele and distribute to another set. Thus, as intermediaries they cannot be eliminated because they would leave two diverse sets of clients with peculiar needs—those who need to give and those who need to receive.

As the fortunes of agencies and foundations like the United Fund rise and fall, so do tribalism and tribal existence. These agencies are the weathervane of our society. We can tell at a glance how our society is responding to the expansion of tribal corporations by their progress and setbacks. As tribal corporations meet the challenges of modern life, there will be less use for United Fund agencies and their revenues and programs will decline. But if the tendency is away from tribalized existence on the corporate level, these agencies will expand and their revenues will increase. People will need to become more meaningfully involved and will seek out both services and recipients for their funds. Thus such agencies are an accurate indicator of giving and receiving in our society. From them we can take one cue as to what the future holds.

There is another aspect of modern society to which Indian society relates and that is law. The evolution of law is as fascinating as it is complex. The manner in which Indians and law can combine in the modern world depends upon an understanding of the nuances of law.

We first came across law in its original cradle of tribalism in the Old Testament. Torah, law, comes from a root word meaning to extend one's hand as if pointing the way. A careful reading of the Old Testament and its concern for law can reveal—as it does for the Jews—a standard of behavior by which a person can be fulfilled. Thus originally law was not confining or regulating but indicating the way to a better life.

In feudal days law once again rose from the ruins of Roman codification as customs gradually became the laws of England and western European civilization. Only in certain aspects were early laws regulatory or confining. In most cases they were indicative of inter-personal relationships.

The history of America has shown the gradual replacement of custom and common law with regulatory statutes and programs so that law today is more a case of legalizing certain types of behavior and penalizing other types of behavior. We are just passing through the most radical period of law as a confining instrument of social control.

The programs initiated by President Johnson are sometimes looked at as the logical extension of the New Deal concept of government as development agent for social welfare programs. It has been said that the War on Poverty was simply a rehash of the WPA projects and the CCC camps. But close examination of the Economic Opportunity Act, the Economic Development Act, the Model

Cities programs, Urban Renewal, and other Great Society programs will reveal a basic foundation completely foreign to New Deal concepts. All of these programs are founded upon the premise that the federal government must help local efforts to accomplish certain things, but that government itself cannot do those things for local people. Law has thus begun a new cycle of existence as a means to social fulfillment.

Programs of the Great Society point the way toward experimentation by local people in various ways and means of creating a more meaningful existence. They therefore become vehicles for change and fulfillment of potential, rather than payoffs to certain groups who would otherwise refuse to participate in modern economic ventures. While there is no doubt that Great Society programs have political overtones, within certain limits most American citizens can participate in them.

The great fear of minority groups in the 1968 elections was that law and order meant a return to the conception of law as an instrument of confinement and away from the idea of law as an expansion of opportunities. Regulated existence has rarely been able to provide the stability and potential which societies need to survive. When codification has been emphasized, societies have tended to decline because law has traditionally been a means of confinement and oppression.

When law takes on its most creative aspect, customs develop to operate internally within the social structure. The vacuum created by expanding and developing programs and laws gives rise to the need for internal controls by which men can govern themselves. Customs naturally arise to fill this need and custom depends upon participation by all members of society.

A good example of custom is the American system of two political parties as an undefined adjunct to the Constitution. Nowhere does the Constitution outline the need or the structure for political participation. No parties are mentioned. They have arisen through customs which filled in the missing pieces of the Constitution. No one had to follow one path or another. But over the years a significant number of citizens adopted the same customs and the great political processes of our nation took shape.

As the political parties became structured with rules and regulations, additional customs arose which by their solution gave meaning to the unarticulated problems of the process. Thus, for example, for a while the candidate remained at home awaiting the demand of the people that he become a candidate. This custom was overcome by Roosevelt's daring visit to the convention in 1932 and the rise of primaries in the various states.

As we become aware of our customs we will become more able to live in a tribalizing world. Tribal society does not depend upon legislative enactment. It depends heavily in most areas upon customs which fill in the superstructure of society with meaningful forms of behavior and which are constantly changing because of the demands made upon them by people.

One of the chief customs in Indian life is the idea of compensation instead of retribution in criminal law. Arbitrary punishment, no matter how apparently suitable to the crime, has had little place in Indian society. These customs have by and large endured and many tribes still feel that if the culprit makes a suitable restitution to his victim no further punishment need be meted out by the tribe.

Contrats this outlook with the highly emotional appeals to "lawnorder" over the last year and it is easy to see that the white man's conception of criminal law has changed little from the harsh codes of the ancient eastern despots. America's prison population continues to climb as society attempts to punish those guilty of violating its mores. Little is done to restore the victim to his original state. The emphasis is on "getting even" on the victim's behalf by imposing a term of imprisonment on the offender.

With the passage of the 1968 Civil Rights Act, Indian tribes fell victim to the Bill of Rights. The stage is now set for total erosion of traditional customs by sterile codes devised by the white man. Some tribes are now fighting to get the law amended because the law allows reliance on traditional Indian solutions only to the extent that they do not conflict with state and federal laws.

Although the Bill of Rights is not popular with some tribes, the Pueblos in particular, I do not believe that it should be amended. With the strengthening of tribal courts

Indian tribes now have a golden opportunity to create an Indian common law comparable to the early English common law.

Many national leaders have encouraged Indian judges to write lengthy opinions on their cases incorporating tribal customs and beliefs with state and federal codes and thus redirecting tribal ordinances toward a new goal. Over the next decade the response by Indian judges in tribal court may well prove influential in the field of law. Perhaps the kindest thing that could be said of non-Indian law at present is that it combines punishment and rehabilitation in most instances. With a additional push for compensatory solutions Indian people could contribute much to the solution of the problem of crime in the larger society.

The stage is now being set, with the increasing number of Indian college students graduating from the universities, for a total assault on the non-human elements of white society. Ideologically the young Indians are refusing to accept white values as eternal truths. Such anomalies as starvation in the midst of plenty indicate to them that the older Indian ways are probably best for them.

Movements to re-educate Indians along liberal lines only serve to increase the visibility of the differences between their own backgrounds and the backgrounds of the non-Indians. Yet the bicultural trap, conceptually laid for Indians by scholars, does not appear to be ensnaring the most astute young Indian people. Accommodation to white society is primarily in terms of gaining additional techniques by which they can give a deeper root to existing Indian traditions.

The corporation serves as the technical weapon by which Indian revivalism can be accomplished. At the same time it is that element of white culture closest to the tribe and can thereby enable it to understand both white and Indian ways of doing business. As programs become available, tribal councils should simply form themselves as housing authorities, development corporations, and training program supervisors, continuing to do business according to Indian ways. The tribe is thus absorbing the corporation as a handy tool for its own purposes.

Of all the schemes advocated today for the solution of poverty, the guaranteed annual income appears to be the most threatening to ultimate tribal progress. Guaranteed annual income would merely accelerate the inertia which continues to nip at the heels of reservation development. Yet the humanistic basis of the guaranteed annual income is solidly within Indian traditions.

In the old days a tribe suffered and prospered as a unity. When hunting was good everyone ate, when it was bad everyone suffered. Never was the tribe overbalanced economically so that half would always starve and half would thrive. In this sense all tribal members had a guaranteed annual income.

With the basic necessities guaranteed by tribal membership, means had to be devised to grade the tribe into a social ladder. Exploits in hunting, warfare, and religious leadership effectively created status necessary to structure the interpersonal relationships within the tribe. A man was judged by what he was, not by what he owned.

Society today has largely drifted away from accomplishments. Concern is focused instead on "image"—what a man appears to be, not what he is. Thus the 1968 elections saw Richard Nixon cautiously refuse to face any issues which might have taken votes away from him. In previous years the Kennedys made even greater use of image and it will probably never be known exactly what the Kennedys accomplished on behalf of their constituency. People will rather remember Jack and Bobby as they appeared on television.

As Indians continue to appear in modern society other issues will come to be drawn in certain areas. Some tribes have zoned their reservations so that the land is used primarily for the benefit of reservation people. Gradually planners in the white society will come to recognize the necessity of reserving land for specific use rather than allow helter-skelter development to continue unchecked.

Education must also be revamped; not to make Indians more acceptable to white society, but to allow non-Indians a greater chance to develop their talents. Education as it is designed today works to destroy communities by creating supermen who spend their lives climbing the economic ladder. America is thus always on the move and neighborhoods rarely have a stable lasting residency. In the future, minority groups must emphasize what they share with the white society, not what keeps them apart. Black may be beautiful but such a slogan hardly contributes to the understanding of non-blacks. Intensity turns easily to violence when it has no traditions and customs to channel it into constructive paths of behavior. The powwow serves as more than a historical re-enactment of ancient ways. In a larger sense it provides an emotional release heavily charged with psychological and identity-absorbing tensions. This is perhaps one reason why "red is beautiful" has not become a necessary slogan.

Non-Indians must understand the differences, at least as seen in Indian country, between nationalism and militancy. Most Indians are nationalists. That is, they are primarily concerned with development and continuance of the tribe. As nationalists, Indians could not, for the most part, care less what the rest of society does. They are interested in the progress of the tribe.

Militants, on the other hand, are reactionists. They understand the white society and they progress by reacting against it. First in their ideas is the necessity of forcing a decision from those in decision-making positions. Few militants would be sophisticated enough to plan a strategy of undermining the ideological and philosophical positions of the establishment and capturing its programs for their own use.

Nationalists always have the option of resorting to violence and demonstrations. Militants shoot their arsenal merely to attract attention and are left without any visible means to accomplish their goals. Hence militancy must inevitably lead on to more militancy. This is apparent in the dilemma in which the SCLC found itself after the 1966 Civil Rights Bill. Demonstrations had proved successful and so SCLC found itself led on and on down that path, never satisfied. Even after King's death, when SCLC could have changed its goals and techniques, it continued to the disaster of Resurrection City.

But Indian tribes riding the crest of tribal and nationalistic waves will be able to accomplish a great many things previously thought impossible by Indian and non-Indian alike. There is every indication that as Indians articulate values they wish to transmit to the rest of society, they will be able to exert a definite influence on social developments.

At present the visible poverty of Indian tribes veils the great potential of the Indian people from modern society. But in many ways the veil is lifting and a brighter future is being seen. Night is giving way to day. The Indian will soon stand tall and strong once more.

11 ✤ A REDEFINITION
OF INDIAN AFFAIRS

IN MARCH OF 1966 the executive committee of the National Congress of American Indians met in El Paso, Texas, to discuss its program for the future. During the meeting a man named Tom Diamond appeared before us with a ragged little group of people. Fervently he made his plea for NCAI support and assistance for the Tigua Indian tribe of Isleta, Texas. The modern era of Indian emergence had begun.

The year 1688 saw the end of the Spanish rule of New Mexico for nearly a generation. The Pueblos of New Mexico revolted against Spanish rule and pushed the Spanish out of New Mexico back to their river fortress of El Paso del Norte, now Juarez, Mexico. With the retreating soldiers a number of Indians from the Isleta Pueblo were taken. Like human mules they carried the stolen treasures of New Mexico south.

Once at El Paso del Norte, the Tiguas were of no further use to the Spanish and therefore assigned a piece of land on the north bank of the Rio Grande River, where it was expected they would provide a buffer zone against the warlike Mescalero Apaches who dominated eastern New Mexico and western Texas.

Centuries passed. The little group was forgotten. The Bureau of Indian Affairs listed them as a Pueblo group

239

under the jurisdiction of the New Mexico office but little was done for them. Some of the Tiguas attended the government boarding school in Albuquerque and occasionally bureau officials stopped by, but the tendency was to ignore them.

In 1936 President Roosevelt was made an honorary Tigua warrior when he visited Texas. There was no doubt that the Tiguas deserved federal recognition, having once received services from the federal government and having been listed as one of the tribes eligible for such services. But since they were secreted away in the middle of El Paso, Texas, they were soon forgotten. They had not been heard from since the visit by Roosevelt and people assumed they no longer existed.

The NCAI recognized the Tiguas as a surviving tribe of Indians and began to take steps to see if they could be formally recognized. Tom Diamond, an attorney in El Paso who had given his time and money for years in an effort to help the Tiguas, led the struggle to get their status clarified.

Finally in early April, 1968, President Johnson signed into law a bill that officially recognized the Tiguas as an Indian tribe and ceded responsibility for them to the state of Texas. Under the programs of Texas the Tiguas are now enjoying a revival of tribal life with a chance to build a sound economic base for the future.

Ever since Indians began to be shunted to reservations it has been assumed by both Indians and whites that the eventual destiny of the Indian people was to silently merge into the mainstream of American society and disappear. The thought of a tribe being able to maintain traditions, socio-political structure, and basic identity within an expanding modern American city would have been so preposterous an idea had it been advanced prior to the discovery of the Tiguas, that the person expounding the thesis would have been laughed out of the room.

Yet the Tiguas had fought for their tribal existence and been successful. The famed melting pot, that great sociological theory devised to explain the dispersion of the European immigrant into American society, had cracks in it through which, apparently, Indian tribes were slipping with ease.

Discovery of the Tiguas rocked Indian people in several respects. Indians had been brainwashed into accepting the demise of their tribe as God's natural plan for Indians. Yet the Tiguas plainly demonstrated that Indian tribal society had the strength and internal unity to maintain itself indefinitely within an alien culture.

If, many Indian people thought, the Tiguas had survived for three centuries in the middle of El Paso, might not their own tribe also survive somehow? Once accepting the idea that tribes were really entities that had no beginning or end, Indians began to view their problems in a new light. The basic operating assumption of tribes changed from that of preserving the tribal estate for an eventual distribution to the idea that tribes would always manage to survive, that present difficulties were not insurmountable, and that perhaps the Indian community was nationally much larger than people had imagined.

Since 1966 there has been an increasing awareness of tribalism sweeping the Indian power structure. No longer does Indian country begin at the Mississippi. Now it extends from coast to coast. Talk has even begun about contact with the surviving natives of Hawaii.

The NCAI set its sights to contact as many groups as possible in the eastern portion of the United States, hoping to find other groups such as the Tiguas. In due time the Tunicas of Louisiana, the Appalachicolas of Florida, the Haliwas of North Carolina, the Pamunkeys of Virginia, the Wampanogs of Massachusetts, the Coushattas of eastern Texas, the Cherokees of southern Ohio, and the Payson Band of Yavapai Apaches in Arizona were all located.

In many cases knowledgeable non-Indians had learned of the search for missing tribes and come forward with information. In other cases the Bureau of Indian Affairs began to push for recognition of bands which had always been eligible for federal services but which had been caught between reservations during frontier days and preferred to remain among white friends in small towns.

A symptom of the national Indian awakening was the appointment of Judge Lacy Maynor of North Carolina, the distinguished leader of the Lumbee community, as a co-chairman of the First Citizens for Humphrey-Muskie, a coalition of Indian people supporting the Democratic ticket in 1968. Judge Maynor had gained national recognition in 1958 when his Lumbees surprised the Ku Klux Klan at a meeting in North Carolina and sent them packing. But Maynor's appointment as a co-chairman was tacit recognition by western Indians of eastern non-federal tribes as an important segment of the emerging nationwide Indian community.

The awakening of the tribes is just beginning. Traditionalists see the movement as fulfillment of ancient Hopi and Iroquois religious predictions of the end of white domination of the continent. Others feel that American society has now reached the point of maturity where the platitudes of the Constitution can finally begin to take on real meaning.

Anthropologists love to talk knowingly about this movement and call it pan-Indianism. When the first Indian came to Plymouth Colony and chanced to meet another Indian on the way in, a committee of anthropologists was probably trailing him, eagerly observing pan-Indianism at work.

But pan-Indianism exists primarily in the mind of the beholder, as do all anthropological theories. Pan-Indianism implies that a man forgets his tribal background and fervently merges with other Indians to form "Indianism." Rubbish.

Younger Indians are beginning to understand the extent to which the Indian community is being expanded and to many of them it is an affirmation of tribalism over individualism. Traditions, which kept the Tiguas together and which are holding the Tunicas and other tribes in the ways of their ancestors, are now beginning to become of primary importance.

The mechanized concepts of image, relevancy, feasibility, and efficiency are now being seen as gimmicks by which white America fools itself into believing it has created a culture. In reality, it has used these plastic devices to avoid the necessity of having a real culture. Tribal existence is fast becoming the most important value in life. Consideration of other ideas takes second place to tribalism.

The federal tribes of the southeastern United States, always separated by distance and ideology, recently moved in the direction of a southeastern coalition of tribes. The Choctaws of Mississippi and the Seminoles and the Miccosukees of Florida recently banded together with the Eastern Band of Cherokees of North Carolina to form an inter-tribal council to work specifically on their problems.

As federal policies change and become clarified, there is little doubt that the southeastern United States will experience a great Indian revival, bringing the focus in Indian Affairs to philosophy rather than program considerations.

While tribal societies are beginning to awaken, assert themselves, and contact others in the rural areas, urban Indians have been developing a new nationalism for themselves. In January of 1968 representatives of twenty-six urban Indian groups met in Seattle, Washington, for the first of a series of consultations on problems of off-reservation Indians.

The Seattle conference was attended by a number of reservation Indians who were suspicious of the gathering. In the late 1950's the off-reservation Colvilles were organized by a white man for the specific purpose of selling the large Colville reservation. The land is valued at one hundred million dollars and the critical issue has been division of the money among the non-reservation people. Mistrust ran rampant throughout the meeting, especially among the attending reservation people who feared it would result in a massive movement against the reservations. Consequently the meeting ended with both groups preparing for the next confrontation.

At the annual NCAI convention in the fall of 1968 the subject of urban Indians was cussed and discussed at length. Several resolutions attempting to define policy with respect to off-reservation Indians were offered. Finally a compromise resolution very general in nature was passed.

The fears of reservation Indians were perhaps justified when one considers what the organization of unsuspecting off-reservation members of a tribe could do to reservation programs. But reservation people need not fear the urban movement among off-reservation people. Urban centers are inter-tribal and the chances of one center having a majority of one tribe are practically nil.

Furthermore, urban Indians have become the cutting

edge of the new Indian nationalism. For centuries they have been going into town and remaining there. Now they are asserting themselves as a power to be reckoned with. Urban Indians frequently return to their reservations, if only for a vacation or weekend, and until recently they were content to think of themselves as temporary residents of the city in which they lived.

Over the past decades the empty stores, church basements, and rented halls they had been meeting in for social activities have become newly purchased Indian centers, complete with staff and programs. From a once-a-month dance to an ongoing program of social services, the spectrum of Indian centers appears endless and continually in transition. The eventual list of cities in which Indians have organized may one day pass the one hundred mark.

The large midwestern cities of Chicago and Minneapolis represent the most comprehensive development of urban Indianism. With a long history of capable leadership from both white and Indian communities, people in these two cities have set up the procedure for total Indian renaissance. Fund-raising drives have provided financial support for their programs. In Chicago the two Indian centers own buildings and have achieved relative financial stability. In Minneapolis, settlement houses have served as rallying points and been used by the urban Indians to spread into neighborhoods in all parts of the city.

Both cities are characterized by the organization of many smaller groups of Indians who participate in city-wide programs. Indians in these cities have found that tribal differences do not merge into a general blur of Indianism. Tribal backgrounds are too strong for even an Indian melting pot. So the people have built their organizations on tribal differences.

Clubs have been organized by tribe. Thus Minneapolis has the Twin Cities Sioux Council, the Twin Cities Chippewa Council, and others. The tribal clubs support the overall program of the urban center and in turn have their own programs in which ideas unique to the particular tribe are emphasized. Overall membership in the entire program is much broader and more active than when tribes were indiscriminately merged into one amalgam.

From the consultation at Seattle, Indians of other cities

came to an understanding of what was possible for urban people. Many left Seattle determined to reproduce in Tulsa, Denver, Rapid City, and Omaha what had been done in Minneapolis, Chicago, and Oakland. And many of the conference participants were surprised to discover that they all felt a real desire to get into the fight for better legislation to help the reservation people protect the reservation homeland from further encroachment.

Even the eastern cities—traditional homes of tribes thought long since vanished—have begun the task of organizing themselves. The second urban meeting in Tempe, Arizona, saw the attendance of a group from New York City. Eventually Cleveland, Cincinnati, Boston, and Washington, D.C., are also expected to have urban Indian centers.

When one realizes that the majority of Indian people live in urban areas, the extent of the new movement becomes clear. The cities are beginning to furnish the catalytic agents for total national organization. A decade ago organization was primarily according to tribe; off-reservation people had not yet begun to seek each other out. Few even suspected that very many other Indian people resided in the city in which they lived.

Now it is becoming painfully apparent to government agencies that reservation people are the least of their problems. Demonstrations against Bureau of Indian Affairs offices have taken place in three cities. More are being planned by young urban Indians sent to the cities to receive job training. Soon bureaucrats will be asking for transfer to isolated reservations instead of cities where the young militants are sure to make their lives miserable.

The Vice President's Council on Indian Opportunity, set up in April, 1968, by order of the President, is now in contact with the urban Indians who have formally organized as American Indians United. Problems are being outlined and possible solutions discussed by the two groups.

Chicago has seen the rise of Indian nationalism by younger people. In addition to the established centers and clubs, young people have started to move the urban Indian structure toward a more militant stance in regard to urban programs available through the mayor's office. Denver has recently seen the organization of another Indian club that is avowedly more militant with regard to programs being administered by the city. Omaha has a group of younger Indians which threatens to begin to move city Indians toward community involvement.

Because there is such a mushrooming movement among urban Indians, old ideas and traditional policies have become woefully outmoded. In the past, tribal councils have largely determined national Indian policy. Many times the Bureau of Indian Affairs has been able to apply pressure on certain tribes to hold back militant stands by Indian people. It learned to effectively play one tribe against another until the tribes were confused and disheartened. Then it would appear to compromise and tribes would eagerly agree to whatever was placed before them. When one recalls that every tribe had to have approval of the BIA to lease its lands, to travel, to get legal counsel, it is a wonder that tribes have been able to get anything done.

While the BIA still has to approve basic tribal operations, it no longer has the resources to keep track of everything happening in Indian Affairs today. Other agencies are continually calling conferences which take tribes from one end of the country to another. Pressuring individual tribes has become too risky because of the great competition between government agencies to appear more active than competing agencies.

Urban Indians have a great advantage over reservation people. They have no restrictions on the way they raise or spend money. The bureau has no means by which it can influence urban Indians at all, it must be by offering them something. Urban Indians have nothing to lose and everything to gain, so initial success breeds deeper thought and more comprehensive planning for the next go-round.

Nor do the emerging non-federal eastern Indians have anything to lose. In many cases, in many states, they are busy compiling the documentation to prove their claims. The tribes of Maine are moving incredibly fast in pressing their claims against Massachusetts. And Massachusetts may have its hands full with other tribes such as the Wampanoag and Narragansett before it is finished with Indian people.

The great weapon which the eastern tribes have is invisibility. No one believes they exist, yet back in the statutes and treaties lies the key to their eventual success. The Montauks are a good example. At the turn of the century the tribe was thrown out of court because the Montauks lacked standing to file suit. They were wards of the state of New York. Well, people argue, if they were wards of the state of New York, what has the state been doing for them?

At present there is tremendous potential awakening in the cities and among the non-federal tribes of the East. At least three-quarters of the national Indian population lives in the cities and eastern United States. A new coalition of eastern Indians and urban groups could force a radical change in existing federal policy toward Indian people. These people generally vote more than reservation people. When they organize for political purposes, they will be able to exert more influence than they have at present.

Many non-reservation Indians are scattered in states and Congressional districts that have yet to produce a Senator or Congressman who has taken an interest in Indians. When these groups organize for effective action they will begin to make Indian affairs a concern of interested non-Indians who would like to assist Indian people. Thus there is every indication that eastern and urban people will be able to bring up issues which reservation people have not been able or willing to raise.

Tragically, Indian Affairs within the Bureau of Indian Affairs is today exclusively oriented toward individual reservations. Little concern is shown for program development on a regional, state, or inter-area office basis. Thus the BIA is extremely vulnerable to unexpected pressures from regional groups which combine urban concentrations or urban centers and reservations.

Urban Indians may very well endorse proposals of reservation people without a thought for the larger issues which are emerging in the cities. Employment is inevitably bound to housing, which in turn is bound to credit availability. Concentration of simple issues designed for upgrading reservations may not take into account the complexities of the urban situation.

The nomadic tendency of Indians could conceivably

limit the possibilities of upgrading programs and policies for all Indian people. It is almost impossible to keep an accurate census of Indians in a city. Some surveys taken in Denver indicated that only one-quarter of the people listed at a certain address in the fall were there that same winter. They had vanished, moved, gone back to their reservations, or moved on to another city.

Similar attempts to count reservation people have produced almost identical results. Programs designed to provide employment on certain reservations may be woefully out of touch with the nomadic tendencies of the people of that reservation to move back and forth.

Some attempt should be made to coordinate movements of Indians to coincide with ongoing programs in both reservation communities and urban centers. One such attempt is being made in the Midwest. Whether it proves successful or not will depend primarily upon the ability of the urban Indians to articulate the problem to their reservation cousins and the ability of these urban people to understand national trends.

Sioux City Indian Center was funded this spring to do work in organizing the Indian people in the surrounding four states of South Dakota, Minnesota, Iowa, and Nebraska. These states have small concentrations of Indian people in their larger towns. Many of these people go back and forth to the neighboring reservations of Yankton Sioux, Santee Sioux, Flandreaux Sioux, Winnebago, Omaha, Sac and Fox, and Lower Brule. Sioux City will be the focal point of a regional effort to coordinate employment, housing, education, and organization of the Indian people in this area.

With careful planning a large number of Indian clusters can be built up in neighboring towns and smaller cities such as Sioux Falls, Worthington, Minnesota, and Des Moines, Iowa. In a very short time an integrated balanced Indian community, which will encompass an area of some fifty thousand square miles, can be built. From the focal point will come directions for economic development by which a self-sufficient Indian community can be stabilized.

Concentration simply on reservation problems in this area would produce little if any tangible results. Employment is primarily available in the cities and towns. Development of the reservations as centers of employment is absurd because of a multitude of problems. But development of those same reservations as enclaves of residential and social stability makes a great deal of sense.

Combining urban and reservation goals must, therefore, be led by urban people who are much more aware of opportunities for specific developments. If urban Indians can take the time and trouble to plan for the future, they will gain a strong influence over Indian Affairs locally and eventually nationally.

There is an added danger to urban Indians from their involvement with the militants of other minority groups, particularly the black power movements. Spectacular success in achieving national publicity has attracted a great many urban Indians to the black power people. In Omaha and Chicago, Oakland and Los Angeles, young Indians are talking like black militants and beginning to ape their ideas and techniques. Participation in the Poor People's March gave additional impetus toward development of red power movements.

Indians are often told by bureaucrats that "Indians don't act like that." This idea is entirely false and only serves to illuminate stereotypes and make the militants more active. Militancy in certain areas is the only means by which the Indian people can accomplish their goals. But it makes a great deal of difference what philosophy lies at the basis of militancy.

By and large, blacks have rioted and marched for undefined objectives. Cries of "Freedom now!" have provided very little understanding of problems or solutions. Indians who copy blacks simply because they are attracted by the chance to make their names household words are embarking on a disastrous course of action.

During the Poor People's March Abernathy made continuous veiled threats that certain things would happen if his demands were not met. Nothing happened. It was obvious to everyone that Abernathy was conducting a demonstration in a symbolic representation of the poor, not in a real sense. Abernathy could no more have produced on his threats than he could have reached the far side of the moon.

So before urban Indians consider the path of the black

militant they would be wise to insure that they have power firmly in their grasp within the urban Indian community. Otherwise, like the more radical blacks, they will be forced to turn increasingly to violence as a means of backing up their demands.

Blacks have not been denied because of their so-called extremism, but because they failed to consolidate the power that does exist in their hands. No one is going to hand over decision-making authority to people who have no base within the community other than their ability to articulate demands. Blacks have failed to operate for power positions in their own communities, and Indians must not make that mistake.

And although important, consolidation of power is secondary to the comprehensive examination of goals and techniques. Indians must first understand the position they occupy in urban and national affairs. Then they must become aware of the weak points where leverage and power can be combined to provide a means of pivoting the power structure that confronts them. Only then can they apply their power to the situation and contemplate significant results.

When one examines the history of American society one notices the great weakness inherent in it. The country was founded in violence. It worships violence and it will continue to live violently. Anyone who tries to meet violence with love is crushed, but violence used to meet violence also ends abruptly with meaningless destruction.

Consider the history of America closely. Never has America lost a war. When engaged in warfare the United States has always applied the principle of overkill and mercilessly stamped its opposition into the dust. Both Grant and Eisenhower made unconditional surrender their policy. No quarter, even if requested. Consider Vietnam, where the United States has already dropped more bombs than it did during the last world war—a classic of overkill.

Consider also the fascination of America's military leaders with the body count. It is not enough to kill people, bodies must be counted and statistics compiled to show how the harvest is going. Several years ago every effort was made to keep the ratio of enemy killed to American fatalities at a certain proportion. Yes, violence is America's sweetheart.

But name, if you can, the last peace the United States won. Victory yes, but this country has never made a successful peace because peace requires exchanging ideas, concepts, thoughts, and recognizing the fact that two distinct systems of life can exist together without conflict. Consider how quickly America seems to be facing its allies of one war as new enemies.

The United States operates on incredibly stupid premises. It always fails to understand the nature of the world and so does not develop policies that can hold the allegiance of people. It then alienates everyone who does not automatically love it. It worries about its reputation and prestige but daily becomes more vulnerable to ideologies more realistic than its own. This country could be easily influenced by any group with a more comprehensive philosophy of man if that group worked in a non-violent, non-controversial manner.

Ideological leverage is always superior to violence. People are always open to ideas even though they may appear to reject thought itself. Few people will allow themselves to become victims of irrational behavior, however, and violence and militancy are animalistic shortcuts to non-existent ends. Having once made a convert, the struggle ends and the convert is committted to realization of the ideology. But having once beaten a man to the draw, the winner is always subject to others who want to test his skill.

For Indians to walk the steps of the black militants would be a disaster. The problems of Indians have always been ideological rather than social, political, or economic. Simply to invite violence upon oneself for the sake of temporary concessions seems ridiculous and stupid.

It would be fairly easy, however, with a sufficient number of articulate young Indians and well-organized community support, to greatly influence the thinking of the nation within a few years. The white man asks only the opportunity to chase the almighty dollar. Whoever can take the burden of thinking from him is worshiped and praised beyond belief. Thus did Americans immortalize John Kennedy who did little to solve America's problems but seemed as if he thought about them a great deal.

Consider also the strange case of Lyndon B. Johnson. He brought to fruition more programs and opportunities than any other President in history. Yet he never presented the image of a thinker. Johnson was unable to attract the intellectual community to his side. And he never gave the impression that he had deeply considered the problems on an intellectual or philosophical level. People therefore felt that if they themselves had to confront the issues that the President must be the cause of those problems.

So it is vitally important that the Indian people pick the intellectual arena as the one in which to wage war. Past events have shown that the Indian people have always been fooled about the intentions of the white man. Always we have discussed irrelevant issues while he has taken the land. Never have we taken the time to examine the premises upon which he operates so that we could manipulate him as he has us.

A redefinition of Indian Affairs, then, would concentrate its attention on the coordination among the non-reservation peoples and the reservation programs on a regional or area basis. In that way migrations to and from urban areas could be taken into account when planning reservation programs. There would therefore be a need for the Department of the Interior to redefine its service function. Present regulations restrict Interior services to Indians living on trust land. Only these people are eligible for health, education, and trusteeship services. An urban Indian can become eligible for bureau services simply by returning to the reservation for a decent period and establishing residence. Often he spends as much time and money establishing his eligibility as the services he eventually receives are worth.

Because the bureau is restricted in its services to reservation Indians, little progress is made in uplifting the total Indian community. The result is the continual return of people from the urban areas, adding to the burden carried by the reservation programs.

Interior also concentrates its efforts on a few selected reservations, which have influential lawyers from big law firms in Washington, D.C. The majority of the organized tribes, which are too poor to afford full legal counsel, receive very little from the Department of the Interior. It is these little groups which fall victim to schemes developed by competitive bureaus within Interior, such as the Bureau of Reclamation which is always looking for Indian land to take for a development project of its own.

It is doubtful if Interior will initiate change. The department is ridden with career men who have spent their lives defending the traditional way of doing business. Change has never been Interior's forte, whether under Democratic or Republican administrations. More likely would be the possibility that as urban Indians begin to work out new policies and programs with the Vice President's Council on Indian Opportunity, Interior will grudgingly begin to adapt its policies to conform to the new currents moving in national Indian circles.

The most useful thing Interior and its component bureaus could do in the immediate future is to begin contracting with tribes and Indian centers to provide a comprehensive national program for development and training. A tribe or number of tribes could combine with an urban center to provide a reservation-city program of training and employment placement. In this way people could be trained in a city to take over specific jobs existing on the reservation and reservation people could be given pre-urban orientation before they left the reservation. In either case an Indian agency, the tribe or urban center, would be aware that they were receiving training and could expect employment, housing, and services when their training was finished.

Since a majority of Indian people now reside off reservation and are involved in work in the private area, Interior's most fruitful approach would be to seek out projects which it could initiate in cooperation with tribes and urban centers. It could hold a series of conferences between selected tribes and urban centers, suggesting specific contracts it might issue to them jointly to solve particular problems. Interior already has legal authority for such a move under an old law called the "Buy Indian" Act which gives preference to purchases made directly from a tribe.

Using such an approach, Interior might cushion the shock wave that appears inevitable as non-reservation people become more active. People and funds might be better channeled into projects that have the support of the Indian people in both areas. Ultimately, the federal government has responsibility for all Indian people. Whether or not Interior will take an aggressive stance in program development before Indians take the initiative and put Interior on the defensive is a question to be answered by the present Secretary of the Interior.

Udall proved a tremendous disappointment to the Indian people in his years as head of the Interior Department. Too many times he was totally unresponsive to Indian proposals. When the tribes suggested an advisory council so that tribes and Interior could make plans jointly, Udall refused to act. Yet he had advisory committees for some of his other agencies, notably National Parks. Udall also continued to pack the Indian Arts and Crafts Board with non-Indians who cared little for the development of Indian arts and crafts. Allegedly a great conservationist, Udall promised the Pyramid Lake Paiute tribe water for its declining shore line on the lake. Then he failed to deliver any significant amount of water and would not make any effort to clarify the tribe's rights to water in the lake.

A new Secretary could begin programs on a national scale that would give the tribes almost total control of reservation programs. Expanding the scope of services would mean less decision-making in government and more by Indians. The natural movement in Indian Affairs now exerting itself could fill the vacuum that exists in bureau programs.

A good example of this is the old relocation program. Originally conceived by the bureau in the 1950's as a means to get Indians off the reservation and into the cities, the program was renamed "Employment Assistance" in a feeble attempt to make it seem contemporary. This program could be expanded threefold by use of the contract method of operation since bureau offices in the relocation cities could be closed.

Churches must also shed their ineptness at facing modern problems. The rise of native religions in the past two decades has clearly put the churches on notice that their days as supreme religious authorities are numbered. Urban areas are showing a great deal of interest in native religions. In St. Paul, Minnesota, an urban chapter of the Medicine Lodge religion holds forth. Religious confrontation in the Great Lakes area may not be far away. With the exception of the Oneidas, Christianity may completely disappear among the Indians in that area.

Churches should acknowledge the relevancy of the Old Testament social forms if they mean to keep abreast of modern religious developments in Indian Affairs. As more urban centers appear on the scene, social-religious functions will begin to merge as Indian people give up differentiated social forms for an integral tribal existence. Even within the white church, men are forsaking the orthodox concept of the ministry for socially oriented functions comparable to the worker-priest movement of France.

Creation of new forms of ministry would place churches in the vanguard of social change within the field of Indian Affairs. Previously, churches have used the paid ministry as the representative of the organized church. Now they must acknowledge and support the informal channels of social activity by which the new Indians are reorienting their people. The informal, yet recognized, ministry would bring new blood into the churches and enable them to understand social fusion into tribal forms of the future.

I strongly doubt that American Christianity has the foresight or flexibility to embark on new paths of action. It has always been torn between being *good* and being *real* and generally chosen to be *good*.

The future indicates vicious struggles between those that have traditionally dominated Indian Affairs and those of the new movement. The Association on American Indian Affairs, Indian Rights Association, and other white interest groups have seen their best days despite the fact that they presently raise enormous sums of money which are apparently spent on some type of Indian program. For the better part of two generations these whites have not hesitated to make policies and direct programs on behalf of Indians without bothering to consult Indian people on the matter. Those days are vanishing swiftly. For the new Indian groups in the major cities will come to dominate news and programs relating to Indians in the respective areas. It is these new groups which the public will have to face and negotiate with.

National Indian organizations must also take cognizance of the new Indian movements. No longer will the NCAI be able to make simple appeals for membership and support on the basis of unity. Urban Indians, under the new American Indians United, will swiftly move into the lead position in Indian Affairs, determining the trends and issues which will attract both urban and reservation Indians alike.

Urban Indians will have the benefit of city libraries, night schools, all of the communicative tools of modern life. They will be able to focus on simple issues with simple answers in the same manner as the Civil Rights movement once made "We Shall Overcome" a national issue of integration.

Any national Indian organization of the future must contain a number of membership categories that operate by function or area of interest. The simplistic membership by tribes will no longer support political movements in national Indian affairs. As urban groups achieve organization for political purposes, they will begin to hold the balance of power on a statewide basis. This will be particularly true in Nevada, California (if not true there already), and Minnesota.

In many cases tribal clubs organized under large Indian centers will be wealthier and stronger and contain more people than does their tribal council on its home reservation. It is not inconceivable that people from the larger tribes, Sioux, Cherokee, Chippewa, and Navajo, will have a national urban organization. Individual Indians are now examining the method used by ACLU in building its branch offices. ACLU underwrites the creation of field offices and returns a percentage of income raised by a field office to the local branch. Eventually the local branch builds a sufficient income to operate its own programs.

State organizations of all Indians will be the wave of the future. It will no longer be possible to distinguish reservation from non-reservation people or to play off one tribe against another. Urban Indians will create a new sense of unity as they fight for equal representation in inter-tribal organizations. Their voting power will be sorely needed by reservation people as the population of reservations declines and that of non-Indians in the states continues to rise.

As programs become statewide the power and influence of urban Indians will continue to rise. Indians will begin to seek total development of reservation recreational facilities for their weekend and vacation use.

If the Bureau of Indian Affairs and the Congressional committees do not fight the broadening of Indian concerns into these areas, hitherto undefined and unexplored, much of the confusion and indecision now characterizing Indian programs will be cleared up. Total expenditures on Indian programs will decline as Indians rely more and more upon their own resources.

Indians will become fiercely independent of federal sources of funds as they exercise their new-found ability to operate as an independent force. Once freed from the confining definitions of rights and privileges of the past, Indians will embark on a series of community development projects that are based upon new concepts of tribalism.

If Congress initially funds experimental efforts by tribal-urban combines, traditional programs which provide basic services to Indian people will disappear. The momentum of development will carry programs completely into the private sector of life. Thus there is everything to gain and little to lose for Congress to extend eligibility for funding to non-federal Indians in the next decade.

Tribalism is the strongest force at work in the world today. And Indian people are the most tribal of all groups in America. They are also in the most advantageous position of any tribal people in the world. Using modern technical knowledge and having tremendous natural resources, Indian people can combine urban and rural life in a nationalistic continuum. An understanding of the forces and ideas brought forward by Indian people to solve particular problems during the next decade should prove to be useful information for solving similar problems elsewhere in the world.

The eventual movement among American Indians will be the "recolonization" of the unsettled areas of the nation by groups of Indian colonists. This process began several years ago when a group of Cherokee Indians, business and professional people from Los Angeles, moved from southern California back to Tahlequah, Oklahoma. They arrived at the old Cherokee capital and immediately blended into the existing Indian community virtually without a trace.

In Canada there has been a similar development. Several years ago a group of Ojibway moved off the reservations, purchased some land, and set up a corporation for community development. They began to get contracts for pulp wood from some of the papermills in the area. Now they own their own homes, a piece of land suitable for further development and expansion, and a great deal of machinery for their pulp wood business. Further experiments are planned by other groups in Canada.

In both cases the economic base for the new community was carefully analyzed and studied before the project was undertaken. Knowledge of modern economic mores and understanding of the strengths of tribal society enabled the people to project the type of recolonization that would be most likely to succeed. Both did.

The feasibility of such colonies is very much dependent on the rejection of the consumer mania which plagues society as a whole. The Indians had to determine whether continued treadmill consumption of luxuries was equal in value to a more leisurely and relaxed life. While certain benefits of urban or reservation living had to be surrendered, both experiments have shown that tribalism can be used in a redefinition of Indian life which has contemporary significance and strength.

Recolonization will call for a revival of Indian social and legal patterns. Rugged individualism will have to be reinterpreted to coincide with traditional Indian beliefs and practices. Some property must be held in common, personal property will remain the same. The corporate structure appears to give the best potential for development and use of small corporations as tools of development and recolonization will be highly favored.

Tribes already have corporation charters under the Indian Reorganization Act. Some urban centers have incorporated as non-profit organizations. The next logical step is a corporation for development purposes in which both reservation and non-reservation people participate. These corporations would be formed to explore ideas of development outside either reservation boundaries or urban centers.

It is at this point that the traditional Indian customs will come to predominate among the operations of Indian people nationally. Tribalism looks at life as an undifferentiated whole. Distinctions are not made between social and psychological, educational and historical, political and legal. The tribe is an all-purpose entity which is expected to serve all areas of life. The new corporations will not simply be development corporations. Rather they will be expected to cover all areas of life from small business to scholarships.

Where ordinary white corporations serve to produce income from capital invested, corporations will not do so in the new Indian scheme. Rather they will serve to coordinate community life. Earnings will be used to provide services ordinarily received from various governmental agencies. As economic independence becomes greater, independence in other areas of life will follow. Indians can thereby achieve a prosperity not seen since the landing of the white man.

Knowledgeable anthropologists will probably tear their hair out reading this chapter. According to the scholars, community Indians should have vanished long ago. The thought that Indians might retribalize, recolonize, and recustomize will short many a fuse in the universities. But the urge is present. The concepts are being discussed, in places the idea is being tested; and when the urban Indians have achieved a certain amount of political awareness and made their presence felt in national Indian affairs, it will happen.

"Indianness" has been defined by whites for many years. Always they have been outside observers looking into Indian society from a self-made pedestal of preconceived ideas coupled with an innate superior attitude toward those different from themselves. Many times anthropologists and sociologists have acted as if we couldn't do anything if they didn't first understand it and approve of it. Those days are also gone.

"Indianness" never existed except in the mind of the be-holder. Tribal social forms have always existed but they have been buried during past years by the legal entangle-ments of the federal government. Consequently Indians have come to believe that their problems were soluble by conformity to white culture (if there is one). Now that In-dian people have realized that their problems are legal and not cultural, legal solutions will be found through political action, and Indian people will not only be free to revitalize old customs, but also to experiment with new social forms.

Tampering with the present legal status of Indian tribes will only bring change faster and tinge it with potential violence. Disenfranchised people, bitter from their termi-nation experience, will provide the core of a violent urban Indian constituency if the present policy is contin-ued. If the federal policy, however, contains provisions for self-determination of Indian groups wherever they happen to be, options for non-federal people will provide such a strong pull to the urban areas that people will willingly leave the reservations to join the new movements. This will speed development of self-sufficient projects and hurry the process of colonization.

There is, in fact, little need for more funds. The great need is for reorientation of existing expenditures to sup-port projects of non-federal people. With much of the money now being spent in the Indian field going mainly to keep a dribble of young Indians on relocation, there is in-credible monetary waste. This is no urgency in the pro-gram which can be felt by the Indian people themselves.

The more support that can be given to retribalizing of the people, the better chances are to avoid violence. Para-doxically, a greater sense of urgency in retribalization will tend to curb possible violence. Nationalism must be the ally of future policies. New policies must not be directed at breaking tribal ties because they will break upon the rock of the tribe.

As Indians become more and more aware of what they are doing the pressure on leadership will become less and less. In turn, the group will be stronger and more demo-cratic and produce better leadership. The potential for de-velopment is unlimited but actual progress can be ham-pered by a number of factors. One is what the black community will be doing during the same time. At present the key words are "law and order." All political candidates have used these words in their campaign speeches. Everyone understands that "law and order" are synonymous with repression of the black community. If the black community is severely repressed, it will accelerate movement in the Indian community. The natural tendency of Indians to withdraw will force them back upon themselves and act as a catalyst in hastening the time for recolonization.

Like all redefinitions, many factors of varying importance may change present projection. Crucial to the change in Indian Affairs is the ability of tribal people to understand the implications of movement over a long period of time. Any movement which begins to exert a significant influence in America, is subjected to publicity. Too much attention from the press can radically change conceptions and goals simply by making the process appear commonplace.

But hopefully, enough Indian people will take the time to reflect on their situation, on the things going on around them both in the cities and on the reservations, and will choose the proper points of leverage by which Indian renewal can be fully realized.

12 ❖ AN AFTERWORD

WRITING THIS BOOK, as I have, has placed me in a certain position in Indian Affairs from which, unfortunately, I shall not be able to retreat. At least not very soon. One reason I wanted to write it was to raise some issues for younger Indians which they have not been raising for themselves. Another reason was to give some idea to white people of the unspoken but often felt antagonisms I have detected in Indian people toward them, and the reasons for such antagonism.

When one writes a book, or at least tries to write a book, a great deal of one's soul is surrendered and placed in print for all to see. Thus, to quote my old friend Clyde Warrior, "I've sold out." At least in many ways.

But there is more to the story than that. Indian people today have a chance to re-create a type of society for themselves which can defy, mystify, and educate the rest of American society. Yet they mill around like so many cattle, not bringing to the surface the greatness that is in them. If nothing else, this book should make enough people take sides either defending it, which will be that valiant few, or condemning it, which will be spearheaded by my friends in the anthropology classes into whose hitherto exclusive domain I have intruded and hopefully given a new sense of conflict to Indian Affairs.

I apologize only for not having documentation enough to reveal some of the real scandals that are occurring today in the Congress and churches in regard to Indians. Someone more clever than I will bring them out some day.

It would be well, before going further in my own evaluation of Indian Affairs, to give enough of my background to provide a context by which this book can be better remembered and perhaps make it possible to understand my conclusion.

As long as any member of my family can remember, we have been involved in the affairs of the Sioux tribe. My great grandfather was a medicine man named Saswe, of the Yankton tribe of the Sioux Nation. My grandfather was a Yankton chief who was converted to Christianity in the 1860's. He spent the rest of his life as an Episcopal missionary on the Standing Rock Sioux reservation in South Dakota. So earnest was his work that he was called the Phillips Brooks of the Indians and his statue was placed in the Natonal Cathedral in Washington, D.C.

My father was an Episcopal missionary for thirty-seven years in South Dakota, retiring only last year. He had worked among our people all his life and ended his church career as the Archdeacon of the Missionary District of South Dakota.

I often considered the ministry when I was younger. But as I watched the frustrations of my father within the Episcopal Church I decided that Church life was totally irrelevant to Indian needs. Time after time my father would advance a plan by which the church could be made stronger in South Dakota. Each time, white church administrators vetoed the plan, primarily because it was a plan that had been advanced by an Indian.

Over the years I observed that Indian clergy were shunted aside when it came time for promotions. Indians could spend an entire lifetime in the Episcopal Church and never achieve any advancement. Whites, on the other hand, were often made superintendents of missions within a couple of years after they had graduated from seminary.

But I was intrigued with the whole spectrum of Christian theology and so, after a hitch in the Marine Corps and graduation from college, I attended the Augustana Lutheran Seminary in Rock Island, Illinois, for four years, getting a B.D. degree there in 1963. My years at Augustana were very happy. The Lutherans welcomed me with great warmth. I was allowed to take any courses I wanted in any sequence I wanted. So I spent my time there working in a body shop at night, attending school in the daytime, and generally soaking up whatever theological doctrines caught my fancy.

From my time at Augustana, I began to see that within a broad Christian framework many social systems could become valid and human-oriented. Most of all I was intrigued with the Swedish Lutheran studies in Old Testament books. It seemed to me that Lutheranism, at least on the continent, was about to break through into a new theological position which would be of great significance to the modern world.

The only people in the modern world comparable to the Hebrews that I could see were the Indian tribes. Like the Hebrews they had been shunted aside by more powerful people and made to taste the bitter dregs of an alien culture. Yet, like the four-hundred-year sojourn in Egypt, Indians had managed to maintain their culture and basic social life.

After graduation from Seminary I got a job with the United Scholarship Service in Denver, Colorado. The USS was a private clearing house for scholarships for American Indian and Spanish-American college students. I was hired to develop a program to get scholarships for Indian students in eastern preparatory schools and over the year I met many of the creative people in the eastern educational establishment. Schools such as Exeter, Andover, Kent, Mercersburg, and Lenox eagerly responded to the program and soon we had a number of Indian students in eastern schools and more scheduled to go the following fall.

In August of 1964 I went to Sheridan, Wyoming, to meet a teacher from Exeter to show him around the All American Indian Days celebration there. Meeting in conjunction with that celebration was the annual convention of the National Congress of American Indians. I wandered around the convention naïvely, trying to get introductions for my teacher friend with some of the tribal chairmen attending the convention.

The NCAI was undergoing one of its periodic purges and was looking for a new Executive Director. More of a pawn than an active candidate, I ended the week as the new director. The NCAI was deeply in debt. Tribal and individual membership was at an all-time low. I was so reluctant about taking the job that I accepted temporarily and asked that a further meeting be called two months later to see if they still wanted me as director. I was hoping in the meantime that tempers would have cooled and that I could gracefully bow out of the picture.

Two months later I had the job. But the tribes had done nothing to build up the organization which was one of the conditions I had set before I would take the job. The next year was incredibly difficult. Tribes held back as much as possible, figuring the organization wouldn't survive and unwilling to risk even a hundred dollars in dues to pay debts.

Several times the NCAI was so far behind on its debts that we considered closing it and declaring bankruptcy. But each time we were ready to close, a few devoted tribes would give more money and we would weather the crisis. In February we owed some $1,100 in back rent and were within hours of storing everything pending final closure. But the Colorado River tribe of Arizona, stalwart tribal members of long standing, wired in $1,000 and we were able to keep open.

By June of 1965 we were several thousand dollars behind and in desperation I sent out letters announcing the closing of the organization. Immediately the Sioux tribes responded with special contributions telegraphed in and we managed to weather the disaster. Coeur d'Alene, a small tribe in Idaho, through the hard work of Mrs. Leona Garry, the chairman's wife, raised over $1,000 during the summer to keep us in business. But things were incredibly difficult. In August our total income was $63.00.

Finally we arrived at the annual convention, weary but alive. Tribal membership had increased spectacularly that fall before convention time and we had the third highest number of tribal members in the history of the organization.

The year 1966 was also lean. In March we had to close our large office, store everything we had in an $80.00-a-month room, and operate by telephone. But gradually memberships were coming in and through the interest of the Field Foundation we received a grant to do research in the field on Indian economic resources. This field work, centered in Denver, enabled us to keep in closer contact with tribes so that eventually we pulled the organization through and set up our Washington headquarters again. By convention time we were setting all time membership records for the organization.

I served another year and then entered law school at the University of Colorado in September of 1967. By that time the NCAI was doing well financially, had managed to bring together nearly a hundred tribes nationally, and fought and beaten the Interior Department in a number of skirmishes.

Many Indians look at the director of the NCAI as a superhuman who can do all things equally well. Others view him as an eternal foul-up forever "making money" on Indians. Neither is the case. The job is very taxing emotionally. Each director sees opportunity after opportunity go down the drain because the tribes don't respond to strategy on a national level. Time after time we would recommend that certain areas of legislation or program be undertaken by the tribes. Each time there would be such little response that we wondered if our mail was being delivered.

There is a constant temptation when one is director to forget about Indians and issues and present a good "image" of Indians nationally, hoping that somehow the tribes will respond with enthusiasm to new frills and fancies. Other groups seem to have a great deal of success in following this course, but it has been a disaster for Indians. The historical image of the Indians is pretty well set, we are the bad guys who burned the wagon trains and images are the white man's game. For the Indian, symbols are reality: what a man appears to be, he is. Consequently, when an NCAI director glorifies himself hoping to attract national publicity for Indians, he is simply a gloryhunter in the eyes of Indians. And the tale of Custer should suffice to show how Indians feel about gloryhunters.

Although I felt I had been able to achieve a good national consensus of the tribes in support of the NCAI, I also felt that other tactics had to be created if Indians were to fight and win the battles looming on the horizon. Much of the success of the NCAI during the time I was director was not my doing but the result of the hard work by organization members who truly wanted a strong national organization. One man or one tribe cannot create anything. At least in Indian country he can't. Rather the success of the NCAI was, I felt, the result of the loyalty of the people from Colorado River, Fort Hall, Flathead, Standing Rock, White Mountain and San Carlos, Pyramid Lake and Hoopa Valley. Other tribes and individuals too numerous to mention had begun to take responsibility and move the organization into new fields.

Two things turned me to the field of law. In August, 1966, we invited Jack Greenberg of the NAACP Legal Defense Fund out to Sheridan, Wyoming, to talk with us about the legal problem with which the black community had so successfully overturned the old Supreme Court doctrine of Separate but Equal in the case of *Plessy v. Ferguson*.

Greenberg talked with us the whole afternoon. Patiently he explained how each case taken by the Legal Defense Fund had led to another until *Brown v. Topeka Board of Education* had produced the desired holding, overturning *Plessy* and making equality a legal reality.

As I sat there listening to Jack I could visualize a national legal program for Indian people similar to that which had served the black community so well. I could see us piling case upon case, precedent upon precedent, until we had forged out a new definition of Indian rights by which our Indian communities could live in peace from encroachment from any source.

But I realized that without any Indian people willing to undertake complete training in law and having a comprehensive knowledge of all tribes, such a program would not be able to get off the ground. At the time, the idea of a legal program seemed quite remote and so I forgot it for a while, although I suggested it to a number of tribes to get their reactions.

The following May I was making a field trip through the Southwest, trying to get the smaller more isolated tribes to join the NCAI. Group after group listened patiently and then decided not to join or to postpone their decision. I came to realize very quickly that these people were worried about their own reservations. The idea of joining a national organization headquartered in Washington, D.C., was simply too remote and abstract for them.

So I began to ask them about their reservation problems. In no time I learned to my horror that these tribes were without legal counsel, had no idea what their rights were, and had no way to find out such information. Each small tribe I visited made me more depressed. The problems appeared to be insurmountable. Yet these people were trying their best for their little tribes.

The primary problem, as far as I could ascertain it, was that policies and laws made years ago had handicapped these people for decades. Laws such as the Indian Reorganization Act, while quite effective for larger tribes, had had little influence on the lives of these people. It was as if they had been placed in an isolation ward for the last half century.

I believe that the solution to many problems affecting Indian people can only come through intensive work with such small tribes. They are basically one community unit, whereas larger tribes may consist of a number of small communities. If a course of action can be shown to work with a small tribe, chances of its succeeding with a larger tribe are much greater.

When I finish law school I hope to start a program which will assist smaller tribes and Indian communities to achieve a balanced program in which their rights are clearly outlined. This may take extensive research into past legislation which has shunted them aside in favor of railroads, reclamation districts, mining ventures, and other development schemes of America's past. It will probably also take a great deal of basic organizational work before any lasting benefits can be achieved. But I have talked with enough leaders of small tribes to feel that they would respond with enthusiasm to anyone who could bring them necessary technical skills to begin working out their problems.

Many people deride attempts to create one national Indian voice. Many of those who ridicule us do so because they have a large vested interest in maintaining the myth that Indians are confused and don't know what is "best" for them. Others get a satisfaction out of being the person who "understands" Indians.

This book has been hardest on those people in whom I

place the greatest amount of hope for the future—Congress, the anthropologists, and the churches. They have been largely spinning their wheels either emotionally or programmatically. And it's past time when people who have that amount of influence can afford to spin their wheels.

If I were asked to make a list of the useful anthropologists, it would be very short. But this group of people could be critical in helping American society to understand the concepts involved in equality—real equality. I believe that they should offer themselves as volunteers to the various tribes and apply their skills in research to real problems. Who really gives a damn if the Oglalas were a great warrior band of the Sioux? That won't help to solve the problems that exist today. I would like to see anthropologists volunteer to appear before Congressional committees on behalf of the tribes when serious legislation is being considered and bring the special skills they claim to have to the defense of the tribe involved.

I can also see that we are getting more and more favorable voices in both the Senate and House committees that pass Indian legislation. Such men as George McGovern, Lee Metcalf, and Paul Fannin in the Senate and Richard White, Ed Edmondson, and others in the House of Representatives continue to push for the fairest possible legislation for Indian people. Tribes should begin to realize who their friends are and give better support for the progressive members of Congress who are willing to take a chance on Indians.

Above all I am hopeful that the churches will give up this passionate desire to steal sheep from each other's folds and get down to the business of helping Indian people. If, as they claim, Christianity is for all people, why not let the Indian people worship God after their own conceptions of Him? Why insist on making Indian people conform to a type of Christianity that went out with King Arthur?

As long as white missionaries continue to preach stilted abstractions learned in seminary while our people starve, the churches occupy a demonic role in the life of the Indian people. We must have immediate termination of the religious trusteeship into which we were placed a century ago.

But I have never been able to recall when the churches understood the world in which they lived. I remember arguments against integration in 1964 and in favor of self-determination. In 1968 churchmen try to argue self-determination when we are talking recapitalization. The same churchmen who were angry at me for questioning God's will for integration now berate me for suggesting a different course today. I have no realistic hopes that the churches will become real. It is tragic because they could do so much to alter the confusion that exists today among the minority communities.

I worry more and more about the Indian people. It seems as if our leadership is severely handicapped in facing the modern world. Representation of Indian people should be a post of heavy responsibility. Yet so many of our younger leaders appear to relish only the publicity and shun the arduous tasks of organization from which real power and influence come.

The modern world appears to be more than a match for our present leadership. The temptation to be militant overcomes the necessity to be nationalistic. Anyone can get into the headlines by making wild threats and militant statements. It takes a lot of hard work to raise an entire group to a new conception of themselves. And that is the difference between the nationalists and the militants.

Clyde Warrior, who died in 1968, was a true Indian nationalist. He was a gentle person who attempted to use shock treatment to get Indian people to stand up for themselves. Few Indians understood him. The white press used Clyde as an example of an Indian Stokely Carmichael. Perhaps the world will never know to what extent Clyde was able to influence Indian people. But Clyde refused to join the Poor People's March because he knew the difference between nationalism and militancy. I hope that other Indian people will understand the difference in time.

I make no claim that this book represents what *all* Indian people are *really* thinking. Or that Indian people should follow the ideas presented in this book. But many things I have written have been logical extensions of things I have heard other Indian people say. I have tried to cull out of my experience in Indian Affairs the various spheres of influence which appear to manipulate Indian people. I have taken extreme positions in regard to them because too often Indian people are so polite that they refuse to insult anyone by bringing up the fact that he is giving them a hard time.

Robert Thomas tells a famous story concerning the Cherokee who had a white man kill his children, steal his wife, sell his cattle, and burn his farm. The Cherokee chased the man for ten years and finally caught him. "Are you the guy who did all those things," the Cherokee asked. Yes, the white man admitted, he was the one.

"Well, you better watch that crap," the Cherokee warned.

And that is my greatest concern for the Indian people. That we will be so damn polite that we will lose everything for fear of hurting someone's feelings if we object to the way things are going.

I believe that as Indian people we should leave the past glories to historians and embark on an aggressive program of rebuilding our tribes. Thus I do not intend to spend much time speaking to YMCA's, women's groups, and conferences in the future. Other people can do this job much better than I.

I want to search out the sheep missing from our national Indian fold and help them to get moving with the rest of the tribes. Perhaps we will not finish the job of rebuilding in my lifetime. Certainly Clyde Warrior, Quentin Markistum, Arvid Miller, and many of the great Indian leaders of our times have not seen the final victory. But it is our duty to do what we can while we are here.

Interested white people often ask what they can do to help Indians. Many have done a great deal for Indian people. And many more would help if they knew how. Indians, I believe, have passed the point where they reject assistance because of their nationalistic momentum. I would suggest that the best help non-Indians could render would be to support the two most important national Indian organizations. If we could be assured that we have adequate financial resources to determine our own future by receiving strong support for our work, then it would be up to us to provide our own solutions.

These Indian organizations are the National Congress of American Indians and the League of Nations—Pan Am Indians. These organizations represent opposite points of view. The NCAI supports the modern tribal council as organized under various federal laws. The League of Nations–Pan Am Indians works for tribal government by traditional Indian chiefs and clans. Until we resolve the two opposing points of view we will not be able to move forward as a united people. It is critical that we finally arrive at a universal understanding of what an Indian tribe is or should be.

I conclude my comments by reminding the Indian people of the great war chief of the Oglala Sioux—Crazy Horse. Crazy Horse never drafted anyone to follow him. People recognized that what Crazy Horse did was for the best and was for the people. Crazy Horse never had his name on the stationery. He never had business cards. He never even received a per diem.

When he was dying, having been bayoneted in the back at Fort Robinson, Nebraska, Crazy Horse said to his father, "Tell the people it is no use to depend on me any more now." Until we can once again produce people like Crazy Horse all the money and help in the world will not save us. It is up to us to write the final chapter of the American Indian upon this continent.